HOW
WEAPONS
WORK

HOW WEAP

ONS WORK

edited by Christopher Chant

Marshall Cavendish London & New York

Published by Marshall Cavendish Publications Limited,
58 Old Compton Street,
London W1V 5PA
© Marshall Cavendish Publications Limited 1976
© Marshall Cavendish Limited 1974, 1975, 1976
Some of this material was previously published
in *How It Works* and *War Monthly*.
Printed in Great Britain by Redwood Burn International
ISBN 0 85685 196 5
Designer Jim Bamber
House editor Renny Harrop
Previous page : The USS Henry Clay nuclear powered
submarine clearly showing its immense power as it
runs at speed on the surface. It is armed with
sixteen Poseidon missiles each carrying ten
nuclear warheads.

Christopher Chant worked as assistant editor on Purnell's History
of the First World War and of their History of the Second World War.
He was then editor of the Orbis/Marshall Cavendish publication,
Encyclopedia of World War I. Included among the titles of the
numerous books he has written himself on aircraft are *Ground Attack*,
Kursk and *Aircraft*.
Martin H. Brice worked for twelve years at the Imperial War
Museum, London, in several departments. He was involved in the
preservation of HMS Belfast and is the author of *The Tribals* and *The
Royal Navy during the Sino-Japanese Incident*.
Kenneth Macksey — served in the Royal Tank Regiment for 27 years
and saw active service in the Second World War. On leaving the Army
in 1968 he became deputy editor of Purnell's History of the Second
World War and then of their History of the First World War. He is
among the leading writers on armoured warfare with his *Tank, Tank
Warfare* and the *Guinness Book of Tank Facts and Feats* besides being
the biographer of the great tank pioneers, General Hobart in *Armoured
Crusader* and his latest, highly praised book about General Guderian —
Guderian, Panzer General.

Involvement in this book has been particularly fascinating for me, both as editor and as the author of the chapter on aircraft, for it explores in detail those aspects of weapon design and function which are all too often glossed over or ignored in other books about modern military hardware. For while it is quite correct to examine weapons by the ultimate parameters of their battlefield performances, it is just as interesting and illuminating to see not only what these weapons can do, but also how they do it. This is the real object of the book : an illustrated examination of how weapons work, set within the context of a short history of each basic type of weapon on land, sea and air.

I should also like here to thank Martin Brice and Kenneth Macksey for their contributions on naval and tank warfare respectively. By inclination I am concerned mostly with air warfare, but I found both these chapters of great interest, and feel sure that the book will prove of interest and use to laymen and specialist alike.

Christopher Chant

CONTENTS

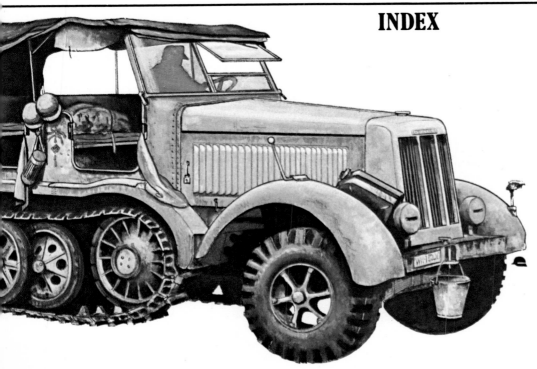

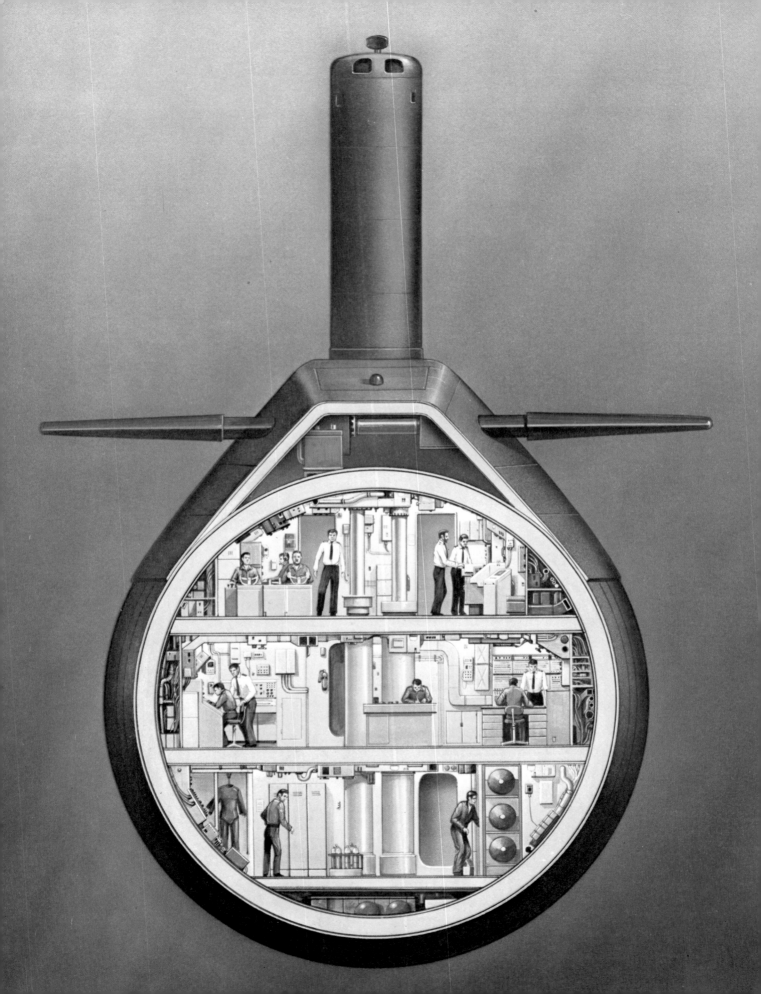

INTRODUCTION

The subject of weapons is constantly brought to our attention by the inclusion, in both the press and on television, of references to their use. So that the mention of the death of a soldier in Northern Ireland or the sale of a vast consignment of armaments to a Middle Eastern power seem commonplace. Such references mean very little until one thinks about their implications. One man, using a SAM 7 Strela, hand-held, anti-aircraft missile, is capable of bringing down a 'jumbo jet'. A Polaris submarine has a greater destructive power than the entire sum of the bombs dropped during World War II. Moreover, it is worth noting that the manufacture and sale of armaments provide a considerable source of revenue for many industrialized nations.

A 'weapon' is defined in the *Concise Oxford Dictionary* as *material thing designed or used or usable as an instrument for inflicting bodily harm.* This implies that a weapon is a small thing, used by one individual against another. Although this may have been accurate enough in the early days of 'weapon technology', it now stands in need of considerable revision.

At the bottom of the military scale the individual soldier still has his personal weapon, such as a rifle, intended for use against other individuals; slightly higher up the scale

Below: An illustration of Greek Fire taken from a Byzantine manuscript of the 10th century. The swivel tube can clearly be seen in the illustration and it is apparent that the burning material is being ejected with some force.

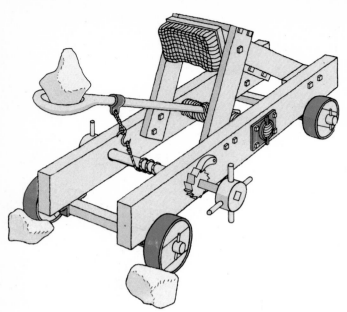

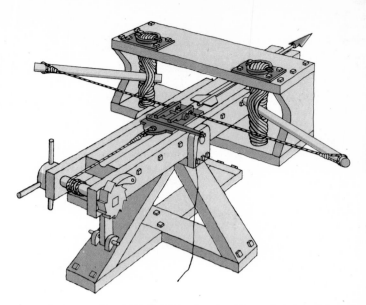

Left: A mangonel, a simpler development of the original ballista adapted for throwing stones. The padded cushion is to stop the arm from smashing itself on the frame. Some versions had slings.
Right: A dart throwing ballista of the classical period, reconstructed from the descriptions of ancient writers. It is made of wood reinforced with bronze, and uses twisted sinew as its source of power. There is a windlass and ratchet to wind it up, and an ingenious trigger which releases the string by pulling a bar out from under two pivoted 'fingers', allowing their other ends to rise.

are what may be described as 'team weapons', used by a small crew to fight other small crews, such as a tank; and finally there are a multitude of 'mass weapons' designed for deployment against mass targets, such as nuclear weapons.

The major change in mass weapons has occurred since the end of World War II, and was brought about by the rapid advances in electronic technology. As well as improving the actual battlefield performance of weapons, these developments have also enabled complex weapons, or rather what should in reality be called 'weapon systems', to be used to full effect by smaller crews (and even individuals) than was previously possible. The new generation of one-man, shoulder-launched, anti-aircraft missiles is an example of this. The individual user has merely to raise the whole weapon package to his shoulder, sight on the previously detected target, press the trigger and discard the shell of the package once the missile is on its way. Previously, the same results, or rather efforts to produce the same results, would have needed a large number of men and a considerable quantity of equipment — a light anti-aircraft gun, with a crew of two or three men, the gun's towing vehicle with a crew of two, three or four loaders and fuse setters, plus a number of other crew members under the command of a senior non-commissioned officer or a junior officer. Thus at the cost of higher development and production expenses, and a higher ratio of support troops, the individual fighting man has been made more self-sufficient than his predecessors.

Weapons may be broadly categorized into two classes, shock weapons and missile weapons. The former are wielded by the user for the most part, and secure their effect by the impact of a fairly large mass striking the object at a relatively slow velocity. The latter, as the name implies, are thrown or mechanically propelled at the object, and secure their effect by the impact of a fairly small mass striking the object at a relatively high velocity.

Before the development of gunpowder weapons to a considerable degree of efficiency, the struggle between the two categories of weapon was fairly evenly balanced. Technical improvements in the weapons of either category, coupled with the tactical skill to use them, ensured a temporary predominance for that category. Thus from the earliest days of weapons until the middle of the 17th century, the balance between shock and missile weapons was relatively stable. From the middle of the 17th century, however, there have been rapid improvements in missile technology which have not been equalled by those in shock technology, and as a result the former has become the predominant military type, with a few important exceptions.

The first pre-historic weapons were in all probability stones and sticks, wielded in the hand as clubs, or thrown as crushing missiles or spears. The invention of flint-knapping made considerable advances possible, such as cutting edges on hand-held shock weapons like axes and knives, and sharp piercing points on missile weapons such as spears. Further developments in stone technology produced sophisticated versions of these early weapons. The slashing sword was produced by fitting small flint slivers along a piece of wood, and mechanical propellers for 'spears' were introduced in the form of the spear-thrower and the bow, the arrows of which are in essence miniature spears. At the same time the sling, capable of hurling a small stone at a considerable velocity, seems to have made its first appearance.

Further advances were limited by a lack of new materials, until the discovery of metals. Although copper could take an edge, it was too soft for military use. The Sumerians of Mesopotamia, however, discovered that copper alloyed with tin produced a fairly hard substance (bronze) that could be worked easily, took an edge and was capable of being resharpened. By about 1700 BC the use of bronze had spread to Egypt and the new technology swiftly spread over the Mediterranean area.

Bronze was used principally for shock weapons such as swords, with stone still retained for the heads of missile weapons such as the bow and throwing spears. At much the same time, protection against both shock and missile weapons, previously obtained from hide and animal bone, began gradually to be supplemented with, and then replaced by bronze.

The Egyptians, chief users of the bronze weapon, controlled much of the eastern Mediterranean until the advent of iron weapons, introduced by the Hittites at about 1400 BC. Although iron had been known for long before this date, it was only when the Hittites discovered how to smelt iron and mix carbon with it (in the form of charcoal) that the working of iron became a practical possibility. It enabled weapons far harder and sharper than bronze ones to be produced. Gradually the science of iron-working spread over the eastern Mediterranean and Middle Eastern lands, leading to the widespread use of iron weapons by about 1000 BC. It should be noted, however, that the design of weapons altered little, the main improvements being in their manufacture, strength and sharpness; all attributable to the use of iron instead of bronze.

The first 'professional' standing army appeared in Assyria at about 1250 BC, and from this date onwards considerable progress was made in military art, mostly as a result of tactical improvements and innovations rather than weapon technology. Early iron weapon technology

Above : The longbow, after a 15th century French painting. Left : The windlass crank, shown here being operated by a Genoese archer, made the crossbow a much more powerful weapon.

11

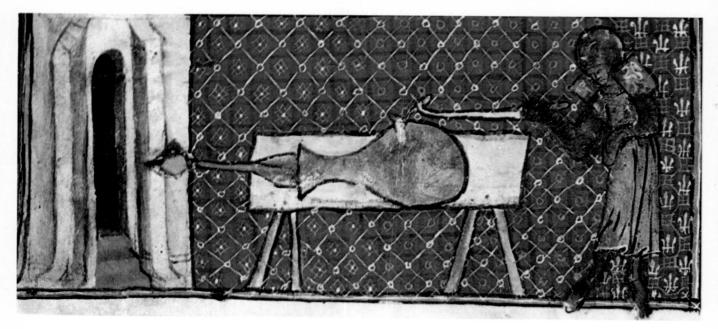

Above : The earliest illustration of a cannon, from the Milemete manuscript of 1326. A flame is being applied to the touch hole and the 'iron pot' is about to fire an arrow.
Above right : This German drawing of 1450 depicts a firemaster, on the left, who is supervising the pounding of gunpowder. Each man pulls down a heavy wooden beam mounted on a spring into a trough, where it crushes the ingredients which will be made into gunpowder.
Below right : The firemaster, in another picture from the same work, is overseeing the weighing and mixing of the essential ingredients to make up the composition of gunpowder. The ingredients are then mixed together in a moist, pasty state. A rope fuse is being fitted to each completed 'grenade'.

reached two high points with the armies of Alexander the Great (*circa* 325 BC) ; and the Roman armies of the period about the beginning of the Christian era.

The subsequent 'Dark Ages' were marked in the military field by the forgetting of the tactical sophistication of the Greeks and Romans, and by the failure to make any significant technological improvements. With the emergence of Western Europe from the Dark Ages towards the end of the first millenium AD, tactical innovations once again became the norm. In the 'tactical arms race' that marked European history between 1000 and about 1450 AD, the chief problem was the struggle between missile power and mobility, and protection from missiles combined with shock effect. The latter type was best exemplified by the increasingly heavily-armoured knight on his armoured warhorse, armed with thrusting spear and sword. The former reached its peak with the English longbow, probably the best missile weapon invented before the age of gunpowder. The almost total superiority of mobile missile power over unwieldy shock power was clearly demonstrated by the terrible defeat inflicted on the cream of French chivalry by the English longbowmen at the Battle of Crécy in 1346.

The see-saw battle between 'iron age' missile and shock power was to continue for some time to come, but the invention that was to revolutionize warfare had already been in existence for some time. This was gunpowder, first invented in China and initially mentioned in a European manuscript in 1301. The first mention of a gun (in this case, a piece of artillery) was in 1326, and gunpowder weapons seem first to have been used at Crécy 20 years later.

Early artillery weapons were very inefficient, firing imperfectly shaped stone or metal balls from unwieldy and inaccurate muzzle-loading guns. By 1453, however, heavy guns were useful siege weapons, where their lack of mobility was unimportant. In this year the great city of Constantinople fell to the Turks, mainly as a result of the large-calibre guns built for them by a renegade Hungarian.

Early experiments with breech-loaders were not successful, and the basic European artillery piece became the smooth-bored brass muzzle-loader, produced in a bewildering number of calibres and weights. As production techniques improved in the 16th and 17th centuries, guns became fairly accurate and improved in range, but full advantage of these factors could not be taken without adequate sights and a mechanical means of absorbing the recoil of guns. The lack of the latter meant that the gun had to be relaid after each shot, which was time-consuming and caused considerable inaccuracy.

The 18th century saw considerable advances made in the design of carriages and trails for guns, with consequent improvements in mobility, but the advent of the modern type of gun came in the 19th century. Round solid shot was by this time almost universally supplanted by the pointed, cylindrical shell filled with high explosive; adequate sights had been invented and perfected for service use; mechanisms to absorb the recoil of the gun without disturbing the gun carriage, and then of returning the gun to its original position had been introduced; and a practical system of breech-loading, which allowed a one-piece round of propellant and shell to be used, had been universally adopted. All the basic elements of modern artillery were ready for development into the weapon that was to play so prominent a part in both world wars.

Gunpowder also had an immediate effect on personal weapons, but for some time this effect was small. Individual guns, essentially scaled down artillery pieces fitted with handles for the firer, appeared shortly after the middle of the 14th century. In purely military terms, these early handguns were more of a hindrance than an asset, for they were wildly inaccurate, heavy, and very time-consuming to load, during which time the firer was virtually defenceless against any adversary except another gunman. Technical improvements did take place, but the handgun, in its muzzle-loading form, did not achieve any real prominence until relatively light smooth-bore muskets fitted with an efficient firing lock were introduced in the last quarter of the 17th century. The widespread introduction of the flintlock musket and volley-firing at the beginning of the 18th century marked the end of the highly-organized shock-tactic pikemen who had dominated European wars since the beginning of the 15th century. Volley firing was a system involving three ranks of men who moved around in sequence. The front rank fired, the middle rank prepared to fire and the rear rank reloaded. The missile power of massed musketeers also started the decline of horsed cavalry as a major battlefield weapon. Various types of cavalry (more or less heavily armed and armoured on large or small horses) were tried in the 18th and early 19th centuries, but their major use in European wars seemed to be reconnaissance rather than involvement on the major battlefields. Many generals, however, were loathe to see the departure of the *arme blanche*, and horsed cavalry formations featured prominently in all European armies until after World War I.

The smooth-bore muzzle-loading musket reached its peak in the Napoleonic wars at the beginning of the 19th century, lingered on for about another 50 years, but was then replaced by the breech-loading rifle. The rifle was

Top : A carronade gun-crew about to fire their weapon. The gun captain, with pricker and powder horn, will jerk the trigger-line of the gun-lock. One loader has the rammer and sponge while the provider uses a hand-spike to adjust the gun traverse. The other loader holds the lint-stock with its lighted slowmatch taken from the tub behind. If the flintlock mechanism fails, he can apply his slowmatch to the firing vent.

easier to load, more accurate and possessed of very considerably improved range. It was not until the 2nd Boer War (1899-1902) that the true impact of rifles on infantry tactics was realized. The same is true of what may be termed the automatic rifle (machine-gun), whose battle-field dominance was first revealed in the Russo-Japanese War (1904-5).

Modern warfare, heralded by the introduction of these new weapons, has produced its own special problems, and some of the solutions attempted (tanks, rocket-launchers, grenades and landmines, plus special forms of artillery) are described in subsequent chapters, together with the course taken in the development of 'conventional' weapons of land warfare since the turn of the present century.

The history of naval warfare presents a different picture. From the earliest time ships were used principally as a method of moving men and supplies, and of taking wars afloat. Ships were used as moving 'land platforms', loaded with troops who would fight what was effectively a land battle at sea, firing their missile weapons if the range was right, or engaging in a shock battle if two opposing vessels were brought together.

The introduction of the ram in classical Greek times altered this. For the first time the ship itself was a weapon, intended to disable or destroy the enemy's ships by ramming their sides with its own hard, pointed ram bow. Until the advent of gunpowder weapons, these two basic types of battle (the land battle at sea and the ramming battle) remained all that a ship could achieve in the purely military sense. The gradual adoption of improved cannon, however, allowed ships to fight each other with missile weapons, although shock tactics were still employed.

The wooden battleship, fitted with about 100 guns of varying calibres, 50 on each side, reached the peak of its usefulness in the Napoleonic wars. The object of naval battles at this time was to catch the enemy where he had least protection from thick timbers and least offensive armament, either the bow or stern, with the full weight of one's own broadside at short-range, and so batter the enemy into submission or destruction.

Naval warfare, however, was revolutionized by two things. The advent of steam power, which allowed higher speeds regardless of the presence of wind or its direction, and breech-loading guns of large calibre. The introduction of shell-firing, muzzle-loading guns had already started the revolution towards smaller numbers of 'great guns' on trainable mountings, combined with an ever-increasing thickness of armour plate to protect the ship's vital portions from enemy shell-fire. However, the arrival of breech-loaders at last led to the development of the present-day type of warship, with its guns mounted on the ship's centre line in fully enclosed, trainable turrets.

By the end of the 19th century the variety of basic warship types had proliferated, and the submarine's emergence as a practical fighting ship, its main weapon the new and very potent torpedo, meant that naval warfare could take on a three-dimensional aspect. This aspect was confirmed by the appearance of aircraft as a practical and useful adjunct to the older weapon in World War I, and the introduction of the first aircraft-carriers.

Since World War I, the relative importance of the various types of warship to each other has fluctuated, and there has been considerable tactical development. The ships themselves, however, have remained basically similar to their World War I counterparts with the two exceptions of powerplants and armament. In the latter field the guided missile has gradually taken over from the gun as the ship's most powerful and important weapon.

Where modern warships differ from their predecessors, however, is in the extent and sophistication of their various detection systems. Whereas World War I ships had to rely on their lookouts' eyes for detection of enemy warships, and primitive hydrophones for submarine detection, today warships bristle with underwater, surface and air detection equipment. Information is fed to an array of computers which take much of the effort out of decision-making. This same dependence on electronic improvements to men's basic detection and decision-making equipment also marks today's land and air forces.

The one wholly new weapon to emerge during the 20th century is, of course, the aircraft. (The first true aircraft flew on 17 December 1903). Balloons had been used for aerial observation as early as the Battle of Fleurus in 1794, and in the 19th century in the American Civil War (1861-5), the Franco-Prussian War (1870-1) and in various colonial wars fought by the British in the last quarter of the 19th century. Logical development of the spherical balloon into the cigar-shaped dirigible, combined with petrol motors to provide propulsion, produced the Zeppelin type of lighter-than-air craft which caused so

Below : This private from Company K, 8th Louisiana Infantry Regiment is holding a calibre .58 Springfield rifled musket with an 18in bayonet.

Above: A rather romantic picture of the effectiveness of a cavalry charge during the Boer War. In reality, the machine gun in the foreground would have brought such a charge to a rapid end.

much discussion during and after World War I. However, as a military weapon, the airship was of limited use, its vast size and vulnerable gas tanks making it extremely hazardous to fly in combat.

The true master of the skies was destined to be the heavier-than-air craft, which sustains itself in the air by aerodynamic lift rather than the 'buoyancy' of lighter-than-air craft. Progress with aircraft was swift during World War I. In 1914 no specific types of aircraft existed; anything that could fly was used for reconnaissance and artillery spotting. By 1918 a whole range of aircraft was in existence. These varied from small, single-engined fighters intended to keep the skies clear of enemy planes, through various reconnaissance and spotter types and light and 'heavy' bombers to the giant German bombers produced in the closing stages of the war.

Between the two world wars the development of fighting aircraft was steady. By the beginning of World War II most of the important combatants had air forces equipped with monoplanes fitted with retractable undercarriages. These were vastly superior to those of 1918. Moreover, whereas aircraft in World War I had been mostly adjuncts to the land forces, by World War II air power had evolved into an independent strategic weapon, with the British and Americans in particular conducting energetic and, at times, very effective campaigns against Germany and Japan from the air.

More radical changes were on the way by the end of World War II, however, in the form of guided missiles and electronic aids (the German V-2 and the radar detection and jamming gear deployed by Great Britain, the United States and Germany in particular), and a new method of propulsion (the jet engine pioneered by Great Britain and Germany).

The development of jet aircraft has been very rapid in the last 30 years, but the most spectacular advances have been in the field of avionics, the airborne electronics that consume more than half the aircraft's 'flyaway' cost and provide it with all the detection, control and jamming gear to enable it to fight in the type of war any future conflict will be.

The avionics side is also of key importance in the development of guided missiles, both the small, infra-red homing missiles used by fighters to destroy other aircraft, and the vast intercontinental ballistic missiles with their inertial guidance systems and multiple nuclear warheads.

Weapons, then, fall into three basic categories: before the invention of gunpowder, after the invention of gunpowder, and after the invention of the internal combustion engine. Each of these three periods had been significantly shorter than its predecessor, but of significantly greater impact on world history. The weapons of the pre-gunpowder age limited men to killing with shock or short-range missile implements that severely restricted their ability to wage any but relatively insignificant wars in terms of racial survival. The weapons of the post-gunpowder age gave men far greater destructive potential, with their ability to kill considerably extended. The weapons of the post-internal combustion engine era have opened up the possibility of racial destruction by weapons of enormous power and range, self-guiding and self-locomotive.

SMALL ARMS & AMMUNITION

The term 'small arms' is properly defined as the type of weapon carried and used by the individual fighting man, although by common usage this definition has now been extended to include the machine guns used as organic weapons by infantry units. We are here concerned with the firearms that have over the last five or six centuries come to replace the variety of spears, bows and cutting weapons used for millenia before that by individual soldiers.

The early firearms were singularly inefficient weapons, expensive to produce and uncertain in their military applications; it might indeed be said that the most important aspect of these early firearms was the psychological impact that the use of 'new technology' made on opponents. Time, however, brought advances in the reliability and accuracy of weapons, leading to the introduction of new tactics, and culminating in the development of volley-firing by massed ranks of infantry. With this last progression the development of the relatively short-ranged musket type of weapon had reached its peak.

Small arms development from that point concentrated on the enhanced accuracy of rifled barrels, and speed of fire. Advances in the field of ballistics and in industrial capabilities made rifling a matter of course, and the invention of the modern magazine and bolt action made rapid fire possible towards the end of the 19th century. Since then there had been further rapid advances in the production of self-loading weapons, and in the invention of fully automatic weapons such as the machine gun and sub-machine gun, giving small units of infantry the capability of producing the same volume of fire as that of a battalion of infantry only a century before.

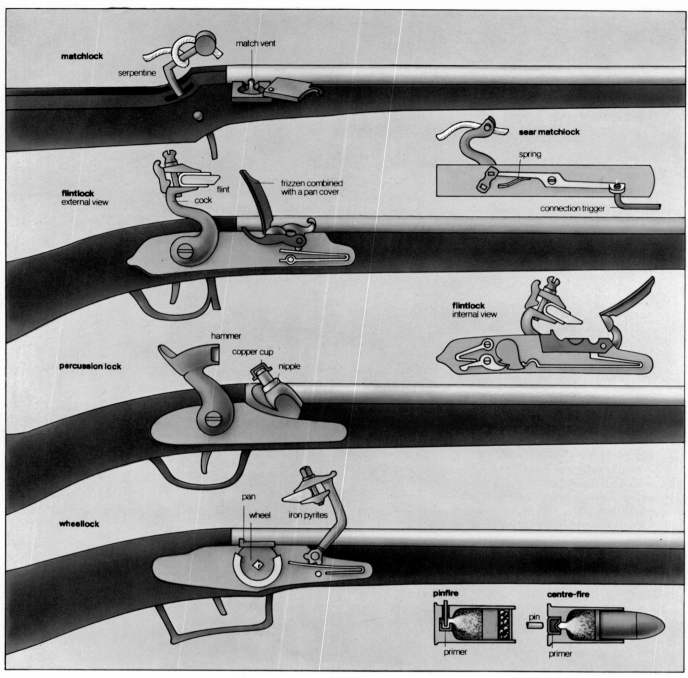

matchlock
serpentine
match vent

sear matchlock
spring
connection trigger

flintlock
external view
flint
cock
frizzen combined with a pan cover

flintlock
internal view

percussion lock
hammer
copper cup
nipple

wheellock
pan
wheel
iron pyrites

pinfire
primer

centre-fire
pin
primer

Six types of firing mechanism.
Matchlock : In the early serpentine matchlock, a length of burning match held in a hole in the head of the serpentine (red) is pulled down to light the priming in the pan next to the match vent.
Sear matchlock : The match holder is spring loaded and held away from the priming by the sear (yellow) until released by the trigger.

Flintlock : The external view shows it cocked, the internal view fired. The trigger releases the spring loaded cock (red), which brings the flint down, hitting the frizzen to strike a spark and lift the cover of the priming simultaneously.
Percussion lock : A copper cup containing impact sensitive priming is struck by the falling hammer ; a channel in the nipple transmits the flash to the main charge in the barrel.

Wheellock : Earlier than the flintlock but out of the main line of development. The wheel, protruding through the bottom of the pan, is wound up on a spring. Pulling the trigger lets the wheel spin and brings a piece of iron pyrites down to strike a spark.
Pinfire cartridge : The pin is struck to detonate the primer.
Centre-fire cartridge : a separate pin (part of the gun) strikes the primer set into the cartridge. Still in use today.

SMALL ARMS
Firing mechanisms

Firing mechanisms first appeared on small arms about 1400. Previously, small arms as well as artillery were fired by a separately applied red-hot coal or rod, or piece of rope soaked in some combustible material.

Matchlock The earliest mechanism was the matchlock, of which there were three types that came into general use between the fifteenth and seventeenth centuries. The first was the serpentine, in which the mechanism consisted of an S-shaped arm, pivoted at its centre to the side of the gun stock at the rear of the barrel. The upper part of the arm gripped a length of rope impregnated with a combustible substance and kept alight at one end, called the match. The lower end of the arm served as a trigger: when pressed it brought the glowing tip of the match into contact with a small quantity of gunpowder, which lay in a horizontal pan fixed beneath a small hole in the side of the barrel at its breech. The hole was known as the vent. This priming would ignite and its flash pass through the vent and ignite the main charge in the barrel.

The second type of matchlock was the sear matchlock, in which the match holder was under spring pressure, held away from the priming until the lever beneath the grip of the stock was pressed, bringing it down into the pan. This device was mounted on a long flat plate, inset into the side of the stock, known as the lockplate. Inside, the arm was linked to an intermediate bar called the sear which was connected to the lever; it was the sear against which a small spring pressed.

The final improvement in the matchlock was the tricker lock, or trigger lock, which appeared in the last quarter of the fifteenth century. It had a modern form of trigger, with a trigger guard, which acted vertically against the right-angle section of the sear, which was turned into the stock in a recess, and brought the match holder down to the priming against spring pressure.

The development of the matchlock meant that the soldier or hunter could keep his eye on the target while shooting, instead of watching the pan to make sure he was touching the powder. The matchlock had disadvantages, however; it had to be kept lit all the time, which was dangerous around powder and it was difficult to use in wet or windy weather.

Wheel-lock The wheel-lock was developed early in the 16th century. Its intricate parts, working on the principle of a modern cigarette lighter, were mounted on a large lockplate with the wheel roughly in the centre, its upper edge coming through a slot in the bottom of the pan. Ahead of the wheel, pivoted at the front of the lockplate, was a large arm called the dog, which held a piece of iron pyrites in its jaws at one end, called the doghead. The dog was held in position by a V-shaped spring beneath it. The lock was spanned (made ready to fire) by using a tool resembling a piano tuner's key called a spanner. This was placed over a square external end of the wheel spindle and turned about three-quarters of a turn, until the sear caught in a notch on the inner surface of the wheel. The wheel spindle was linked to the mainspring by a short

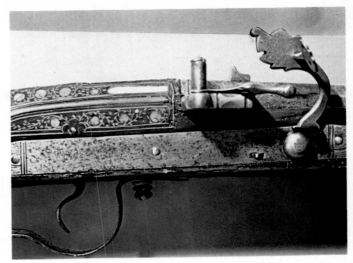

Top : A German 17th century 'trigger lock' matchlock gun. The match holder was brought down to the pan against spring pressure when the trigger was pulled, igniting the priming. This model has a pivoted cover to protect the charge in the pan until needed. The match was kept constantly lit.
Above: 18th century Spanish flintlocks. Pulling the trigger caused the cock, holding a piece of flint, to fall against the steel, opening the pan and striking a spark which ignited the priming, firing the piece.

chain. Priming was placed in the pan, over the wheel, and the pan cover closed. To fire, the dog was pulled back onto the pan cover and the trigger pulled. The wheel revolved rapidly, the pan cover flew back, and the wheel made sparks on the pyrites, igniting the priming.

The wheel-lock, while reliable, was complicated and therefore expensive. It did not, for these reasons, replace the matchlock in general usage, being reserved for wealthy sportsmen and certain troops.

Flintlock The flintlock was the most important development in firing mechanisms until the metallic cartridge breech loader.

The true flintlock (there were regional variations), called the French lock, appeared around 1610 and was in general use by the 1650s. The pan cover was combined with a nearly vertical hardened iron plate on its rear edge, called the steel or the frizzen. It was pivoted just ahead of the pan and held open or closed by a V-shaped spring mounted on the lockplate beneath it. The S-shaped arm, which held a piece of flint in its jaws, was called the cock

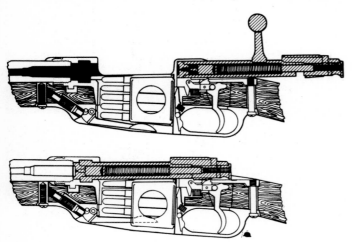

Above: Cross section view of a typical bolt action rifle. In this case the German 7.92mm Model 1888 frequently called a Mauser, and also a Mannlicher it actually combines the magazine of the Mannlicher with bolt features of the Mauser Model 1871/84. The rifle uses a five round clip which functions as part of the magazine and drops out when the fifth round is chambered.

and fitted over the squared end of a tumbler at its lower end. Inside the lock the mainspring bore against the front of the tumbler, while the sear engaged in notches cut into the rear edge of the tumbler. The notches positioned the cock at full cock or half cock. When firing, the pan was primed and the cover closed. The cock was brought to full cock and the trigger pulled. The mainspring pushed smartly down on the tumbler, which was released by the disengagement of the sear by the trigger; the cock was carried downwards and the flint struck on the face of the steel. The steel was forced back on its spring, opening the pan, and the priming was ignited by the sparks made by the flint on the steel.

Percussion lock Although first designed in 1805 by a Scottish clergyman, Alexander Forsyth, the percussion lock was not in production until after 1820, when the copper cap was perfected. Its extreme simplicity and its virtually waterproof design made possible the revolver, known to earlier gunsmiths but rendered impractical by the firing mechanism. The internal works of the lock were the same as the flintlock, but the external parts were reduced to an S-shaped hammer with a cupped nose. Into the breech of the barrel a hollow cone or nipple was threaded; over the end of the nipple was placed a cup-shaped copper cap containing a primer which exploded when struck by the falling hammer. The flash of the cap passed through the channel in the nipple and ignited the charge in the barrel.

Metallic cartridges Breech loading was as old as the earliest firearms, but was not practical for small arms until the development of the self-contained cartridge.

The first self-contained cartridge was the pin-fire, developed in France in the 1830s. It was a paper-cased cartridge with a pin sticking out of the end of it. The pin rested on the cap and was struck by the falling hammer to ignite it. The subsequent explosion of the charge caused the sides of the cartridge to expand against the walls of the barrel forming an effective seal. The centre-fire cartridge made its commercial appearance in England in 1862, and quickly superseded the pin-fire. The cap, now called the primer, is placed externally in the centre of the base of the cartridge, where it is struck by the firing pin of the hammer.

Metallic cartridge breechloaders continued to use a separate lock as the firing mechanism, although many designs were produced between 1860 and 1890 attempting to consolidate the breech-opening and firing mechanism. The external hammer was popular into the 1890s, but during the 1880s the hammerless lock, in which the tumbler was re-designed to strike the firing pin from inside the lock through the rear of the breech, became popular and continues so today on double-barrelled sporting guns and rifles. Several falling block designs for single-shot rifles combined the firing and breechloading mechanisms, but the most popular combination design has been the bolt action. The bolt is a tube with a handle on the side; the handle sticks out of the side of the rifle. A coiled mainspring inside the bolt acts against the shoulder of the firing pin. Turning the bolt by means of the handle to open and close the breech causes the bolt to bear eccentrically on the sear and to be cammed into the cocked position, although some early designs had to be cocked manually.

Revolver

A revolver is a firearm in which a series of barrels, or a cylinder with a series of chambers bored centrally through it, revolves about a central axis. In this way each barrel or chamber, containing a cartridge, may be presented to the firing mechanism in turn. In the case of the cylinder containing the chambers, each chamber is lined up with a single barrel as it reaches the firing mechanism. The revolver can be a pistol, a shoulder gun or a machine gun, and the first specimens appeared before the close of the sixteenth century. These early models were nearly all pistols and today the term revolver is taken generally to mean a particular type of repeating pistol.

In the earliest models it proved extremely difficult to ignite the charges. Matchlocks and flintlocks did not work well in any position other than upright, and designers had immense problems to overcome in ensuring that the priming charges did not fall out of their respective pans when the cylinder rotated. Great ingenuity was displayed in producing repeating priming systems which poured fresh charges of powder into each pan as it came to the top and lined up with the barrel, but none of these was consistently reliable, although the Collier revolver of 1818 came very close to being ideal. The Collier pre-dated most of the innovations which were credited to other inventors in the next sixty or seventy years, but it was never manufactured in any numbers and now only a handful survive in museums.

Pepperbox revolver The development of a practical revolver became possible when the percussion cap method of ignition was invented. With percussion caps, the cylinder could be loaded with powder and bullet, primed with caps and carried in the pocket or holster with reasonable certainty that each chamber would fire when the trigger was pulled. For simplicity most of these early percussion revolvers were what is now called the 'pepperbox' type because each chamber was also its own barrel, an arrangement which resembled a pepper shaker.

Above: Puckle's gun of 1718. Apart from its flintlock firing mechanism it had many features in common with the first Gatling gun introduced nearly 150 years later (below).

Above : When the trigger is squeezed it rotates on its axis (A), lifting the trigger lever into contact with the hammer which also rotates and compresses the main spring. Eventually the lever is no longer in contact with the hammer (B) which is now released and forced by the main spring into contact with the bullet. The trigger is returned to its original position by a spring.

1. Main spring
2. 'Hand' pivoted on trigger lever
3. Ratchet
4. Hammer (uncocked)
5. Rear sight
6. Bullet in chamber
7. Revolving cylinder
8. Barrel
9. Front sight
10. Empty chamber
11. Cylinder stop
12. Trigger lever
13. Trigger
14. Trigger spring
15. Frame
16. Stock

Development of modern types One man can be said to be the 'father of the modern revolver' and he is Samuel Colt. His models of 1836 laid the pattern for all subsequent revolvers and since then the multitude of designs which have appeared all over the world have been little more than variations upon the basic Colt. When the metallic cartridge was invented in the 1860s revolvers became extremely popular.

The present day revolver still closely resembles the original Colt, but there are many improvements, particularly in respect of strength and general resistance to rough treatment. Internally there are detailed changes, but the principles are the same. There are now two broad divisions of revolver types: the single action and the double action. Most early designs were single action, but now this style is retained only for target weapons or replicas. In the single action revolver the hammer has to be pulled back by the shooter's thumb to cock the hammer and rotate the cylinder round to the next chamber. Then all that is needed to fire is a light pull on the trigger. In the double action mechanism the trigger not only fires the shot, but it also cocks the hammer and rotates the cylinder in the first part of its backward movement. In the process of performing these actions it usually travels a fairly long way and the pull is quite heavy. This long and heavy trigger pull means that the weapon is difficult to hold to an accurate aim and so the double action system tends to be used for close-range shooting only. Many modern double systems can also act as single action if the hammer is cocked by the thumb so that the firer has the best of both systems, at the cost of a little extra complexity.

These combined mechanisms are extremely ingenious. In order to fire a chamber the trigger has to complete several functions in the correct order. It must unlock the cylinder, cock the hammer, rotate the cylinder, lock the cylinder again, release the hammer to fire the cartridge and finally withdraw the hammer slightly so that the cylinder is not jammed by the firing pin. A few revolvers have no thumb-piece on the hammer and are meant to be fired double action at every shot. These are usually special-purpose revolvers, where the designer tries to eliminate items which might catch in the firer's clothing.

Nearly all modern revolvers are six-chambered, because this is a suitable number to accommodate the popular sizes of pistol cartridge. Five chambers are often found on small pocket models and in the past there have been revolvers with up to 12 chambers, but these were impractical. Loading is by one of two methods: either the cylinder drops out to one side on a pivoted arm, or 'crane' or the barrel and cylinder unlock and tilt forward, exposing the back of the cylinder and the chambers. With each type an ejector expels the empty cases in one movement and the shooter simply has to drop in six fresh ones.

A great deal of ingenuity has been wasted in attempting to close the small gap between the cylinder and barrel which allows some of the propelling gas to escape every time the revolver fires. The additional complexity has never been found to be worth the effort.

The greatest asset of the revolver is the fact that it is the most reliable repeating weapon ever made. The mechanics of it are so simple that it is almost impossible for it to jam, and if a cartridge fails to fire, all the shooter has to do is to keep on pulling the trigger and another cartridge will be brought round to the hammer. With an automatic pistol the failure of one cartridge jams the gun.

Other applications The revolver principle has also been applied to weapons other than pistols. In the days of the first metallic cartridges there were several revolver rifles, but they failed because the rotating cylinder is not suited to firing a powerful cartridge and other mechanisms were better. But in the machine gun the revolver principle proved to be very suitable. Doctor Gatling grouped a number of barrels round a central axis in the same way as with the pepperbox. He then arranged a simple hand crank to turn the barrels and a cam system to open and close the bolts on each as they rotated. As a barrel reached the top of the circle a cartridge was dropped into its feed-way, and on the way down the bolt closed it into the breech and locked. At the bottom the barrel was fired and the bolt pulled open on the way up again and the empty case ejected. It was very simple and the rate of fire depended on the speed of turning the crank.

The same principle is employed today in the Vulcan aircraft gun. Nowadays the barrels are rotated by an electric motor and the ammunition is fed in by another motor but the rate of fire reaches the extraordinary figure of more than 6000 rounds a minute, at which speed the sound of firing is one continuous blast of noise.

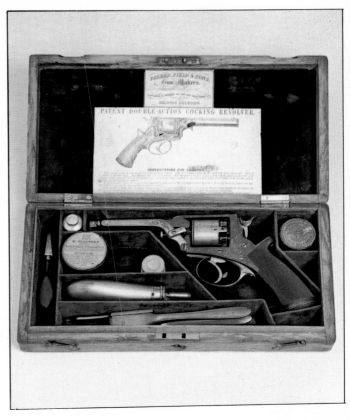

Above: A Tranter percussion revolver in its case with powder flask, maintenance tools and lubricant for the mechanism.

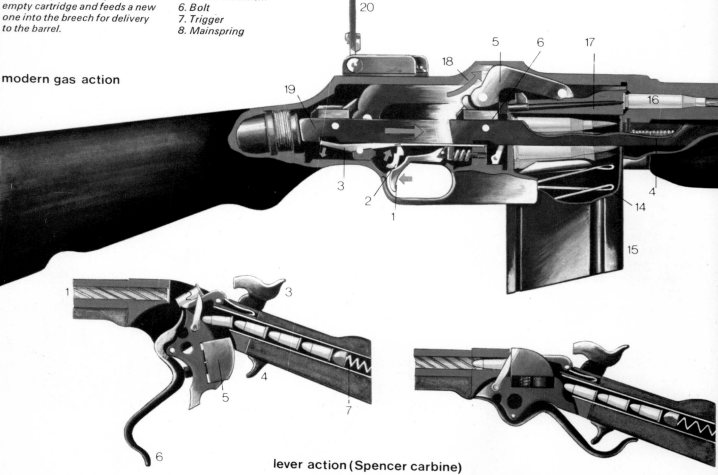

Below: A Browning gas action automatic rifle. Whe the trigger is squeezed it raises the connector, which in turn raises the sear, depressing the end of the sear and disengaging the slide. Driven by the piston spring the slide moves forward and the bolt lock is forced up into a locked position. The slide, still moving forward brings the hammer into contact with the firing pin which strikes the cartridge. The bullet passes by the gas port, allowing pressure in the barrel to force back the piston. The slide now recoils, unlocking the bolt lock. Meanwhile the cartridge is withdrawn by an extractor in the bolt mechanism. The bolt action rifle is unlocked by turning the bolt handle up and pulling back the bolt mechanism. The cartridges are dropped into the magazine. When the bolt is pushed home it chambers the top cartridge and cocks the piece. On squeezing the trigger, the mainspring is released and forces the firing pin against the cartridge. On retracting the bolt, the cartridge is automatically ejected.

In a simple lever action rifle, depressing the lever ejects the empty cartridge and feeds a new one into the breech for delivery to the barrel.

modern gas action
1. Trigger
2. Connector
3. Sear
4. Piston spring
5. Bolt lock
6. Hammer
7. Bullet
8. Gas port
9. Barrel
10. Front sight
11. Rifling
12. Gas piston (forward end of slide mechanism)
13. Gas cylinder
14. Spring
15. Magazine
16. Cartridge
17. Firing pin
18. Recess
19. Slide
20. Rear sight

lever action
1. Barrel
2. Cartridge
3. Hammer
4. Trigger
5. Breechblock
6. Lever
7. Spring fed magazine tube

bolt action
1. Barrel
2. Cartridges
3. Firing pin
4. Magazine
5. Bolt mechanism
6. Bolt
7. Trigger
8. Mainspring

Rifle

A rifle is a firearm which imparts a spinning motion to its projectile for greater accuracy. This spinning motion is caused by spiral grooves (rifling) cut into the inner surface of the barrel which engage with the projectile on its way to the muzzle. The rotation thus acquired continues during flight, giving gyroscopic stability which equalizes the tendencies to erratic flight caused by irregularities in the shape or density of the projectile.

The principle of rotational flight for projectiles is ancient: arrows and javelins were caused to spin in flight long before the first guns were made. Rifled barrels appeared soon after guns became small enough to hold in the hand, and the first ones were the work of unknown inventors in central Europe, probably Austria or Germany, in the late 1400s.

For the next three centuries it was mainly sportsmen who used rifles, though small numbers were introduced into armies. These rifles were of course all muzzle loaders, and the drawback to the muzzle loading rifle lay in the difficulty of getting the ball to fit the rifling, and of clearing the rifling grooves of powder fouling. Most muzzle loaders used a tight fitting bullet which was rammed or even hammered down the barrel, an operation which took some time.

The breech-loading systems which were invented in the 1860s changed the whole aspect of rifling. It was no

modern gas action

lever action (Spencer carbine)

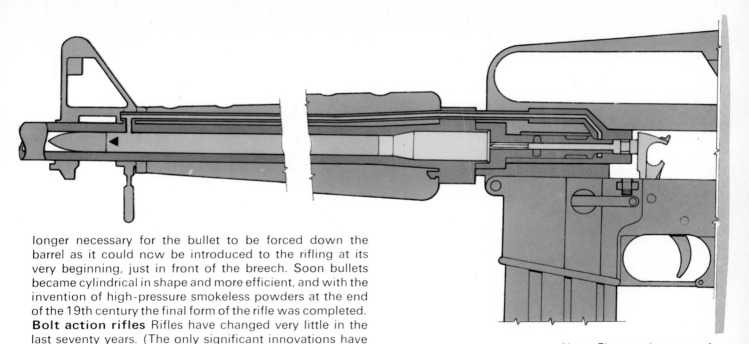

longer necessary for the bullet to be forced down the barrel as it could ncw be introduced to the rifling at its very beginning, just in front of the breech. Soon bullets became cylindrical in shape and more efficient, and with the invention of high-pressure smokeless powders at the end of the 19th century the final form of the rifle was completed.

Bolt action rifles Rifles have changed very little in the last seventy years. (The only significant innovations have been the self-loading systems and even smaller calibres.) All the older rifles were hand operated and they used a variety of mechanisms, some of which have survived today. By far the most practical mechanism, and also one of the earliest to be used, is the bolt action. With this type of action the breech is closed by a device very similar to

Above : The operating system of the M16. As the bullet moves down the barrel, some of the gases are channelled back through a stainless steel tube and into the bolt-carrier. This is forced back and given a twist to disengage the locking lugs from the barrel extension. The carrier then pulls the bolt back against a spring, which supplies the energy for the bolt to operate the firing pin. Spent cases are withdrawn from the chamber by an extractor on the bolt, and are ejected through the opened dust-cover.

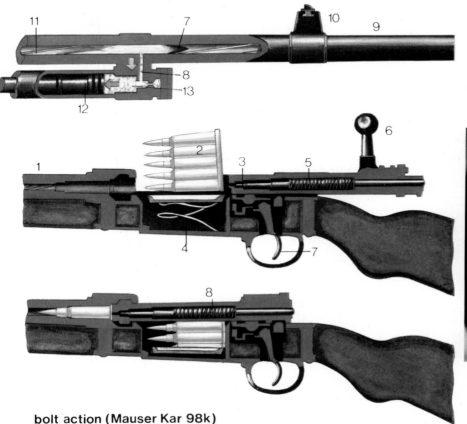

bolt action (Mauser Kar 98k)

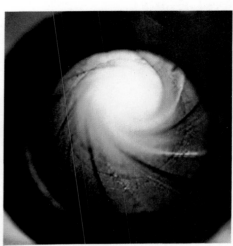

Above : Inside view of a rifled barrel, showing the 'lands' – the spiral ridges and grooves of the rifling.

the domestic barrel bolt found on household doors. This rifle bolt has a small hole drilled through its length to accommodate the firing pin. The action is arranged so that on opening the bolt the firing pin is withdrawn and cocked, ready for the next shot.

The first bolt action rifles were all single-shot, each cartridge having to be put into the bolt-way and the empty case pulled out and discarded. It was not long before repeating rifles were made, in which there was a magazine of several rounds of ammunition and a system of feeding

A corporal of the US 101st Airborne Division. The standard weapon during World War II was the .30in M1 carbine.

the rounds successively into the breech. Enormous ingenuity was displayed in the design of repeaters, but once again the bolt system has proved to be the best and simplest for general use. A magazine is placed below the bolt and the rounds pressed upwards by a spring. As the bolt is pushed forward by the shooter it strips a cartridge off the top of the magazine and runs it into the breech. An extractor pulls out the empty case. Speed of firing is entirely dependent upon how fast the shooter can operate the bolt.

Bolt action rifles are used in large numbers for sporting and target shooting, and a few are retained by armies for sniping. Practically all these rifles are of a similar size and weight, being about 10lb (4.5kg) together with ammunition, and they all shoot bullets of 0.30in (8mm) calibre or thereabouts. A rifle of this type can fire a bullet to a range of well over 2000 yards (1800m) and will be capable of hitting a target 2ft (60cm) square at half a mile (800m), while a precision competition rifle will do even better.

Self-loaders Normal military rifles are no longer hand-operated and all use some type of self-loading system which only requires the firer to pull the trigger. The mechanism is operated by the force of recoil or, more usually, the gas generated by the propellant powder. The firer has only to take a fresh aim and pull the trigger after each shot, and he can thus shoot far more rapidly for less effort than he can with a hand-operated rifle. Self-loading systems are more complicated and more expensive than hand-operated ones, but for military needs this is worthwhile.

There is a general move in all modern military rifles towards smaller calibres and lighter weapons. The British army rifle in 1880 was 0.45in (11.4mm) calibre. The present US army rifle is half that calibre, 0.223in (5.56mm) and half the total weight. It is likely that military rifles will become even smaller, though the limit must soon be reached.

Sights However accurate a rifle is, all the effort is wasted if the rifle is not pointing in the right direction. The sight is a very important part of any rifle, and as with any other precision instrument, quality costs money. For short range general shooting a simple arrangement of an open vee-shaped notch at the breech and a post at the muzzle will usually suffice; but for any shooting demanding a degree of accuracy the sights have to be finely made and carefully fitted. The modern target shooter uses a complicated set of sights with vernier screw adjustments which permit him to allow for different ranges and different conditions of wind. In addition there are coloured filters which ease the strain on the eye in varying conditions of daylight, and the size of the backsight notch or aperture can be altered, as can the foresight shape and size.

At night or in darkness ordinary sights are virtually useless but there are devices which allow almost normal vision even in these conditions. Light intensifiers or passive night sights have special lenses which can pick up the tiny amounts of star or moonlight, intensify or amplify these until the image is bright enough to be seen with the naked eye. Other special sights, such as the Russian N2P2 can detect infra-red radiation which is invisible to the human eye and use this to produce an image.

Shotgun

A shotgun is a smooth-bore weapon which fires a charge of small shot or pellets. It is primarily used for shooting flying birds or small ground game such as rabbits. The shotgun launches a large number of pellets which spread out to form a distinct pattern in the air, and this pattern allows the shooter to be less exact in his aim than if he were firing a rifle. The effective range is usually quite short, not much more than 30 metres or yards, and the pellets fall to the ground in a couple of hundred metres. The danger area is therefore quite small.

Most shotguns fire about 1oz (28g), or slightly more, of lead pellets. These pellets are graded in size by a numbering system which is more than two hundred years old. The smallest size has the highest number, which in practical terms is 8 or 9. The largest has the lowest number, and this is about 3. For most game shooting size 5 or 6 is preferred. With number 6 shot there are 280 pellets to the ounce (10 per gramme).

The usual criterion of the quality of a gun is the number of pellets that it can fire into a circle 30 inches (76cm) in diameter at a set range, usually 30 metres. A good gun, firing $1\frac{1}{8}$oz (31.9g) of number 6 shot, should put 240 pellets into the circle. This allows for one pellet every 3 square inches, and means that anything inside that circle is certain to get at least one, if not more, pellets. One pellet is sufficient to kill most birds and small animals.

The bore of a shotgun is described by a number which is the number of spherical lead balls of a size to fit the bore that will add up to 1lb (454g) in weight. Thus, the diameter of a bore which would accept a ball 1/16th of a pound in weight, namely 1oz, is a 16 bore: 12 balls to the pound, a 12 bore, and so on. The method is very old and universally used. The popular 12 bore is actually 0.729in (1.852cm) in diameter.

Shotgun barrels are usually tapered internally. A parallel sided barrel is called a 'cylinder'. One with a taper is said to have a 'choke'. Choking a barrel makes the shot fly in a closer pattern and so improves the chance of hitting at longer ranges when the shot from a 'cylinder' barrel would have spread so widely as to pass around the target. Choking does not increase the velocity. Double-barrelled shotguns rarely have the same degree of choke in both barrels. The right hand one, which is always fired first, has less choke because the target is nearer; the left barrel is fired second and has more choke for greater range.

Semi-automatic guns have a magazine and are re-loaded and re-cocked by the shooter moving some part of the gun with his hand. Usually it is the front hand guard which is pumped to and fro, giving rise to the nickname of 'pump' guns or 'trombone' guns. Self-loading guns use the same principle as a self-loading rifle and employ recoil or gas-action to operate the mechanism. Shotgun magazines can hold up to 5 cartridges.

Shotgun cartridges are all parallel sided cylinders, made of cardboard or plastic, with a thin brass base. They generate low pressure, by rifle standards, and the usual muzzle velocity for the shot is just above the speed of sound. This means that the barrels can be made quite lightly, and a good double-barrelled gun weighs less than 6 pounds (2.7kg).

Above: Shotguns have a unique loading method, known as 'breaking', in which the barrel is pivoted forward and downward. This action also serves to eject the spent cartridges.
In some shotguns the barrels are mounted alongside each other while others have their barrels positioned one on top of the other. On semi-automatic guns the bottom barrel becomes the magazine, holding up to five cartridges. It is loaded by pumping the front hand guard to and fro. This operates the loading and cocking mechanism and led to the use of the nickname 'pump' guns.

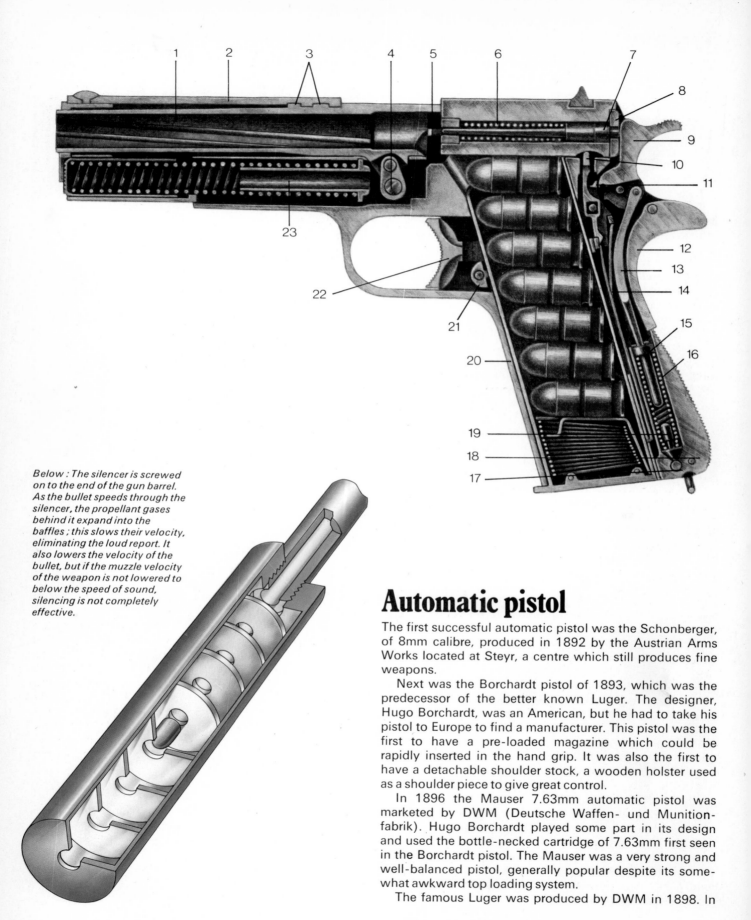

Below : The silencer is screwed on to the end of the gun barrel. As the bullet speeds through the silencer, the propellant gases behind it expand into the baffles ; this slows their velocity, eliminating the loud report. It also lowers the velocity of the bullet, but if the muzzle velocity of the weapon is not lowered to below the speed of sound, silencing is not completely effective.

Automatic pistol

The first successful automatic pistol was the Schonberger, of 8mm calibre, produced in 1892 by the Austrian Arms Works located at Steyr, a centre which still produces fine weapons.

Next was the Borchardt pistol of 1893, which was the predecessor of the better known Luger. The designer, Hugo Borchardt, was an American, but he had to take his pistol to Europe to find a manufacturer. This pistol was the first to have a pre-loaded magazine which could be rapidly inserted in the hand grip. It was also the first to have a detachable shoulder stock, a wooden holster used as a shoulder piece to give great control.

In 1896 the Mauser 7.63mm automatic pistol was marketed by DWM (Deutsche Waffen- und Munition-fabrik). Hugo Borchardt played some part in its design and used the bottle-necked cartridge of 7.63mm first seen in the Borchardt pistol. The Mauser was a very strong and well-balanced pistol, generally popular despite its some-what awkward top loading system.

The famous Luger was produced by DWM in 1898. In

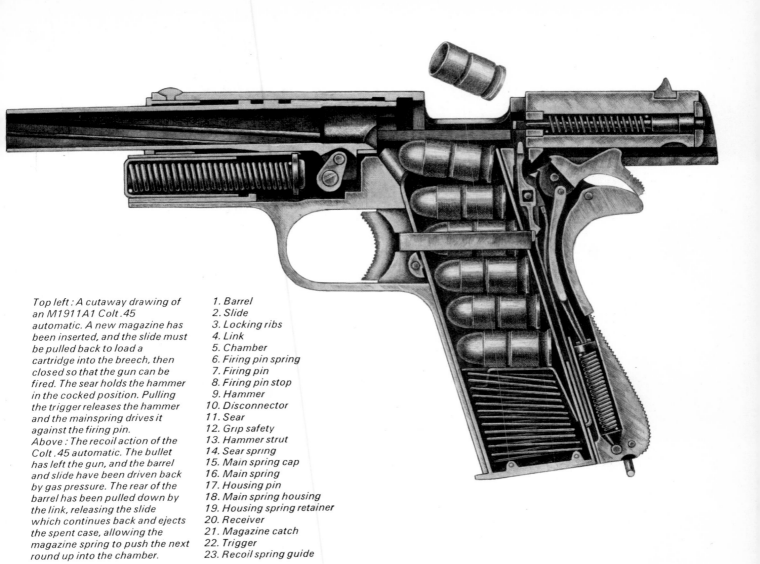

Top left: A cutaway drawing of an M1911A1 Colt .45 automatic. A new magazine has been inserted, and the slide must be pulled back to load a cartridge into the breech, then closed so that the gun can be fired. The sear holds the hammer in the cocked position. Pulling the trigger releases the hammer and the mainspring drives it against the firing pin.

Above: The recoil action of the Colt .45 automatic. The bullet has left the gun, and the barrel and slide have been driven back by gas pressure. The rear of the barrel has been pulled down by the link, releasing the slide which continues back and ejects the spent case, allowing the magazine spring to push the next round up into the chamber.

1. Barrel
2. Slide
3. Locking ribs
4. Link
5. Chamber
6. Firing pin spring
7. Firing pin
8. Firing pin stop
9. Hammer
10. Disconnector
11. Sear
12. Grip safety
13. Hammer strut
14. Sear spring
15. Main spring cap
16. Main spring
17. Housing pin
18. Main spring housing
19. Housing spring retainer
20. Receiver
21. Magazine catch
22. Trigger
23. Recoil spring guide

1908 the 9mm Parabellum became the standard German military cartridge; this was also used in the Luger and remained in service until the end of World War II in 1945.

In 1903 the Colt Hammerless .32 Automatic Pistol, designed by John Browning, appeared and was subsequently copied by a large number of manufacturers in Germany, Belgium and Spain.

The famous Colt .45 automatic of 1911 became the standard side-arm of the US Forces and is still in service. The self-loading pistol is now in favour as a military weapon, and many high quality weapons have been produced, such as the Walther P38 and the Swiss SIG 210. Automatic pistol magazines contain six to fourteen rounds, depending on the size and calibre.

To prepare for firing, the slide is fully pulled back, allowing a round to be placed in the chamber. It then moves forward, and the barrel is locked onto the slide by ribs on the top slotting into recesses in the slide. When the trigger is pulled the hammer is released and drives the firing pin forward through the breech face. The bullet moves down the bore and the gas pressure pushes the cartridge case back hard against the breech, which forms part of the slide. The slide goes back but is connected to the barrel, which recoils with it.

The underside of the barrel has a link connected to the non-recoiling frame. As the barrel goes back the link rotates and drags the rear end of the barrel down. The ribs on the barrel come out of engagement with the slide and the slide continues to recoil on its own; it extracts and ejects the empty case, feeds in a new round and springs forward to reconnect with the barrel. It carries the barrel forward and the weapon is ready to fire again. The trigger mechanism includes a 'disconnector', so that in order to fire the next round the trigger must first be released and then pressed again.

The advantages of the automatic may be summarized as: larger ammunition capacity than the revolver; quicker reloading, provided a loaded magazine is available; higher muzzle velocity and lightness and compactness.

Its disadvantages are its mechanical complexity, which means unreliability under adverse conditions, such as mud or sand in the mechanism; its closed mechanism which makes inspection difficult and detracts from safety; and its need for more frequent maintenance.

Sub-machine gun

The sub-machine gun, machine pistol, or machine carbine—all different names for the same weapon—is a light hand-held weapon which fires pistol ammunition both automatically and semi-automatically.

The first appeared in World War I, an Italian design known as the Villar Perosa. This idea was expanded by the Germans who quickly produced the Bergmann in 1918. The next development was the famous Thompson, which became famous as a gangster weapon in the 1920s and 1930s.

World War II gave enormous impetus to the sub-machine gun, and they are now used by every army throughout the world.

Operation All sub-machine guns work on the blowback principle. The gun has a heavy bolt and a powerful recoil spring behind it. This bolt is pulled back by hand and held by the trigger sear. On firing it flies forward and collects a round from the magazine, pushing it into the chamber. On the face of the bolt is a fixed firing pin; as the round enters the chamber it seats into place and the fixed firing pin crushes the cap and fires the propellant. The mass and momentum of the bolt holds the case in the chamber until the bullet has left the muzzle, and then the bolt begins to move backwards under the influence of the energy from the cartridge case. By the time the case is pulled clear of the chamber the barrel pressure has dropped to a safe level and the bolt is now compressing its recoil spring. At the rearward limit of its travel it is either held by the sear until another shot is required, or it flies forward again to repeat the cycle.

Only low powered rounds can be used since more powerful ammunition would require an enormously heavy

Above : The Russian PPSh-41 sub-machine gun, designed by Shpagin. Used extensively in World War II, it fired 7.62mm ammunition, 71 rounds being carried in a circular magazine.

Below : The Sterling sub-machine gun, which superseded the British Sten gun, incorporates a 30-round magazine feeding from the left and a collapsible butt, and weighs about 6lb (2.7kg).

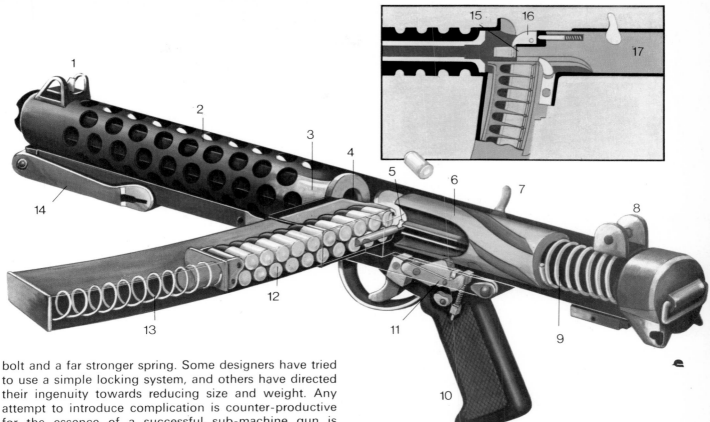

bolt and a far stronger spring. Some designers have tried to use a simple locking system, and others have directed their ingenuity towards reducing size and weight. Any attempt to introduce complication is counter-productive for the essence of a successful sub-machine gun is simplicity, cheapness and low weight. Their effective range is about 100 metres and they are not intended for precision shooting.

Ammunition All sub-machine guns fire pistol ammunition. The Thompson was made for the American .45in ACP rimless cartridge, which has been the standard US Army pistol round since the beginning of the century. In the Thompson models this ammunition was held in a circular drum of 50 rounds or a 20-round box magazine. The Soviets and their allies standardized on the Russian 7.62mm pistol round, which fires a fairly light bullet at a reasonably high velocity. The wartime Russian sub-machine gun, the PPSh-41, carried 71 rounds in another type of circular drum, similar to the Thompson, or 35 in a box magazine. The other European nations have, almost without exception, used some form of 9mm ammunition, generally 9mm Parabellum. The magazines for this round have been simple boxes and the only vagaries have been in the direction of the feed.

All these magazines hold twenty or thirty rounds, though some manufacturers offer other sizes to suit the customers' requirements.

The original sub-machine guns were made in the traditional gun style with long wooden stocks, bodies machined with solid sights, and often long barrels and complicated trigger mechanisms. Modern guns are made from steel pressings and plastic and in most models the only machining is in the bolt and barrel. This type of gun is cheap, costing less than half as much as a rifle, and with a comparatively short service life. Almost all designs now have folding butts and a few are so compact that when folded the weapon is little larger than a big pistol.

Above : A Sterling sub-machine gun ; simple and robust, it is blowback operated. When a round is fired the propellant gas pressure accelerates the bullet, and also the case and bolt, in opposite directions. The empty case, held against the bolt by the extractor, is carried back until it strikes the ejector.

1. *Foresight*
2. *Barrel casing*
3. *Barrel*
4. *Chamber*
5. *Ejector*
6. *Bolt*
7. *Cocking handle*
8. *Backsight*
9. *Return spring*
10. *Pistol grip*
11. *Trigger mechanism*
12. *Magazine*
13. *Magazine spring*
14. *Butt (shown folded)*
15. *Firing pin*
16. *Extractor*
17. *Bolt*

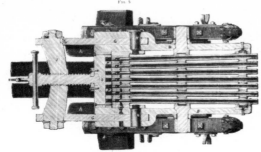

FIG. 5.—SECTIONAL PLAN OF FRENCH MITRAILLEUSE.
(WITH THE CARTRIDGES IN THE BARRELS AND THE CLOSER SCREWED HOME.)

Top : A cutaway view of a French machine gun used in the Franco-Prussian war of 1870, showing seven barrels loaded and with the breech screwed shut.
Centre: The American Gatling gun of the late 19th century.
Bottom : Sir Hiram Maxim is depicted with his most famous invention, the fully automatic machine gun, or Maxim gun.

Machine gun

The first really successful rapid fire gun was that of Dr. Gatling. It was a multi-barrel weapon with the barrels rotating around a central axis and each firing in turn. It was first demonstrated in 1862 and eventually was used all over the world, remaining in service with the United States Army until 1911. It was manually operated and the complete cycle of operations was carried out by the operator rotating a crank.

Late nineteenth-century colonial campaigns had shown what an MG (machine gun) could do to native troops moving in the open, and the Russo-Japanese War of 1904-5 updated the lesson for more advanced troops. In particular it showed the enormous advantage a very small dug-in MG-equipped force had over a much larger one without the weapon. Both Russians and Japanese used European guns and both fought from entrenchments. In many ways this war was an ideal dress-rehearsal for 1914 yet scant notice was taken by many who should have known better.

The German Army studied employment of machine guns with great interest. In 1908 the Military Estimates allotted 14 million marks (£700,000) to MG development and production of guns was pushed ahead as fast as possible. By the end of 1908, every one of the 200-plus infantry regiments in the German Empire had its Maschinengewehr-Kompanie (MG Company) of six guns under the centralized control of the regimental CO, i.e. the MGs were not parcelled out among the three battalions as was the practice everywhere else. There were also an increasing number of MG Abteilungen (detachments) at the disposal of army corps commanders. By 1914 Germany had more machine guns (12,500) in service than Russia, Britain and France put together.

A peculiarity of World War 1 was that very nearly all armies used one machine gun system. This was the Maxim, and its universal application was a monument to the original inventive genius of a self-taught American electrical engineer—Hiram Stevens Maxim.

The Maxim gun differed from all its predecessors in that the power to carry out the cycle of operations, that is feeding, chambering, locking, firing, unlocking, extraction and ejection, and cocking, all came from energy contained within the propellant and needed no external source of energy, such as hand operation. Maxim's gun was sold all over the world, and was used by all the major powers. It was operated by the recoil of the barrel and lock (breech block) caused by the gas pressure. This principle is still used in a high proportion of modern machine guns and it results in a sturdy weapon with a high rate of fire. It has proved to be particularly successful when used in armoured fighting vehicles because there are no toxic fumes emitted in to the crew compartment.

After the success of the Maxim gun in the Russo-Japanese War, minor design modifications were made and it was mass produced at the arsenal of Spandau, near Berlin. The arsenal labelled its products with a brass plate giving type, year of manufacture and the name Spandau. British soldiers seeing captured weapons assumed that Spandau was the gun's name and so an early Great War legend was born.

To give some idea of how effective this MG deployment could be, the 27th US Infantry Division was pinned down all day on 29th September 1918 by MGs alone. On 20th November 1917 51st Highland Division went 'over the top' but was unable to advance for several hours because of only three German MGs.

The German Model 1908 Maxim of 7.92mm (.312in) calibre was more correctly known as Maschinengewehr 08, or sometimes schweres Maschinengewehr 08, the main authorized abbreviation being MG08. The MG08 was heavy; the gun alone weighed 58lb 5oz (26.4kg) and it was mounted on a clumsy and rigid mount of consider-able complexity called the Schlitten or 'sledge'. This added another 70lb (32kg) so that the complete gun with 7½ pints (4litres) of cooling water, sledge mount, a couple of spare barrels and a spare lock tipped the scales at 137lb (62kg). Not surprisingly a small cart was needed to carry it all. The so-called 'sledge' mount was also intended to be a crude toboggan that could be dragged by the crew for short distances. It was rarely used and of no help in trenches or mud. The intention behind the mount was good because it could be adjusted for height so the MG08 could be brought into action behind any reasonable piece of cover, as well as propped up behind a trench parapet. But that was probably the only advantage of the Schlitten; among its drawbacks was a limited traverse.

The Germans were forced to lighten the MG08 so that advancing infantry could carry it with them. The lighter gun was the MG08/15 – the 1915 version of the 1908 pattern. The outline was different, the barrel casing lighter and a wooden butt, pistol grip and trigger were fitted together with a bipod. With an empty water jacket the gun weighed 39lb (17.7kg), still too heavy for a really mobile

Above: A German heavy machine-gun post in 1914 armed with a 1908 Maxim of 7.92mm (.312in) calibre. This gun was usually mounted on a 'Schlitten' or sledge. The sledge added another 70lb (32kg) in weight so that the complete gun weighed 137lb (62kg) and needed a small cart to transport it. Between the wars, the German army moved away from heavy machine guns towards lighter weapons such as the MG34 and MG42, which could be easily carried by one soldier.

Top: US 2/Lt. Val A. Browning fires his father's invention – the calibre .30 Browning M1917 MG on 5 October 1918 only a week after the gun first saw action. Above: An 8mm Hotchkiss of the French 246th Infantry Regt. on AA mount. In 1914-18 French Regt. machine guns multiplied six times.

gun but an enormous improvement on the 08 model.

In 1916 yet another MG08 modification was tried. The sledge mount was replaced by a better tripod. Finally, in 1918, a 36lb 12oz (16.5kg) version of the 08/15 was introduced but suffered from barrel heating and was not a great success.

Russia took the Maxim in 1904 and kept to much the same basic design until 1950. The Great War model was the 1910 version which had steel barrel casing instead of the M1904's bronze — bringing the gun's weight down from 63lb (28.5kg) to 40lb. Even so it was a massive weight to haul around and the mounting made it a miniature field gun with a tiny shield and little wheels. This was the Sokolov mounting, named after its inventor Colonel Sokolov. It is still found in a few Communist countries.

The Maxim gun was followed by the guns designed by Browning, another American. Although Browning's first commercial machine gun, the model of 1885, was gas operated he was most successful with his 0.3in (7.6mm) recoil operated machine gun, presented in 1917. The American army adopted his machine gun as soon as it appeared, and it has been developed both in its original calibre and in 0.5in (12.7mm) calibre. It is still widely used in the larger calibre all over the world.

Britain had adopted the Maxim in 1889, but soon altered the basic layout. All early production models were made for Maxim at the Vickers works in Crayford, Kent, so this firm acquired a unique knowledge of the gun. By 1904 there was an improved version called the Vickers-Maxim. It soon became the Vickers. Higher grade steel and aluminium were substituted where possible, saving a third of the weight. The toggle mechanism was turned around and lightened. A slightly higher rate of fire was achieved, with no reduction in reliability or service life. However, plenty of pure Maxims were also made by both Vickers and the Royal Small Arms Factory, Enfield, Middlesex. Most were ordered by the Navy, but in the 1914 confusion over weapon procurement the two types continued and Enfield built Maxims until 1917. In most respects both Germany and Britain used the same MG throughout the war.

The British front-line gun was the gas-operated Lewis, developed in 1911 by Colonel Isaac N. Lewis, US Army, built in Belgium, and made under licence at Birmingham, Warwickshire. It was quicker and cheaper to make than the Vickers; six could be turned out for the same manufacturing effort as one Vickers, and it was given to the battalions of the expanding British Expeditionary Force. The Lewis gun introduced a new concept of MG use and became ideal for the front-line trench, easy to move about, easy to conceal, and capable of being operated as well as carried by one man. In fact the Lewis was the first widely-used infantry light machine gun (LMG). By 1918 each squad had one. This dramatically increased battalion firepower and made British infantry far more formidable than German, who had no comparable gun. There were drawbacks to the Lewis. It was susceptible to dirt and mud, the variety of its wilful stoppages and jams became a well known barrackroom moan, and the circular 47-round drum magazine took time to reload. But it worked, and the troops had confidence in it and that mattered most.

It also performed well as an aircraft gun with a 97-round ammunition pan and was one of the few MGs used both for forward shooting from the pilot's cockpit as well as on a flexible mounting in the observer's seat.

It survived the war, remaining in infantry service until replaced by the Bren LMG in 1939. The crisis of 1940 brought 50,000 Lewis guns out of store, mainly into Home Guard and Merchant Marine service for the duration. Although never held in the same affection as the Vickers, it was just as important.

The French Army never adopted the Maxim, partly because of an unwillingness to pay the required royalties and partly because they thought their own design to be equally good. This was the 1897 'Hotchkiss', named after the St. Denis firm which built the Austrian-invented gun its American chief designer had improved upon. The gas-operated and air-cooled Hotchkiss was the antithesis of the Maxim, but no lighter or smaller. The most noticeable feature was the ammunition feed system which used metal strips to hold the 8mm (.315in) rounds. Each strip held 30 rounds and acted like a belt, fed in horizontally from the left. In fact the strips could be joined together to make a continuous bar of up to 250 rounds. Despite severe criticism of this strip feed by other nationalities, the French never found any trouble with it and the gun was most reliable and robust.

The lighter form of machine gun used by infantry is considered best operated by the simple ducting of gas from the barrel to drive back a piston which unlocks the breech block and carries it to the rear. Gas operation, as it is called, has been used to power many famous guns such as the Lewis, the Bren, and the current American M60 machine gun. It permits a light, reliable weapon which, unlike a recoil operated one, allows adjustment of the power to cater for such contingencies as dirt getting into the mechanism.

The light machine gun used by infantry seems unlikely to change much in its essential characteristics but it is of interest to note that the larger 20mm type machine gun and those used in armoured vehicles appear to be reverting to the idea of using external power for their operation. This is shown in such weapons as the Vulcan 20mm gun and the latest experimental armour machine guns produced in America by Hughes, which are electrically powered

Development When peace came in 1945 few countries were concerned with further weapon development and for some time armies retained the equipment that they had used during the war. However events caused nations

Above : A Lewis gun on a British AA mount in early 1916 on the Somme.
Below : The Lewis .303 Light Machine Gun. Drum-fed and air-cooled, it was an American invention (1911) mainly used by the British Army. Range : 2,000 yards with auxiliary sights. Rate of fire : 500-600 rpm.

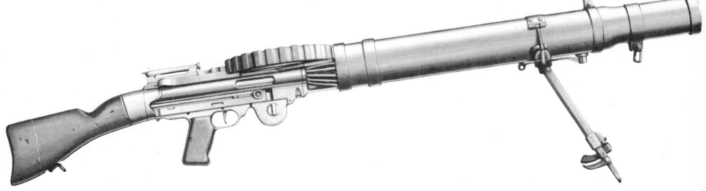

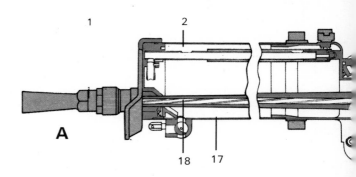

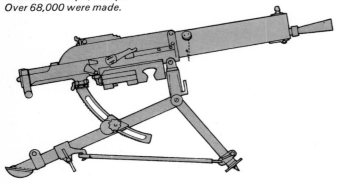

*British Vickers M1912 Mk 1 on
Mk 1VB tripod. Length 45½in;
Weight 40lb; Ammunition
250-round fabric belt; .303in
rnds; Cyclic rate of fire 450rpm;
Muzzle velocity 2,450fps.*

*US Browning M1917 on
M1917A tripod. Length 38½in;
Weight 32lb 10oz; Ammunition
250-round fabric belt, .30in rnds;
Cyclic rate of fire 500rpm;
Muzzle velocity 2,800 fps.
Over 68,000 were made.*

*Austrian Schwarzlose M1907.
Length 42in; Weight 44lb;
Ammunition 250-round fabric
belt, 8mm rnds; Cyclic rate
400rpm; Muzzle velocity
2,050fps. Schwarzlose means
'smokeless'. It needed only one
spring to the 14 of the Maxim.*

MAXIM COMPONENTS

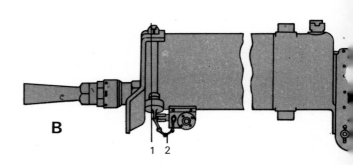

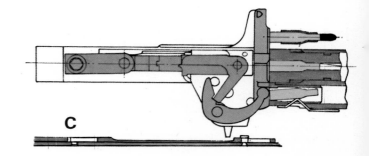

A Section of Maxim
1. Muzzle booster
2. Steam tube
3. Feed block
4. Side cams
5. Cover spring
6. Rearsight
7. Safety catch
8. Handle grip
9. Trigger button
10. Trigger mechanism
11. Crank   ⎫ Toggle
12. Connecting rod ⎰ Lock
13. Tumbler
14. Trigger (lock)
15. Firing pin
16. Ejector tube spring
17. Barrel water jacket
18. Barrel
B. Cocking mechanism
1. Foresight
2. Water emptying plug
3. Adjusting screw
4. Spring box
5. Fusee spring
6. Fusee pulley

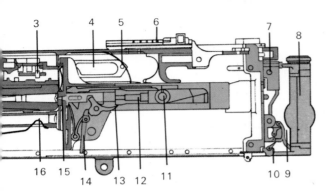

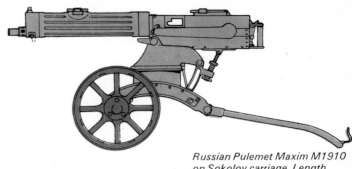

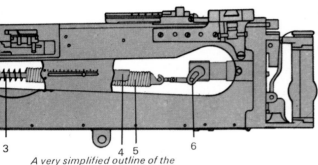

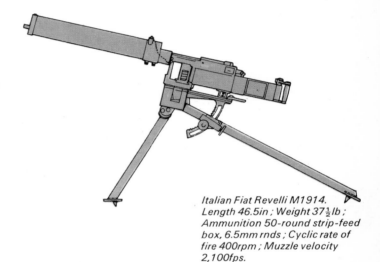

Russian Pulemet Maxim M1910 on Sokolov carriage. Length 43.6in; Weight 52½lb; Ammunition 250-round fabric belt, 7.62mm rnds; Cyclic rate 550rpm.

A very simplified outline of the complex Maxim action. The MG firer pulls the crank lever on the right-hand side of the gun to activate B which sets the lock and loads a round into the chamber when the ammunition belt is pulled across the feed block. Flicking the safety catch the gunner presses the trigger thumb button which by a lever pulls a trigger bar back to free the firing pin (in the lock) which hits the cartridge. Recoil from barrel and muzzle gases force the lock and B back. But the fusee return spring forces the connecting rod, after withdrawing the cartridge, to push the lock forward, feed a new round, eject the old and recock the lock which readies the firing pin. C and D show the lock closed and open.

Italian Fiat Revelli M1914. Length 46.5in; Weight 37½lb; Ammunition 50-round strip-feed box, 6.5mm rnds; Cyclic rate of fire 400rpm; Muzzle velocity 2,100fps.

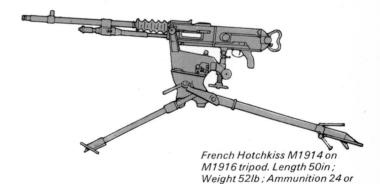

French Hotchkiss M1914 on M1916 tripod. Length 50in; Weight 52lb; Ammunition 24 or 30-round metallic strips, 8mm rnds; Cyclic rate of fire 600rpm.

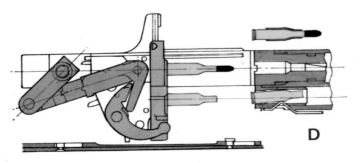

D

German MG08/15 on bipod. Length 46¼in; Weight 39lb; Ammunition 250-round belt, 7.92mm; Cyclic rate 300rpm.

Below right: A German MG42 machine gun which operates on the recoil system, and simplified representations of gas operated and blowback systems. In the MG42 the bolt is driven forward by the recoil spring when the trigger is depressed. The bolthead drives a cartridge into the barrel chamber and is locked in position by the locking piece. A further small movement forward of the bolt (red arrow) fires the round, the barrel and the bolt recoil, and the locking piece releases the bolthead. The cycle is then repeated.

Below : A Gefreiter (lance-corporal) of a Volksgrenadier battalion. He is armed with a 7.92mm MG34 and a 9mm '08' Luger pistol. The pannier carries MG spares and cleaners.

1. Flash hider
2. Front sight
3. Bipod
4. Barrel
5. Feed cover (in open position)
6. Feed arm
7. Feed mechanism
8. Rear sight
9. Locking piece
10. Cartridge belt
11. Bolt
12. Trigger
13. Pistol grip
14. High impact plastic stock
15. Recoil spring
16. Bolt stud
17. Sear
18. Bolt
19. Bolt head
gas operated system
1. Gas cylinder
2. Gas piston
3. Bolt
4. Driving spring
blowback system
3. Bolt
4. Driving spring

to unite and create integrated military forces but this situation meant that standardisation of equipment was important. Both main groups, N.A.T.O. and the Warsaw Pact countries, decided on a standard cartridge, 7.62mm and then proceeded to design their weapons around it.

For general use a light, robust weapon was required and one of the most popular was Belgian-made and this was adopted by many of the N.A.T.O. forces. The MAG (GPMG) general purpose machine gun uses a gas system in which some of the gas produced by the explosion of the propellant is fed back to operate the mechanism for loading, firing and ejecting the cartridges. The bolt, which is locked in position during the time of firing, is based on that used in the Browning Automatic Rifle which saw service in the First World War. The weapon has a rate of fire adjustable from 700-1000 rounds a minute. The cartridges are fed in by means of a belt made up of a series of metal links, and the feed system is based on that used by the Germans on their very successful MG42 machine gun. If a high rate of fire is sustained the barrel becomes so hot that it must be changed but clever design makes this a fairly simple task.

The American M60 also incorporates features from German machine guns but suffers from a number of drawbacks. Changing the barrel is not simple and on the earlier models necessitated the use of an asbestos glove; failure to change a hot barrel is likely to lead to accidents for it can mean that a round in the, breech becomes so hot that it explodes. The M60 fires 600 rounds a minute with the cartridges fed in on a metal link belt.

A change which began in World War II was the replacing of the single shot bolt rifle by self loading rifles, assault rifles and sub-machine guns. Although there are differences, all these weapons are essentially light machine guns intended to be hand held when fired. One of the most used is the Soviet AK47 which has a rate of fire of 600 rounds a minute; Israel developed the Uzi which used the larger 9mm cartridge. One of the most important newcomers was the M16 rifle used by US Forces which takes a smaller cartridge 5.56mm.

The methods of manufacture of most modern light machine guns have undergone considerable changes with the emphasis on cheapness and simplicity. In place of milled or forged pieces most of the weapons are made of die stamped plates, welded into position. Parts such as the butt which were traditionally of wood are now fashioned from plastic, and thin metal sheet is used for items such as the magazine. There have been experiments with disposable magazines but the idea seems to have been dropped. Most weapons are now designed so that they have a minimum number of components which can be dismantled simply and with minimum tools and effort.

The machine gun has proved to be one of the most appalling weapons of war in history. The entire concept of trench warfare in 1915-1918 was produced as an answer to the terrible efficiency of the machine gun. The tank originated as a means of moving across the battlefield in the face of machine gun fire, while aerial battle between aircraft would not be possible without the machine gun.

Above : A modern general-purpose machine gun, which is gas operated.

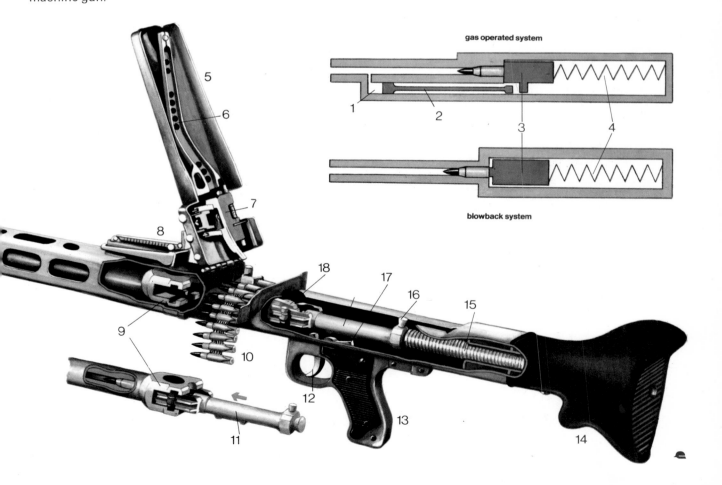

gas operated system

blowback system

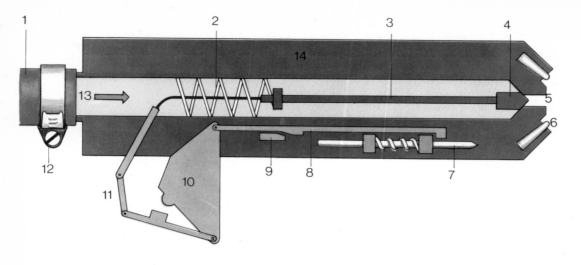

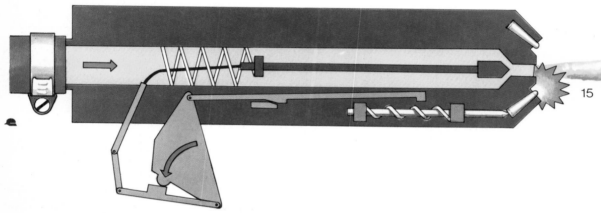

Above and left :The British Ack Pak flame thrower used during World War II. It had a 4 gallon tank sufficient to supply 10 two second shots of flaming oil with a maximum range of up to 50 yards.

1. Hose from fuel tank
2. Pintle valve spring
3. Connecting rod
4. Pintle valve
5. Nozzle
6. Igniter
7. Firing pin
8. Trigger bar
9. Disconnection
10. Trigger
11. Valve lever
12. Clip
13. Fuel under pressure
14. Casing
15. Ignition

Right top: The Ack Pak being demonstrated. The Vulnerability of the operator is clearly shown. Right centre and bottom: The British Churchill tank in action against a strongpoint. This tank, known as the 'Crocodile', carried its fuel supply in a small trailer towed behind the tank which could be jettisoned in an emergency.

Flame thrower

Fire has been used as a weapon of war for thousands of years; Assyrian carvings show towns being attacked with blazing torches. The Greeks had an incendiary mixture which was extremely difficult to extinguish and they kept its formula a secret for centuries; in the Middle Ages arrows with burning tow attached were fired into castles and besieged towns. The modern flame thrower dates from 1901. The German Army experimented with two types of flame thrower (Flammenwerfer) and in 1912 the first Flammenwerfer Regiment was formed. Flame throwers first saw active service in World War I in 1915 against the French troops at Melancourt and the British at Hooge.

In the World War II most armies used portable flame throwers which had a range of about 23 metres or yards. Larger models which were worked by a crew were available, and these could throw the burning oil 80 to 100 metres. The ending of the 'phoney war' in May 1940 was marked by a German airborne attack in which gliders were landed on the Belgian fort of Ebem-Emael and flame throwers used to subdue the defenders.

After the evacuation of the British Expeditionary Force from Dunkirk, drastic steps were taken to protect the south coast of England against the expected German invasion. On those beaches where it seemed probable that invasion forces would land, a petroleum pipe was laid below the high water line so that any oil released onto the surface could be ignited to produce a sheet of flame 100 feet (30m) high. The Germans would have had to penetrate this in making an assault landing, and the smoke from the burning fuel would have made a smoke screen that would have prevented observation of the beaches from the invasion fleet or its supporting aircraft. Another defensive system, rather more widely used, employed a number of nozzles at the high water mark which could produce a defensive wall of flame. If the Germans had managed to effect a landing they would have had to enter defiles and cuttings, leading off the beaches, and these could be flooded with petrol (gasoline) from concealed tanks. These flame traps were ignited electrically or, in the event of power failure, by direct ignition. Inland, large steel petrol barrels were dug into the roadside and after priming could be electrically ignited. There were some 40,000 of these positioned in the verges of the roads leading from the invasion beaches.

The famous 'Molotov cocktail' (a bottle of flammable liquid with a rag at the neck for igniting just before throwing) was invented during the Spanish Civil War. When the Germans invaded Russia in 1941 it was again employed as an anti-tank weapon, but there is little positive evidence of its effectiveness.

The British army was equipped with a portable flame thrower. In operation it acted in the same way as most of the larger equipment. A cylinder contained an inert gas — usually nitrogen — at a pressure of 2000 psi (13.48 bar) and a diaphragm was spring loaded to produce a working pressure of 200 psi (13.8 bar).

This pressure forced a petroleum gel out of its container with sufficient force to project it 50 yards (45m). Pressing the trigger ignited a magnesium cartridge which lit the fuel to produce a jet of flame. If required, the fuel could be projected, unignited, to build up a supply all round the target and then the whole lot ignited with a burst of flame from the back pack. About 10 seconds continuous burning could be obtained, usually employed tactically as 10 one second bursts. The equipment was acknowledged to be efficient, but the user with the large pack on his back felt vulnerable and knew that if he were captured, still wearing it, he could expect short shrift.

When the D-Day invasion of Europe took place in June 1944, the British 79th Armoured Division used the flame throwing Churchill tank known as the Crocodile. The 75mm gun remained but the machine gun was replaced by a flame thrower capable of projecting a tongue of flame about 150 yards (130m). Each of the three brigades of the division had a Crocodile regiment and they operated with great success, particularly in the capture of Bremen.

A smaller flame thrower was mounted on the infantry Bren gun carrier, and the equipment was known as the Wasp. It was used both in Normandy and in Italy where it played a prominent part in the crossing of the Senio in April 1945.

When the Korean War erupted in 1950 the American forces were very much on the defensive, and in an effort to hold up the North Koreans, a new weapon, napalm, was used, This was a petroleum gel with an aluminium based additive which had been developed during World War II. When dropped from aircraft it ignited spontaneously and produced a searing curtain of flame that destroyed villages, vehicles, tanks and most of all, men. It was used again in Vietnam with equally effective results; by that time it had been improved so that even if the victim jumped into a river the gel would continue to burn down to the bone. The use of napalm in Vietnam contributed to demonstrations by anti-war elements in the USA.

The flame thrower as such is a weapon of morale as well as physical effect. It can be used to get men out of strong points or bunkers, as it was in Burma and the Pacific islands, or out of disabled tanks. In a war of fast movement it is less suitable and the vulnerability of vehicles and men carrying it and its limited range makes its use less likely in future.

Recoilless gun

Conventional guns suffer from the disadvantage that when they fire a projectile the gun *recoils*, that is, it moves rapidly backwards. The bigger the projectile and the faster it is fired, the greater the recoil. The reason is contained in Newton's third law of motion which states that to every action there is an equal and opposite reaction; thus as the projectile is accelerated towards the muzzle, the gun is pushed backwards by an equal force. Early guns, such as those in the Napoleonic Wars, had no means of absorbing this force and every time they were fired they jumped back several feet.

The search for a means of reducing recoil began with the first guns, but the only practical answer was to take it up with springs and buffers, which are expensive. Modern guns have highly developed recoil systems which weigh many times more than the basic barrel and breech, and add enormously to the manufacturing cost and time.

The simplest way to eliminate recoil is to put two identical guns back-to-back and fire them at the same moment. The recoil of one will exactly balance that of the other. Unfortunately the idea is scarcely practical for other than a laboratory experiment, but the principle is the key to the present day recoilless guns. The idea was first expanded by an American naval officer, Commander Davis. In 1910 he merged the back-to-back guns into one with a central breech which was loaded by separating the two barrels. He used one charge of propellant and fired a shell out of one barrel and an equal weight of lead shot out of the other. The lead shot, which balanced the shell momentum, travelled only a short distance before it fell to the ground.

It was not an ideal arrangement, but it was used on a few aircraft in World War I. These aircraft were too flimsy to carry a large gun, but the recoil-free Davis placed no strain on the structure when it fired and the lead shot was no danger in the air. The largest Davis fired a 12lb shell, but the idea was dropped after 1918. One of its disadvantages was the great length of the two barrels.

The idea was secretly revived in Germany in the 1930s when a light field gun was required for mountain and airborne troops. Krupp, the German armaments firm, experimented with guns which fired a variety of different substances to the rear. It was soon found that the counterbalance could be something as light as a mass of gas, provided that it was given sufficient velocity. By putting a venturi, or rocket nozzle, at the back of the gun the speed of the gas was enormously increased and could then balance quite a heavy shell. The brilliance of the Krupp design, however, was the fact that it used gas generated by the burning propellant; it is this system which is used today. The gas may flow through one large venturi or several small ones. The variations stem from different manufacturing techniques for the breech and the ammunition, most modern designs using a single nozzle.

In the Davis gun the propellant charge had to be almost twice the usual size, but in the Krupp design the amount of propellant has to be five times the normal. The extra four parts burn up into the gas which is forced out of the nozzle to balance the recoil. Naturally, the cartridge case is very much larger and heavier as a result.

The design of the breech is critical and it requires much care to ensure that the venturi remains closed for about half a millisecond after ignition, to allow a proper start to the burning of the propellant. A closing disc is then blown out and burning continues very rapidly with the gas beginning to flow rearwards and the shell beginning to move forwards. The gun does not move at all.

Weight Since there is no recoil to be absorbed the gun can be made much lighter than the conventional type. The 25 pounder of World War II weighed 4300lb (1950kg). The present day Wombat recoilless gun weighs only 600lb (272kg) yet it fires a slightly heavier shell at the same muzzle velocity as the 25 pounder. However, the Wombat shell and case weigh 60lb (27.2kg) — because of the large cartridge case — whereas the 25 pounder shell and case weighed less than 30lb (13.6kg). If the Wombat were required to fire a barrage of shells for a long time the difference in ammunition weight would soon be apparent to the gun crew and to the re-supply organization.

Backblast Another difficulty is the backblast. It limits the range of the gun since if the barrel is tilted to give a high trajectory the backblast gouges a hole in the ground below the breech. The blast is also hard to conceal since it is powerful enough to blow down vegetation and light structures and gives a brilliant flash and some smoke behind the gun. For these reasons almost all recoilless guns are now used only for short-range anti-tank defence when the barrel can be pointed directly at the target and the large shell is an advantage in penetrating the armour.

Left : A World War I idea, put into practice in World War II, the Bazooka's 2.36in missile knocks out a German tank.
Below : A modern recoilless gun, the Swedish Carl-Gustav M2.

1. Plastic blow-out disc
2. Priming charge
3. Propellant
4. Detonator
5. Firing rod
6. Cam plate
7. Rear end cap
8. Firing pin
9. Venturi
10. Venturi fastening lever
11. Exploder
12. Cutaway of HEAT shell
13. Distance tube
14. Cocking lever
   (shown in locked position ready to fire)
15. Carrying strap
16. Telescopic sight
17. Barrel
18. Front grip
19. Mainspring
20. Trigger
21. Shoulder pad & gun mount
22. Tube supporting
23. The firing mechanism
24. Charge

Below: Development of the recoilless gun.

(A) Two shells fired from a single barrel in opposite directions cancel each other's recoil.

(B) The Davis system: Weight (a charge of lead shot) balances weight of shell.

(C) The modern Krupp system: Gas from propellant escapes rearwards at high speed through venturi.

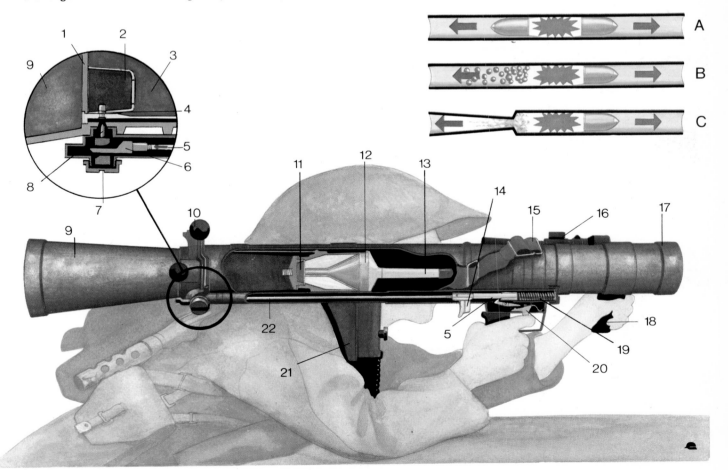

The bigger recoilless guns are dying out, mainly because their comparatively low muzzle velocities make it difficult to hit a moving target at long range and the majority of use is now with small, shoulder-controlled guns which fire out to 400 or 500 metres. The recoilless principle is also used to launch many small anti-tank guided missiles on their initial flight.

The first country to get a recoilless gun in service was Sweden. It appears that the Russians had some form of recoilless gun in about 1938, though no details of it have ever reached the outside world. This gun was apparently used in the Winter War against the Finns and reports of its presence led Sweden to begin work on a 20mm anti-tank recoilless gun in the summer of 1940. It eventually entered service as the 20mm M42, though its existence was kept secret until long after the war. A 37mm M43, a 57mm M43 (both AT guns) and a 105mm M45 infantry gun were later built with the same attention to security.

The most remarkable weapon was the 105mm Salvo Cannon M47, a cluster of 20 105mm recoilless barrels mounted on a five ton Volvo truck chassis. After proving that the idea worked, a service version was developed with 18 barrels on a four-wheeled trailer. A battery of four of these entered Swedish service in 1951 and remained in use for several years. For secrecy's sake, its official title was the '105mm Reserve Barrel Transporter'.

In 1953 the British researchers revealed the results of their labours, the 120mm BAT (Battalion Anti-Tank) gun. It was a heavy gun at 2,200lb (997kg), but it had a massive punch and it was an improvement on the 17pdr which was the contemporary infantry AT gun. In succeeding years the fat has been trimmed from it until the Wombat (developed from Mobat) version weighs only 600lb (272kg) and has the same performance as the original model.

For several years the shoulder-fired rocket launcher held the centre of the stage until people began to despair of ever making a rocket go where it was pointed. With this

disenchantment came a return to the simplicity and accuracy of the recoilless guns. The present level of sophistication is well seen in the *Miniman*, a product of the Swedish Carl Gustav Company, which fires the same 84mm shell as the Carl Gustav recoilless gun. *Miniman* is little more than a glass-fibre barrel carrying the shell and cartridge and a simple trigger unit and sights. The soldier places it on his shoulder, lines up the sights, presses the trigger to fire the shell, and throws the tube away.

After a slow and shaky start the recoilless gun has gone far beyond the wildest dreams of its earliest enthusiasts. It has its faults — principal among them being its appetite for propellant and the backflash that can betray its location — and it is not the universal solution to all problems, as which it was touted in some quarters in the 1940s. But it has its place in the modern armoury, both as a crew-served medium-range weapon and as an individual short-range disposable device.

AMMUNITION

Ammunition is basically any explosive device, from a tiny starter's pistol cartridge to a ten-ton bomb.

The word 'ammunition' is derived from the Latin *munire* meaning 'to fortify' and originally meant fortifications and the tools of war. From this stems a modern definition that ammunition is any military device which includes components filled with explosive, smoke, incendiary (fire producing) or pyrotechnic (illuminating) compositions. Such a definition, however, would exclude many other items, for example shot-gun cartridges, distress and signalling rockets, engineering explosives, chemicals such as tear gas, aircraft ejection seat cartridges, and even fireworks, all of which can be considered as ammunition.

Gun ammunition Ammunition for guns, whatever their size, comprises a propellent charge and a projectile. The two items may be secured permanently together (fixed), supplied as individual items and put together before loading (semi-fixed), or kept and loaded quite separately (separate-loading). The deciding factors are firstly the method of gas sealing or *obturation* adopted, and secondly the gun's barrel size or *calibre.* The charge is sealed off in the gun's chamber either by means of a pad fitted to the breech, or by enclosing the propellant in a cartridge case. Gas pressure from the burning propellant expands the pad or the case to seal off the rear of the charge completely. The projectile fits snugly in the barrel, thereby preventing a forward leak of gas. As the bore size of the gun gets larger so the charge and projectile become heavier and more cumbersome to handle, and it is necessary to load them separately.

A whole round of ammunition comprises the propellant or charge and the projectile or shell. For a typical fixed round the cartridge case is usually made of brass, 70 parts copper to 30 of zinc. The brass is moulded into shape in a series of stages, which toughen and harden the metal. By alternatively working and annealing (at about 600°C, 1112°F) the case can be made thick and hard at the base, to take the initiating cap and primer and to withstand the forces of loading and extraction; softer in the centre section, to expand and seal against the chamber wall; and harder at the nose so that the shell can be firmly crimped to it. Other materials, such as steel, aluminium and plastics, and cheaper methods of construction, are in use, but they have only a limited application.

The propellant may be in the form of small grains, short or long cords, or a solid block perforated by slots or holes to control the speed of burning. It is ignited by the primer. This comprises a small quantity of a very sensitive explosive which is initiated, or detonated, when the striker pinches it between the cup and anvil. The flash is passed to a few grammes of gunpowder, which ignites to set off the propellant.

The shell or projectile has three main components: the high explosive filling, the driving band, and the fuse. Shells are normally forged from a good quality steel, the final shape being the result of three or more operations and some machining to required tolerances. The projectile's shape is determined by a number of factors. For a stable

Above : A magazine clip of ten 7.63mm Mauser automatic pistol bullets. This type of gun, first made around 1895, is the oldest still in regular use and was for many years the most powerful pistol in the world. Some versions were fitted with a wooden stock and used as carbines.

Right : Comparison of artillery and rifle ammunition (not to scale), with details of the detonators, and, below, tracer bullet and shotgun cartridge.

fixed round with explosive shell
1. Fuse
2. High explosive filling
3. Steel shell
4. Driving band
5. Propellant
6. Cartridge case
7. Primer

small arms round with bullet
1. Gliding metal jacket
2. Lead-antimony core
3. Propellant
4. Cartridge case

primer detail
1. Flash holes
2. Gunpowder
3. Metal ball
4. Anvil
5. Sensitive explosive
6. Cup

primer detail
1. Propellant
2. Flash holes
3. Anvil
4. Cup
5. Cap composition

tracer bullet
1. Lead alloy core
2. Tracer compositions
3. Hole

shotgun cartridge
1. Cardboard disc
2. Shot
3. Rolled paper tube
4. Propellant
5. Brass end
6. Cap

flight it should be no longer than five calibres, for low skin-friction it should be smooth, and the base should be streamlined to reduce aerodynamic drag. The driving band is a copper ring forced into a groove cut around the lower section of the body. Its tasks are to provide a good gas seal in front of the charge, to seat the projectile in the bore, and to engage the spiral rifling of the gun barrel to make the shell spin. The shell body is filled with high explosive, for example TNT. This is done by pouring molten explosive into the cavity, taking care to ensure no empty spaces are formed on cooling. A ratio of 15% explosive to total shell weight is normal.

The fuse is fitted to the shell last of all. It is potentially the most dangerous component in the round, and must be designed not to explode during firing, when it is subjected to typical gas pressures of 20 tons per square inch (about 3,000 bar) and accelerations of 20,000 'g'. Yet it must function reliably when the shell strikes the target. Like the cartridge it contains an explosive train: a striker sets off a detonator, the impulse is passed to a less sensitive but more forceful explosive contained in a pellet, and the detonation wave sets off the main filling. Fuses are extremely intricate and are designed to respond to the forces of firing and flight. Their mechanism can be likened to that of a combination lock: it is unlocked by the special signature of the forces imposed by the gun and to no other stimulation.

For separate-loading ammunition, where the gun's breech mechanism provides the rear seal, the charge is composed of sticks of cordite bound together inside a cloth bag. Sewn to one end is an igniter pad holding a few grammes of gunpowder. This is ignited by the flash from a small brass-cased cartridge fitted into a vent in the breech block.

Semi-fixed and separate rounds are necessary on guns where a variety of shell velocities are required, for example to produce a special trajectory to cross an obstacle (such as a hill or forest) behind which the target is hidden. For rounds of this kind, extra charges are packed in several small bags easily removed from the main charge.

Other types of ammunition This basic design of an ammunition round is modified appropriately for other purposes. Small arms rounds do not need gunpowder in the primer, the small amount of cap composition being sufficient to ignite the propellant, and the bullet is made of a lead antimony alloy core coated with a gilding metal jacket. On firing, this jacket, which is slightly over calibre in size, performs the function of a driving band. Armour piercing shells have a core of steel or tungsten carbide instead of lead alloy. Tracer bullets contain compositions that burn in flight, making it possible to see the bullet's trajectory. They are used in machine gun ammunition belts interspersed among ordinary rounds to improve aiming.

For shotgun cartridges, the single projectile is replaced by a quantity of small lead balls (shot), their size and number depending on the range and spread required. As the gun works at low pressures the case need not be made entirely of brass, but only the rear portion holding the cap, which is bonded to a rolled paper tube containing the propellant and shot. The front end is closed by a cardboard disc, and the whole is lacquered to prevent moisture

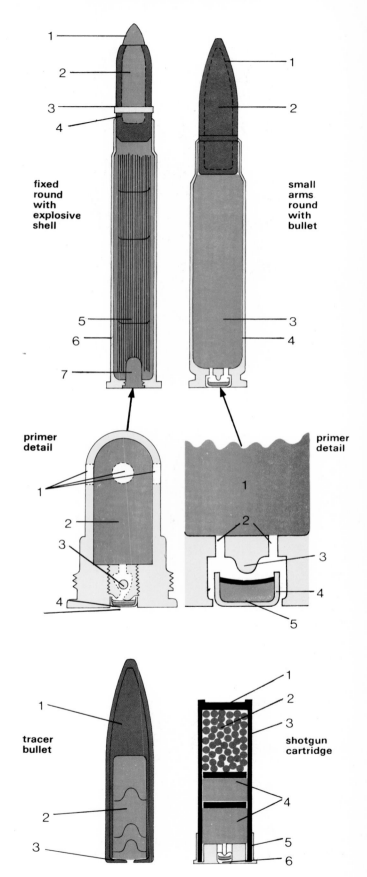

fixed round with explosive shell

small arms round with bullet

primer detail

primer detail

tracer bullet

shotgun cartridge

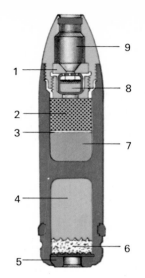

A Mk II shell with high explosive,
incendiary and tracer. All shells
have a tracer composition
though some are simply tracers.
The inclusion of incendiary in
the high explosive compound
gives a very high explosive
temperature – effective for
igniting petrol within the target.
1. Rear disc
2. High explosive filling
3. Waxed cloth disc
4. Tracer composition
5. Base plug
6. Priming composition
7. Incendiary filling
8. Detonator
9. Compression ignition fuse

getting inside. Blank ammunition is normally loaded into brass cases and the propellant, often gunpowder, is merely closed off with a cardboard wad and secured by pinching the nose of the case.

The design of ammunition for guns is complicated by the number of components needed, and the aircraft or hand delivered types are simpler. The aircraft bomb is usually thin-skinned, but contains a substantial quantity of high explosive, from 10 to 16,000 pounds (5 to 7250kg), and the ratio of explosive to total weight is often near 40%. Stability in flight is achieved by means of a tail and good aerodynamic shape. Fuses can be fitted to either or both nose and tail, and can incorporate delayed action so that the bomb functions sometime after hitting the ground.

Grenades may be hand thrown or rifle projected, and may be filled with high explosive, smoke mixtures, or tear gas. Fuses are usually based on a delay train, rather than on impact principles, as space is limited. For rifle projection the grenade is placed in a cup attached to the muzzle, and gas pressure from a special cartridge propels it.

Mines may be mechanically laid or placed in position by hand, and may be designed to cause damage to the target by blast or fragments or both, or may include a shaped charge to penetrate armour plate. The fuse can be made sensitive to a variety of stimuli. Most types, both land and sea, work by simple contact. Non-metallic materials are often used in their construction to prevent them from being found by metal detectors.

Armour piercing shells

The invention of the tank inevitably led to the development of weapons that would pierce its armour plating. Early weapons such as the World War I Mauser anti-tank rifle, which fired a steel bullet capable of penetrating 28mm of armour at 50 yards (45m); and the 2 pounder (pdr), 6 pr and 17 pr anti-tank guns used in World War II, were all of the same type. They achieved their effect by punching a hole in the armour, relying on their mass and velocity for penetration. This is called the 'kinetic energy' attack. Kinetic energy (KE) is the ability of a moving body to carry out work. An important point is that the energy is proportional to the mass of the shell, but also proportional to the velocity squared. Thus doubling the mass of the shell doubles the kinetic energy but doubling the velocity increases the energy four times.

To obtain the maximum effect the kinetic energy must be applied to the smallest possible area of the target and this means a long thin projectile with the maximum mass and minimum diameter, moving as fast as possible. The long, thin, heavy projectile is ideally suited to maintain its velocity as it passes through the air, but inside the gun the maximum muzzle velocity is achieved by having the largest possible diameter shell which will give the biggest base area for the gas pressure to act on. So there is a contradiction in requirement – maximum diameter inside the barrel, minimum diameter while the shell travels through the air and strikes the target.

This contradiction was resolved by the British invention of the 'Armour Piercing Discarding Sabot' (APDS) shell which was first tried in the 6 pdr gun and subsequently the 17 pdr. It has since been used on the 20 pdr, 105mm and 120mm tank guns.

In the APDS shell there is a central core, of small

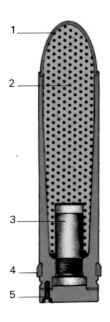

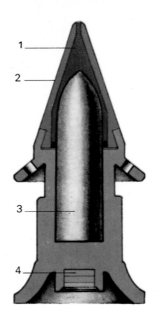

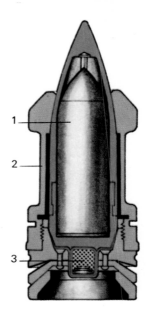

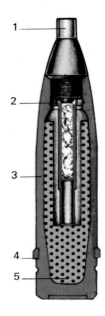

HESH
1. Outer nose casing of aluminium or copper
2. RDX plastic explosive
3. Base fuse
4. Driving band
5. Fixing screws

German APCR
For Tapered Bore
1. Phenolic plastic filling
2. Aluminium alloy ballistic cap
3. Tungsten carbide core
4. Tracer composition

APDS
1. Armour-piercing core of tungsten carbide
2. Plastic or light mangesium alloy sleeve or sabot
3. High-explosive charge

High Explosive
1. Nose cap
2. Fuse assembly
3. Outer casing
4. Driving band
5. High explosive filling

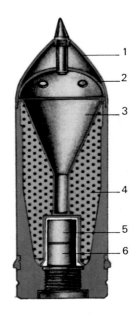

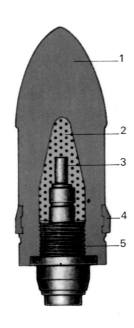

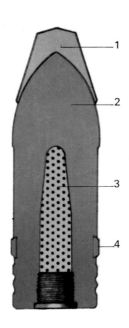

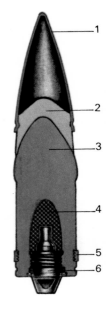

HEAT
1. Nose cap
2. Diaphragm
3. Steel liner
4. PEN/D1 charge
5. Exploder charge
6. Tracer

Armour Piercing
1. Solid shot
2. High explosive charge
3. Detonator
4. Driving band
5. Fuse assembly

Armour-Piercing Capped
(Improving AP shell)
1. Nose cap
2. Casing
3. High explosive charge
4. Driving band

APC+Ballistic Cap
1. Windshield
2. Cap
3. Body
4. High explosive charge
5. Driving band
6. Brass fuse and tracer

diameter, made of tungsten carbide which is a strong and very heavy material. This is surrounded by a light magnesium alloy sleeve, or sabot, which produces a large diameter when the shell is loaded. The force of the explosion breaks up the sabot into sections but the confinement of the barrel holds it together until it reaches the muzzle. The sabot then separates from the core which proceeds towards the target. Thus at impact there is a large kinetic energy contained in a small diameter solid shot and this produces an extremely effective attack on armour.

Unfortunately all kinetic energy projectiles need a large and heavy gun which although acceptable in a tank,

APDS

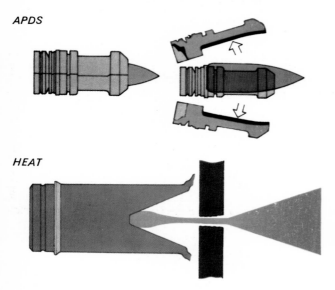

HEAT

Top: Armour-Piercing Discarding Sabot. A high-velocity shell. The discarded tungsten projectile has great penetration.
Above: High Explosive Anti Tank. On impact a lethal jet of molten metal and gas is directed through the armour.

cannot be used by infantry who will have to manhandle their weapons into and out of action. To meet the need for a light launcher, methods of attacking armour other than kinetic energy had to be evolved. Some other form of energy had to be supplied and the answer was found in chemical energy (CE) produced by the detonation of a high explosive (HE) charge in a shell. By this is meant not the explosion produced by a conventional HE shell which relies on blast and fragmentation but a specially designed shell utilizing the controlled application of chemical energy.

The first CE shell embodied the hollow charge, or shaped charge, principle and is known as the High Explosive Anti-Tank (HEAT) round. The front face of the HE filling is hollowed out to produce a cone. A liner of copper or aluminium is placed in front of the cone. When the shell hits the tank the high explosive is detonated by a base fuse and the energy produced is focussed into a parallel sided gaseous jet — like light from a conical reflector. The jet, with the now molten liner carried with it, has a velocity of about 18,000 ft/s (5500 m/s) and although it weighs only a few pounds this velocity produces a very high kinetic energy which allows it to penetrate to a depth of approximately 3 times the diameter of the cone. A modern shoulder-fired 84mm recoilless anti-tank gun will penetrate 250mm (10in) of armour plate.

The effectiveness of the HEAT round depends not only on penetrating the armour but on the energy of the jet, liner and fragments of armour plate which pass through the hole into the interior of the tank to kill the occupants, cause fires and destroy equipment. Unlike the KE round, the effectiveness of the HEAT round is independent of its striking velocity so that a low velocity launcher carried by a single infantryman can be a very effective anti-armour weapon.

An alternative method of using CE is known as HESH — High Explosive Squash Head. In this type of round, a large quantity of plastic HE is carried in a shell. When it strikes the armour plate, the HE filling mushrooms on the armour face, and a base fuse detonates it. This system does not go through the plate — the shock wave from the detonation is transmitted through it. When it reaches the far side it is reflected back, which overstresses the metal on the inside of the plate so that a large 'scab', often a couple of feet across, is detached. This whirls around inside the tank at high velocity causing casualties and damage. The thickness of plate attacked by a HESH projectile is proportional to its calibre and to produce a good scab on a modern tank a calibre of about 120mm is required.

Some countries — including Russia — use another method to defeat armour known as HEAP — HE Armour Piercing. In this the kinetic energy method is used to penetrate the plate and then an HE charge is detonated once it is through.

To obtain long ranges of engagement guided missiles will probably be used. These cannot use the KE effect and so will carry HESH in the larger sizes and HEAT in the smaller. The attack on armour is likely to rely on CE attack by missiles at long range, and KE attack from the high velocity tank gun at shorter ranges.

ARTILLERY

The original definition of artillery referred to the anti-aircraft, anti-tank, medium, heavy and mountain guns used by an army. Today such a definition is insufficient as artillery now includes weapons ranging from the American 20mm Vulcan to surface to surface tactical missiles such as the Russian Frog. Further to confuse the issue, tanks and aircraft now carry out many of the roles previously performed by the gun. However, because both tanks and aircraft have chapters devoted to themselves, in this chapter we will restrict ourselves to the original definition of gunnery.

Above : British 6in 26cwt Howitzer — Weight of gun 26cwt ; Weight of carriage 3.63 tons ; Recoil Mechanism hydro-pneumatic ; Calibre 6in ; Ammunition 100lb shrapnel ; Range 100lb shell 9,500 yards ; Muzzle velocity 1,409fps — 86lb, shell, 1,234fps — 100lb shell.

Gunnery techniques

The history of gunnery goes back to the early 14th century. Early guns were called vasi or pots-de-fer and they were in a vase shaped receptacle; an arrow, with leather wrapped round its stock, was stuffed into the neck of the vase and then the powder was fired by means of a hot iron applied to a touch hole. This method was used with minor improvements for the next 500 years or so.

As with the gun itself, the technique of gunnery developed very slowly after the initial impetus of the invention had slackened. In 1537 an Italian, Nicolo Tartaglia, published a treatise on the subject of gunnery. His diagram of ballistics (the study of projectiles) (see page 00) shows 'the visual line', which is our present line of sight (an imaginary straight line drawn from the gun to the target), and what he called 'the way of the pellet' is what we would describe as the trajectory.

The role of the gun in warfare did not become significant until the 17th century. Cannon were still largely ineffective against large fortifications, and naval battles were still

Above : An illustration from a book published in Germany in 1547 showing gunners calculating the elevation of a piece of artillery using a clinometer (left) and a quadrant marked with shadow scales.
Right : The anti-aircraft gun on the right is aimed at the helicopter whose track is calculated by the gun crew as it flies from AA to A. The gun is fired when the helicopter is at A, but is aimed at B to allow for forward movement of the target during the flight of the shell. The battery of two guns on the left engages the anti-aircraft gun by indirect fire. Information about the target's position is radioed from the helicopter to the battery command vehicle where it is fed into field artillery computer equipment (FACE) which then provides the necessary details for aiming the guns. Alternatively, the helicopter can radio information direct to the gun crew, giving the position of the target relative to the church which they can see. The church thus acts as an aiming point. The tank in the left foreground is being attacked by means of laser-guided shells. An observer illuminates the target with a laser beam and the reflected beam is detected by the shells and guides them on to the target. This tank is firing tracer bullets from a machine gun aligned with the main gun. When the tracer bullets hit the target the main gun will be correctly aimed and can then be fired.

fought on the basis of boarding the enemy ships, although cannon had been carried at sea in great variety (including breech loaders) since the 15th century. Land battles were, until the Thirty Years' War (1618–48), decided largely on the success of the pikes of the infantry and the lances and swords of the cavalry.

It is not enough to point the barrel of the gun straight at the target in order to hit it. That technique would work only if the target were very close and the forces of gravity and air resistance had not had time to take effect. If the target were further away the projectile would drop short, and the gun would therefore have to be elevated above the line of sight to an angle sufficient for the projectile to reach the target.

The distance between the gun and the target is called the range. To achieve a given range each gun has to be set at a different angle because of gun to gun variations in the diameter of the barrel, called the calibre; the length of the barrel; the weight and shape of the projectile, and the amount and type of propellant used to fire it. Even if identical guns use the same propellant to fire identical projectiles, it is extremely unlikely that they will achieve exactly the same range. The minutest variation between guns in wear on the inside of the barrel, for example, can cause a range difference of one or two per cent at the target end.

Once the projectile has left the barrel of the gun its trajectory begins to be affected by wind, air temperature and air pressure; and these will vary according to the different height levels the projectile is passing through. For example, windspeed and direction can vary considerably from ground level to 50,000ft (15,000m) which is the apogee of the trajectory of certain longer range guns. For modern guns, which can fire out to ranges of 15 miles (24kms) and more, it is important that each individual gun should be extremely accurately aimed and that all the guns in the same battery (usually six guns) should perform consistently. To achieve these standards all the variables, such as propellant and meteorological conditions, are carefully measured and recorded and the appropriate allowances made when individual gun ranges are calculated.

Indirect fire Up till the end of the 19th century gunners had mainly engaged targets which they could see. This meant that the guns had to have clear lines of sight to the enemy and they often had to be placed in front of their own infantry. The gun positions were thus very exposed and were vulnerable to being overrun and captured.

During the Boer War (1899–1902) the British gunners began to realize the importance of protecting their guns by concealing them but the foliage they used for camouflage prevented them from getting a clear view of their targets. A system of sighting evolved as a result of this whereby fire could be controlled even though the target could not be seen from the gun. This technique became known as indirect fire, to distinguish it from the established method of engaging a target by direct fire.

When engaging a target by indirect fire, the gunner receives instructions from an observation post, which is sited well forward of the gun position so that the observer has a good view of the area where targets may be expected to appear. The gunner selects an aiming point which he can see and he traverses the barrel of the gun to the right or left (with reference to the aiming point) by the number of degrees ordered by the observer. In World War II artillery officers were trained to pilot light aircraft so that, where appropriate, they could control the guns from the air, giving them a much greater field of view. This technique continues to be used today although the helicopter has now replaced the light fixed wing aircraft.

The indirect fire method of engaging a target is entirely dependent on good communications between the observation post and the guns. The observer passes target information to the guns by radio or by field telephone. The information will usually include a map reference of the target and a bearing to it. At the battery command post on the gun position this information is translated into gun data (range, gun bearing and so on) and passed to the individual guns.

A recent development has been the introduction of small digital computers into the battery command posts. These computers not only carry out, almost instantaneously, the calculations necessary to derive individual gun data, but they also store information about previously engaged targets so that these can be quickly re-engaged if necessary. The computed gun data is passed to each gun by an automatic data transmission system. In the future projectiles containing sensitive guidance systems may be fired from guns. Such a projectile would pick up, during the last part of its trajectory, a laser beam reflected off a target which was being illuminated by a forward observer. The reflection would then guide the projectile to its target, such as a tank, with pinpoint accuracy.

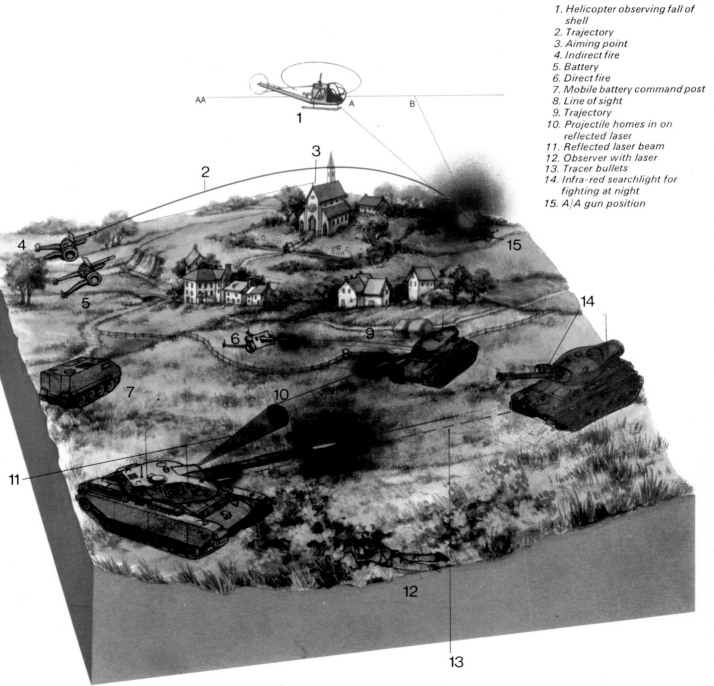

1. Helicopter observing fall of shell
2. Trajectory
3. Aiming point
4. Indirect fire
5. Battery
6. Direct fire
7. Mobile battery command post
8. Line of sight
9. Trajectory
10. Projectile homes in on reflected laser
11. Reflected laser beam
12. Observer with laser
13. Tracer bullets
14. Infra-red searchlight for fighting at night
15. A/A gun position

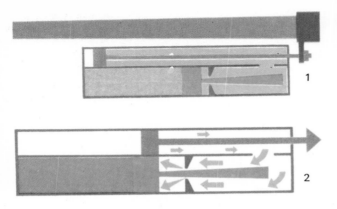

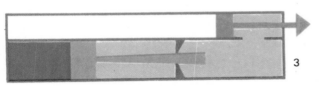

Field gun

A field gun is a piece of artillery used in the field with the army, and is also called a close-support gun. Such a gun must be mobile and cannot fire a heavy shell. It must be capable of rapid change of target, which means today a 360° traverse on a platform, and will usually be a gun-howitzer. (A gun fires with the angle of elevation of the barrel below 45°; a howitzer fires only above the 45° elevation, which gives a high short trajectory, capable of reaching beyond obstacles such as low hills. The gun-howitzer must perform both these functions.)

Until the nineteenth century there had been little development in artillery, and the gun would have been recognized by a gunner from a period two hundred years before. Guns were muzzle loaded; that is, the powder was poured into the barrel and pushed down with a ramrod, a wad was placed over the powder and the shot rammed down on that. If round shot were used another wad might be inserted to keep the shot from rolling out. Between rounds the barrel had to be swabbed out with a wet sponge to remove fouling and burning bits of wad.

After the experience of the Crimean War (1853–1856), rifled breech-loading guns on steel carriages became universal by 1885; dramatic improvements in fuses and powder were made as well. The experience of the Boer War, which began in 1899, was even more valuable.

After the Boer War the Royal Artillery set up committees to make recommendations for a whole new family of weapons, including the field gun. In 1901 British gun-makers were asked to produce designs, and in 1902 selected guns underwent trial. A composite design consisting of an Armstrong wire-wound barrel, Vickers recoil system and ordnance carriage, elevating gear and sights was adopted. An 18 pdr went into large-scale production and by the summer of 1906 seven British divisions had been re-equipped. Some 100 million 18 pdr rounds (20 pound shells) were fired in World War I. The gun had had the buffer-recuperator mounted on top of the barrel and had a unique single-pole trail (rear end) which could be lifted and moved to enable the gun to make a big switch in firing direction.

The French, like the British, placed great emphasis on the mobility and rate of fire of their field artillery, of which the classic piece was the celebrated 75mm, used by the Americans as well as the French. This was an excellent gun, with a high muzzle velocity and capable of a sustained rate of fire of over fifteen rounds per minute with an experienced crew. Unlike the British, however, the French were more concerned with long-range accuracy, and by the end of World War I both German and French field artillery was capable of firing with accuracy up to 10,000 yards or metres. British field artillery seldom concentrated on targets at little more than half this range.

The development of field artillery languished in the two decades following World War I, the real advances in artillery coming in the fields of theoretical research and tactical organization. However, the experience of Germany, Italy and Soviet Russia in the Spanish Civil War (1936–9) once again spurred progress in artillery. The need for mobility was reinforced by the anticipated necessity for field artillery to engage moving targets such as tanks.

Above: The 75's recoil system was an adaptation of the hydro-pneumatic arrangement used for heavy guns. Many attempts had been made to transfer this system to field guns but until the French 75 none had been successful. The 75 had two cylinders beneath the gun, one with a normal piston, the other with a floating piston and a throttling valve. The throttling valve and the exceptionally close fit of the floating piston were the 75's secret.
1. The gun at rest. Cylinders contain oil and air.
2. During recoil. Backward movement of piston in upper cylinder increases pressure of oil in lower chamber, forcing the floating piston forward.
3. Floating piston gradually closes the throttling valve, ending the recoil. Compressed air in lower cylinder forces floating piston back, pushing oil into upper cylinder. The piston there is forced forward and the gun returns to the firing position

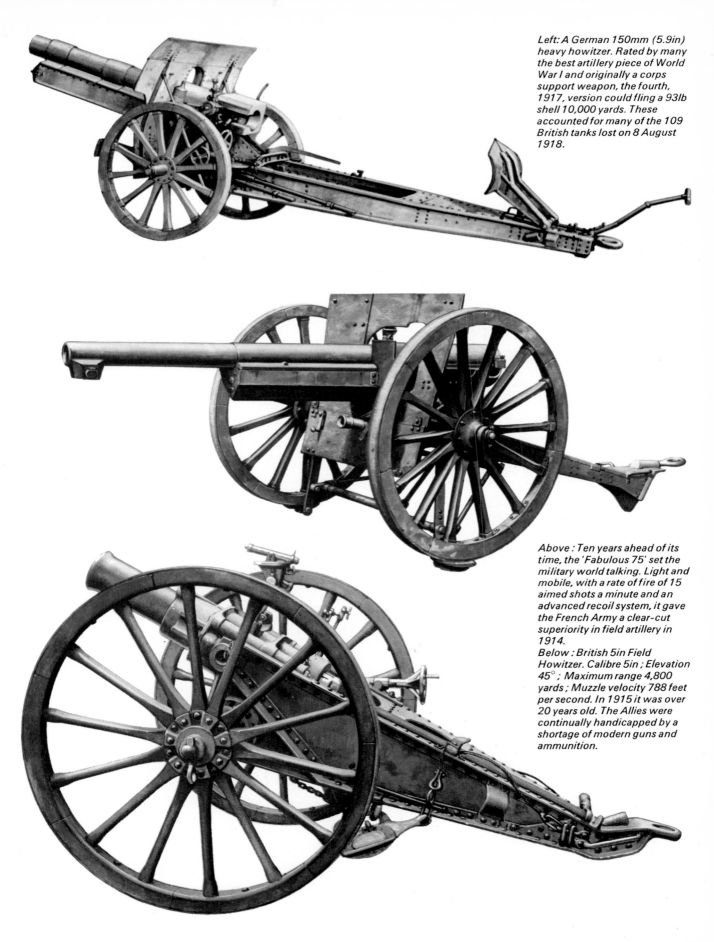

Left: A German 150mm (5.9in) heavy howitzer. Rated by many the best artillery piece of World War I and originally a corps support weapon, the fourth, 1917, version could fling a 93lb shell 10,000 yards. These accounted for many of the 109 British tanks lost on 8 August 1918.

Above: Ten years ahead of its time, the 'Fabulous 75' set the military world talking. Light and mobile, with a rate of fire of 15 aimed shots a minute and an advanced recoil system, it gave the French Army a clear-cut superiority in field artillery in 1914.
Below: British 5in Field Howitzer. Calibre 5in; Elevation 45°; Maximum range 4,800 yards; Muzzle velocity 788 feet per second. In 1915 it was over 20 years old. The Allies were continually handicapped by a shortage of modern guns and ammunition.

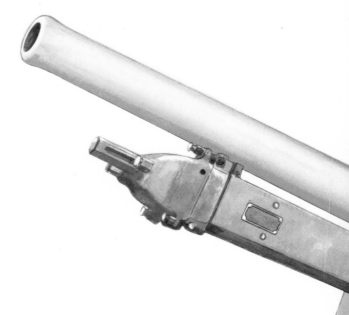

Above left : A Canadian 25pdr
(87mm) field gun/howitzer in
Korea (Oct. 1951).Sgt. i/c on
left holds cordite charge.
Left : A Krupp 105mm light
howitzer. The gun is manned by
Canadians and was one of the
hundreds abandoned on Vimy
Ridge by the retreating Germans.

Above : A 5.5in gun of the
Canadian 12th Bty, 7th Med.
Regt, at Bretteville le Rabet. The
5.5in gun was the standard
medium gun of British and
Commonwealth forces
throughout the 1940s and 1950s.
The uprights alongside the
barrel are spring equilibrators.
Crew – nine, Maximum range –
18,200yd (with 82lb) shell.

Above : The British Army 25
pounder field gun, which was
used as a gun-howitzer and
anti-tank weapon throughout
World War II. It continued in
service until the late 1960s, when
it was phased out after the NATO
countries agreed on a standard
calibre of 105mm. Its normal
range was 12,500 yards
(11,400m) and its rate of fire
4 rounds per minute. It was
crewed by an NCO and five men,
and was towed by a four-
wheeled tractor with its limber.

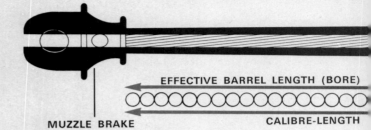

OVERALL BARREL LENGTH

MUZZLE BRAKE

EFFECTIVE BARREL LENGTH (BORE)

CALIBRE-LENGTH

Top: This diagram clears up confusion over calibre, the length and width variety. Muzzle width is shown right and is simply divided into bore length from muzzle to breech face to obtain a calibre length, here 40.

Right and below : The latest British 105mm light gun on its turntable.

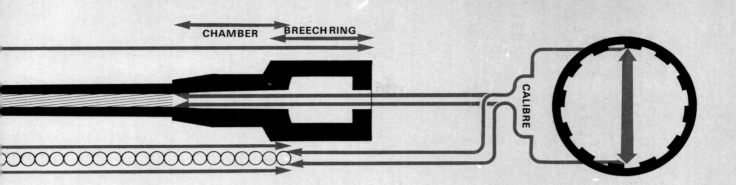

CHAMBER   BREECH RING

CALIBRE

Apart from new materials, which made possible lighter guns and carriages, the ever-increasing use of motorized transport by western armies also offered distinct advantages in the movement of guns both towed and installed in vehicles either wheeled or tracked. The Spanish Civil War also reinforced the armies' natural desire for guns of heavier calibre than the 75mm that had been standard during World War I for field artillery. Thus there emerged a number of good to excellent guns and howitzers such as the British 25-pdr gun-howitzer and 4.5-in gun, the US 75mm pack howitzer, 105mm howitzer and 105mm gun-howitzer, and the Russian 76.2mm, 85mm, 100mm and 122mm guns and 122mm howitzer. These were all excellent weapons, and performed manfully under the most adverse of conditions, both static and mobile, during World War II. Average maximum range for weapons of this type was between 12500 and 15000 yards or metres,

compared with the 10000 yards or metres of World War I guns of this type.

Basically, however, the technology of field guns has not altered significantly since World War I, although there have been considerable advances in the design of the recuperator and in the use of improved metals for construction. This last has made possible present-day weapons, which retain much the same calibres as their World War II counterparts, but which are more mobile as a result of being lighter and also capable of being broken down into easily transportable units. With the type of non-nuclear war now being envisaged, this mobility is a factor of prime importance. The major improvements in current field artillery are therefore attributable mostly to better propellants and the use of advanced technology in such matters as ranging and control, as well as in the production of several new types of shell.

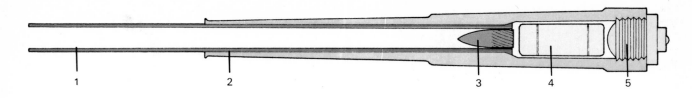

1   2   3   4   5

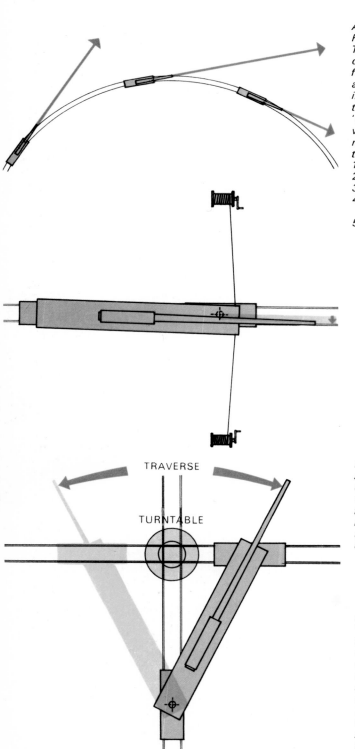

Above : 'Bruce' — named after Rear Admiral Sir Bruce Fraser, Third Sea Lord — reached a range of 62½ miles when it was first fired on 30 March 1943. But after 30 shots the rifling on the inside of the barrel was so worn that the ribbed shells failed to 'catch' in the grooves. The result was that 'Bruce' was unable to make any further contribution to the Allied war effort.

1. 8in liner, 28.3in long.
2. 13.5in barrel, 24.6in long.
3. 8in ribbed HE shell (256lb).
4. 13.5in cartridge (247lb cordite)
5. 13.5in breech of 'Bruce'.

Above : British 13.5in rail guns at full elevation (winter 1940).

TRAVERSE

TURNTABLE

Left top: The Curved Track Aiming System. A method, devised during the American Civil War, that entailed laying or finding a length of curved railway track to increase a gun's arc of fire. A 5½in traverse cost 88ft of track of 500ft radius.

Left centre: Traverse by 'Warping Winches'. This shifted a gun-mounting one or two degrees across the bogies. On curved track it was enough to correct the gun-laying without shunting.

Left bottom: Cross Track Traverse. An ingenious German way of getting a 120° arc of fire. A turntable allows the front bogie to run along a cross-track ; gun rotates about the rear bogie.

Long range gun

Long range guns were developed to allow an army to fire behind enemy lines from a comparatively safe distance. To give a shell enough velocity to travel very long distances a gun must have a long barrel and be strong enough to handle a very powerful propelling charge. This means that the gun must be big and very heavy – so heavy that it becomes difficult to move. The solution was to use the railway and mount the gun on special carriages.

In the early stages of World War I the Germans mounted a number of ex-naval 38cm guns in turrets to protect the Belgian coast. By placing one or two of these on railway mountings they were the first to develop the idea of long range mobile artillery fire. Capable of firing 1,650lb (748kg) shells, they had a range of 16 miles (26km) enabling them to strike behind the French lines.

In 1918, using one of these 38cm guns as a basis, they produced the famous 'Paris Gun'. This was a 21cm gun with a barrel 112ft (34m) long, capable of sending a 264lb (120kg) shell 76 miles (116km), and which, between March and August 1918, dropped 303 shells on Paris. The extension of range meant that the railway-gun had moved out of the heavy tactical support role and entered the super-heavy long-range strategic area.

The problems which the Paris Gun brought into focus were unique. The first problem was range – how do you propel a shell to go 76 miles? The answer was to send it into the stratosphere as fast as possible. Once there the shell coasts through a near-vacuum without the enormous resistance of the atmosphere to slow it down. Eventually gravity pulls it down into the atmosphere and then it falls relatively steeply. To reach maximum range in these conditions the gun has to be elevated to an angle of 55°, to reach the stratosphere as quickly as possible, whereas the angle for maximum range for ordinary artillery is 45°.

The next problem is that while the shell is up in the stratosphere the earth is revolving beneath it, and when the shell finally lands it will miss the target by a considerable amount unless a correction is applied to take this relative movement into account. The extent and nature of the correction depends on how the flight of the shell is orientated in respect to the earth's rotation.

If the shell is fired from east to west then, since the earth is rotating in the opposite direction, the target will be further away in distance over land than the maximum range of the gun. By the time the shell lands the target will

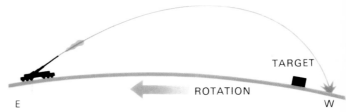

be in range. The reverse is true if firing from west to east. For bearings between these extremes, the correction varies accordingly. This is a considerable simplification of a difficult problem – the formulae for determining the correction are extremely complex.

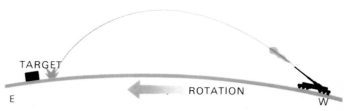

A third problem is the mechanical one. To put a shell into the stratosphere requires a muzzle velocity of over 5000fps (1524mps), otherwise the pull of gravity will force the trajectory to curve before the stratosphere is reached. This velocity demands a large charge of the most powerful propellant and powerful propellants develop extremely high temperatures in the gun which literally wash away the interior surface. Each successive shell seats a little farther into the barrel when loaded because of the erosion and this leaves a greater chamber volume for the charge.

Below : The Krupp railway-mounted naval gun that opened the 10-month struggle for Verdun by hitting the Bishop's Palace at a range of 20 miles and with its sister gun soon cut Verdun's one rail link.

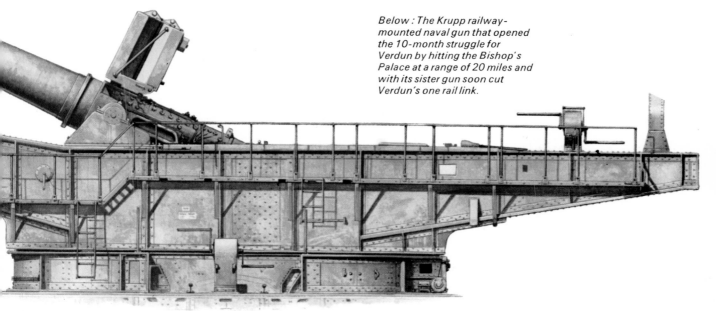

This has to be taken into account otherwise the increased volume would lead to lower pressure and less velocity, leading, in turn, to shorter range. With the Paris Gun therefore, the distance the shell had been rammed had to be measured. The new chamber volume and the weight of propellant needed to reach the desired velocity in this new volume had then to be calculated. The correct amount of propellant for each shot then had to be weighed out and bagged.

Shells are spun in flight to stabilize them. The spin is given by the soft copper driving-band that engages the gun's rifling. But with super-guns, the normal rules do not apply. The enormous pressure needed to send the shell out of a 112ft barrel at 5000fps sets up such a torque (twisting force) as the shell enters the rifling that soft copper shears and fails to spin the heavy shell. The answer was to make the shells with steel ribs on the body, spiralling to match the curve of the gun's rifling. Also,

instead of the 64 grooves normally used with a 21cm gun, 12 deep and wide grooves were cut for the shell ribs to ride in.

The Wehrmacht had 14 different models of railway-gun in service during World War II, but few were used to great effect. A 28cm K5 operated against the Anzio beach-head in 1944 and gained a reputation as a result, but the only other German railway-gun to make a name for itself was the enormous 80cm Kanone, known variously as 'Gustav' or 'Dora'.

On a modern battlefield such weapons would be extremely vulnerable. Their lack of mobility, slow rate of fire and high rate of barrel wear have made them obsolete. Today, close support artillery is mainly guided by weight in order that it may be airlifted either by aircraft or slung beneath a helicopter. The long range gun has now been almost completely replaced by modern surface to surface tactical missiles.

American artillerymen protect their ears from the blast of the 8in howitzer shown at full recoil. The men on the left have an 8in shell on a carrier ready for loading. The shells on the right are having their caps removed and the fuses screwed into place.

Mortar

A mortar is a high trajectory fire weapon in which the recoil force is passed directly to the ground by means of a baseplate. The conventional mortar, as used by the armies of most countries, is muzzle loading and has a smooth bore. It fires a fin stabilized projectile at subsonic velocity, and establishes zones of fire by variation of the charge weight. Range is adjusted by altering the elevation. The high trajectory of a mortar allows the weapon to be placed behind hills, in valleys or in small steep sided pits, and to engage troops in trenches, sunken roads or behind cover.

The mortar was one of the earliest forms of artillery and is known to have been used by Mohammed II at the time of the siege of Constantinople in 1453. It was known in Europe as the bombard and consisted of a metal pot secured to a timber base. It was used for attacking fortresses and cities under siege and also for action against ships close to shore. There was also a naval equivalent. The bombard fell out of favour as other forms of artillery developed and did not come into prominence again until World War I, when trench warfare produced the same effect as a siege. The artillery of both sides refelected this in the quantity of heavy guns introduced in order to inflict damage to the complex defensive lines on both sides. The British were using the Cohorn mortar which had been in existence since 1746 while France produced a 520mm (20.47in) mortar piece on a railway mounting.

Infantry mortar — unlike the heavy artillery mortar, which is centuries older — first appeared in the early stages of World War I.

How to hit an enemy hidden behind a parapet or in a trench became an urgent question for the front-line troops. Sir William Stokes provided the solution by producing a mortar of 3in (7.6cm) diameter, a calibre which is still in favour today.

Construction The great majority of mortars have four main parts: the barrel, the baseplate, the mount and the sight. The barrel is a smooth bore steel tube, and the exterior is also usually smooth, although some mortars incorporate radial finning to assist cooling. The firing

Above : Siege-trains since the 14th century faced the mounting problem of weight as mortars increased in size , due to the need for more and more powerful weapons to overcome stronger and stronger defences. One solution was the British mortar designed by Mallet in 1855. The longitudinal bars clamped the multi-part barrel and breech together. Loading the shell demanded the use of heavy-duty tackle. The 2,400lb shell was hurled nearly two miles by the mortar, which could be broken down into 12-ton sections. Below : A detachment of Garrison Artillery manhandle a British mortar designed by Mallet in 1855.

Below : French 370mm mortar with crane hoisting a 250lb shell.

mechanism is incorporated in a breech piece which is usually screwed into the base of the barrel. In many cases the firing mechanism is a simple stud which sets off the propellant charge of the mortar bomb by impact as soon as the latter has fallen to the lower end of the barrel after loading. In some mortars, however, the firing mechanism is a spring operated device controlled by an external trigger. The baseplate is designed to distribute the downward force of the propellant explosion over as large an area as possible to prevent the mortar from being driven downwards into the ground. The mounting is normally a bipod, but occasionally a tripod is used. The mounting supports the barrel and carries the elevating and traversing mechanisms which are used for aiming. In many mortars a shock absorber is incorporated in the mounting, and this usually consists of one or two cylinders containing springs, although in some heavier mortars a hydraulic system may be employed. These cylinders are interposed between the barrel collar and the bipod, and after the barrel has recoiled and been pushed back by the reaction of the baseplate, the springs ensure that the barrel returns.

The bipod carries a cross levelling device which enables the sights to be kept upright regardless of the slope of the ground on which the mortar is situated. Mortar sights have increased in complexity as the years have passed. Initially they were very simple and consisted of an aiming tube and

Left : A 2in (5.1cm) World War I trench mortar. The spherical head of the projectile is filled with high explosive, and an impact fuse can be seen projecting from its front end. The mortar was fired by a blank cartridge which was loaded into a rifle firing mechanism at the lower end of the barrel.

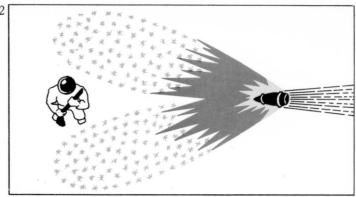

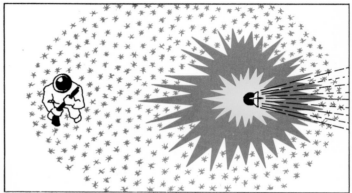

The 'killing area' of an artillery shell (1) is limited by angle of impact. (2) Much of the blast goes too high, or down. By contrast, the mortar's steeper descent (3) gives a more lethal fragmentation pattern (4) and ammunition is cheaper.
The shorter range of the mortar is an advantage in close fighting. The infantryman who fires the mortar can himself see the effect of the bomb and correct for range by rule of thumb. Whereas, with artillery, ranging shots have to be fired, and an observer has to assess, report back and have his assessment converted into firing data before it is implemented by the guns.

a flat plate, which allowed the gunner to relate the direction in which the mortar was pointing to some arbitrarily selected reference point. The modern mortar sight allows the target bearing to be determined and also allows the range and bearing to be recorded so that once a target has been attacked, it can be re-engaged without going through the entire ranging process again.

Characteristics Mortars range in calibre from less than 60mm (2.4in) for light mortars to above 100mm (3.9in) for heavy mortars. A light mortar fires a projectile weighing from 1 to 3lb (0.45 to 1.36kg) to a maximum range of between 500 and 2000 yds or metres. Heavy mortars have a maximum range of about 10,000 yds or metres and fire a projectile weighing 15lb (6.8kg) or more.

The limited number of components and the relative simplicity of the fire control system make the mortar easy to handle and reduces training time. Mortars are cheap and easy to produce. The simple design of the mortar and its sight allows rapid switches of target anywhere within a 360° arc, and the low pressure within the mortar chamber means that a thin walled bomb with a relatively large high explosive content can be used. This, combined with the near vertical angle of projectile descent, provides a good all-round fragmentation and makes the mortar more effective against troops in the open than the artillery gun. The advantages are, however, offset to some extent by the fact that mortars are less accurate than guns.

Variations on the mortar During World War II many new uses were found for the mortar, such as firing smoke bombs for screening infantry movement.

Previously to demand, and get, a smoke screen from field artillery had taken considerable time. Ranging shots had to be fired and an observer had to assess, report back, have his assessment converted into firing data and ordered to the guns. With a mortar, however, the infantryman himself simply reached into a separate box for a smoke bomb and dropped it down the mortar barrel. The man who fired the mortar could himself see the effect of the bomb which was fused to explode on impact and generally filled with white phosphorus to give immediate smoke. He corrected for range by rule of thumb, and maintained fire until he had a suitably thick screen.

After smoke bombs came illuminating bombs for lighting up the battlefield, coloured smoke and flare bombs for signalling by day or night, and even propaganda bombs to shower the enemy with leaflets.

For obvious reasons – low cost, simplicity, light weight – the mortar became a favoured weapon of guerillas from World War II resistance movements to the present day. The reason for this is because by using the mortar one has a light mobile weapon with a fast rate of fire. A well-trained mortar squad can commence action, fire 20 bombs, pack up and be gone before the last bomb has exploded.

Counter-mortar The problem of countering the mortar became more pressing as World War II progressed. Experiments by the British Army showed that it was possible to detect a mortar bomb in flight by using centimetric radar, and towards the end of the war in Europe a number of anti-aircraft radar sets were appropriated for use as mortar detectors. The technique demanded skilled operators, since it meant picking up the bomb in flight and tracking it to determine its trajectory, and then plotting the trajectory backwards until it intersected the ground at the point where the mortar should, theoretically, be located.

The anti-mortar technique of the early 1970s requires much less skill from the operator. Radar locates the bomb in flight and stores its position in a memory data bank. It then locates the bomb a second time, higher up the trajectory, and fixes this position. Using these two fixes and the time interval between, a computer reconstructs the trajectory and calculates the mortar's position accurately to within 25 metres or yards, before the bomb has even hit the ground. By coupling the radar to a data processing system which includes an artillery battery, firing instructions can be produced almost within seconds of detecting the bomb, and retaliatory fire opened before the mortar squad is working properly.

Counter-mortar radar has certainly ended the use of the heavier mortars from static positions, but the lighter infantry versions are still worthwhile. Used quickly, they are not usually the object of radar search, while the very light 50mm models, which act as extended-range grenade throwers, are unlikely to be detected at all.

In the future it seems that light mortars will accompany infantry, so will medium mortars on self-propelled mounts. Heavier mortars, whether owned by regular or irregular forces, stand little chance against counter-mortar radar. With heavier mortars, like the western powers' 81mm, the current trend is to mount them in a tracked armoured personnel carrier to give the mortar greater mobility and to protect the squad from retaliatory fire.

It is this, more than anything else, which has led dissident and guerilla forces, unable to afford armoured personnel carriers, to adopt rockets and recoilless weapons.

Above: Heads down as a German 81mm mortar team operates in Italy in 1943. In order to counteract movement in the loose ground two soldiers grip the supports as the mortar fires. Left: A later development was the 'bouncing bomb' designed by the Germans and used in World War II. On impact, a charge in the head of the bomb is detonated and throws the projectile back up into the air. At a height of about 30ft it explodes, resulting in a highly lethal spread of shrapnel over troops below.

Anti-tank gun

When the British-pioneered tank first appeared in 1916 it was to have a radical effect on battle strategy. The Germans thought that by using the field gun, firing high-explosive shells, they had successfully countered the new invention. They were wrong, but they were not to realise this until they had suffered crushing defeats by tanks in 1917 and 1918. Although it was true that artillery could knock out the thinly armoured tanks, ordinary field guns, with a relatively low muzzle velocity and a large zone of dispersion, could not guarantee sufficient hits in time to avert the counter-measures which the tank's supporting artillery and escorting infantry could mount.

Under the extreme conditions of heavy bombardment, a World War I tank, finding itself in the centre of a concentration of shells, would usually escape a direct hit. The tank's thin armour plating deflected shell splinters and its mobility and firepower gave added protection. Once under attack, the tank commander's first order was for the driver to take cover — the next, to the gunners, was to retaliate.

At the Battle of Amiens in August 1918 the British tanks concentrated on eliminating the German machine-guns, while the infantry silenced the artillery, and in this way each section protected the other. Tactics were varied according to the source of danger and armoured vehicles won tactical and strategic victories at infinitely lower cost in lives than exposed infantry would normally have suffered.

The provision of a weapon to counter the tank was remarkably slow, probably due to the initial German reaction that the tank was merely a novelty with little practical value. The early tanks could be stopped by using normal high-explosive shells fired from field guns, and it became normal practice to site a few guns well forward to act as an anti-tank screen. In 1918, when it began to be obvious that the tank was here to stay, the Rheinmetall company of Dusseldorf produced the first specialist anti-tank gun, a 37mm calibre weapon, low-slung and easily hidden and with a wide traverse so as to be able to follow a moving target. Very few were made before the war ended and fewer still reached the front.

In the post-war years most countries adhered to the belief that tank should fight tank, but slowly it was realized that if an enemy tank managed to evade a defending tank or defeat it, then it could roam round at will behind the enemy's front lines. As a result, some form of anti-tank weapon for the front-line infantry was demanded; most countries produced various forms of heavy shoulder-fired high-velocity rifle, though the 20mm cannon also had its adherents.

During the 1930s the trend of tank design was toward thicker armour, and consequently the development of a heavier-duty anti-tank weapon was required. As a result of this, most nations began to equip their armies with weapons such as lightweight cannon. These were about 37 to 40mm calibre weighing about 1000lb (453kg), firing projectiles of about 2lb (1kg) at velocities sufficient to penetrate 35mm (1.37in) of armour at 500 yards.

The German 37mm PAK 36 was an excellent example of this type of weapon and its general layout was widely copied. The British Army adopted the 40mm 2-pounder;

One of the standard AT guns of the German army the 37mm PAK 35/36 remained in service throughout World War II.

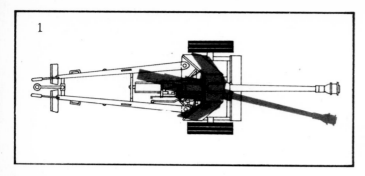

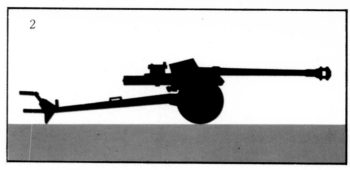

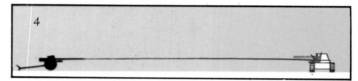

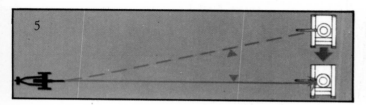

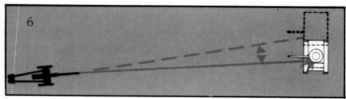

AT gun requirements :
1. Traverse on static carriage (75mm PAK 40).
2. Low profile and flat trajectory. Comparison between AT and field gun necessities :
3. Field gun uses ballistic trajectory.
4. AT gun uses flat trajectory for penetration, and to hit tank where armour is weakest.
5. Field-gun's slow velocity allows tank to move farther.
6. Flat, fast velocity of AT gun more effective.

they also chose to use solid shot, rather than the explosive-filled armour-piercing shell adopted by almost every other nation. In this small calibre the quantity of explosive in the shell (about two or three ounces) was negligible; the manufacturing complications of fusing and filling and the design problem of making the shell function satisfactorily were not considered worth the extra effort.

By 1938, advances in tank design led gun designers to contemplate an increase in calibre. Britain designed a 57mm 6-pounder and Germany a 50mm gun, while the Soviets improved their ex-German 37mm gun by removing the barrel and fitting a new Russian-designed 45mm barrel. None of these, however, was ready by the outbreak of war and in the opening campaigns only the small guns were used.

For Britain the loss of 384 2-pounders at Dunkirk was considerable and production of the 6-pounder was delayed until November 1941. The reason was the need to use the factory capacity to provide sufficient of the tried and tested 2-pounder to re-equip the Army. Germany, with less of a problem, replaced her 37mm gun by the new 50mm PAK 38 late in 1940.

But this was only a temporary respite: again the designers looked at the trends in tank development and began to consider heavier weapons still. The Germans had already begun using their 88mm anti-aircraft gun in an anti-tank role, but this was not a purpose-built weapon and a 75mm gun was proposed to replace the 50mm model. In Britain a 76mm (3in) 17-pounder was proposed. The United States replaced their 37mm gun by obtaining the drawings of the British 6-pounder in a reverse Lend-Lease deal and putting it into production as the 57mm Gun M1. With that in service the USA sought to prepare for the development of the next generation of tanks, and also decided on 3in as a workable calibre, adopting an elderly anti-aircraft gun barrel and grafting it onto the carriage of

Top : The German 75mm PAK 40.
An improvement in Russian tank
armour led to this Rheinmetall-
Borsig model, a scaled-up
version of the 50mm PAK 38.
The 15lb shell travelled at
2,600fps and defeated 116mm of
armour plate at 1,000 yards.
Bottom : A Russian 76mm AT
gun fires from a ruined factory.
Penetration was 108mm at
1,000 yards.
This was the same gun as was
mounted on the Russian T-34
and KV-1 tanks. It was
eventually replaced by more
powerful models as the armour
thickness of German tanks was
increased.

their standard 105mm field howitzer to produce a powerful and effective gun.

Even with these weapons in service the gun's superiority over the tank seemed likely to vanish in time, and a fresh generation of guns went on to the drawing boards. Germany decided that the performance of the '88' was adequate and produced the PAK 43 anti-tank gun in that calibre; the USA looked at their 90mm Anti-Aircraft gun and set about turning it into an anti-tank gun; and in Britain too, an anti-aircraft gun, the 3.7in, was taken as the basis for the 32-pounder anti-tank gun. Finally, Germany developed a 128mm (5.04in) gun firing a 62lb shell which could pierce 178mm (7in) of armour at a range of almost two miles.

With these guns no tank of 1945 — or indeed of the present day — had much chance of survival; but not all these guns got into service. Only two British 32-pounders were made. But even if they had been perfected in time, it is doubtful whether they would have been accepted by the soldiers; the 128mm PAK 44 weighed 10 tons, and the 32-pounder somewhat less — a far cry from the 952lb (432kg) of the 37mm PAK 36 or the 1750lb (793kg) 2-pounder. The German Army had already discovered the penalty of excess weight during the Russian campaign. Many 75mm anti-tank guns had to be abandoned because they were too heavy for the detachments to manhandle.

The other factor which led to the decline in importance of the big anti-tank gun was the war-time improvement in ammunition. At first the guns relied on slamming a steel shot or shell against the tank and punching a hole. As the

tanks' armour grew thicker, the guns had to become heavier so as to be able to fire more and more powerful cartridges to throw heavier shot even harder. But there comes a point — the 'critical velocity' of about 2700ft/sec (823m/sec) — when steel shatters from shock as it strikes. To overcome this, diamond-hard tungsten carbide was adopted, but since this was both heavy and expensive, it became necessary to use it only as the core of the projectile and to built it up to full calibre by lightweight metal surrounds.

Such projectiles developed a high muzzle velocity but soon lost speed in flight. In order to gain the greatest advantage from tungsten, some method of having a light full-calibre shot in the barrel and a heavy small-calibre shot in flight had to be found. The Germans found it by developing guns with tapering bores which squeezed the shot to a smaller diameter, while the British produced the 'discarding sabot' shot in which the lightweight surround was flung off outside the gun muzzle.

These shot developed velocities in the area of 3000 to 4000ft/sec and were the most effective tank-destroyers ever devised, but they demanded massive cartridges and powerful guns. The wartime development of the hollow-charge shell and the recoilless gun, followed by shoulder-fired rocket-launchers, produced a family of weapons which could penetrate armour using low-velocity ammunition fired from lightweight weapons. Mobility was restored to the anti-tank infantryman without much sacrifice of efficiency, and the move away from the heavy anti-tank gun began.

In the foreground an American 57mm anti-tank unit, is in action against the German defences at Monte Cassino.

The German '88'

Probably the most famous of all anti-tank guns was the German '88'. Designed originally as an anti-aircraft gun, it became the most widely used and feared tank-destroyer of World War II.

It entered service in 1933, having been developed by Krupp technicians on loan to Bofors of Sweden between 1920 and 1930. The Versailles treaty restrictions had prevented arms manufacture in Germany, which led Krupps to 'exile' their staff instead of sacking them. But when Hitler came to power the German designers in Sweden returned home, bringing with them the plans for an 88mm anti-aircraft gun. There was nothing unusual in the gun's design, except that the barrel was constructed in sections. This enabled a worn area to be replaced without scrapping the serviceable sections. It also allowed the gun barrel to be manufactured on mass production lines by non-specialized machinery.

Trials and tests followed and as a result the design was slightly modified, again with mass production in mind, the new model being called the 88mm Flak 36. Model 37 appeared after further technical improvements, but the gun's performance was unchanged. It could throw 15 20.25lb (9kg) shells up to 35,000ft (10,700m) in one minute; and although considered only as an anti-aircraft gun it had a ground range of 16,200 yards (14,600m).

At the outbreak of war in 1939, three models, the 88/18, 88/36 and 88/37, were the mainstay of German air defence

systems at home and in the field. But in 1941 the 88mm suddenly appeared as the tank's chief menace in the North African desert. There was no obvious need to use the power of the 88 in this role but the fluidity of desert war favoured tank attacks from any direction and the 24 37mm and 50mm anti-tank guns of the German division were very thinly spread. It occurred to a German officer that the two dozen 88s of the Luftwaffe's Flak Regiment would provide some assistance, and since the balance of air power at that time lay with the Germans they could afford to take a number of the anti-aircraft guns and disperse them cross the divisional front as anti-tank weapons.

By the time the desert campaign had proved the worth of the 88, the Russian campaign was under way, and the unexpected appearance of the Soviet T-34 tank had made

Left : The 88mm in action in Italy in 1944. As the gun is fired, the crew avoid shattered ear-drums by shielding them with their hands and keeping their mouths open in order to equalize air pressure.
Above right : A German gun crew beside the mighty '88'.
Below : The standard AA version of the 88mm Flak 18 gun, as developed by Krupp's designers in 1932. With models 88/36 and 88/37 it was the basis of the German air defence systems.

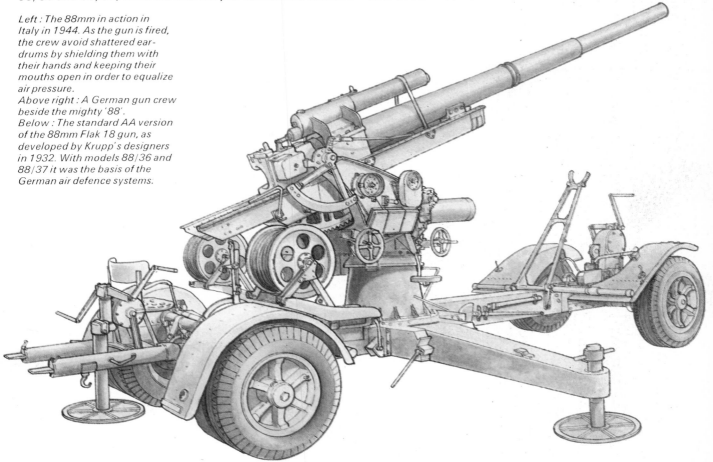

Right : A 12 ton (Sd.Kfz8) prime mover towing an 88 gun. The caterpillar tracks run almost three-quarters of the length of the vehicle giving increased traction and excellent cross-country performance.
The rubber-tyred, pressed steel wheels run on lubricated tracks which are very complicated and require constant maintenance.
The red-brown zig-zag camouflage on the 88mm gun was only used when the gun was situated in a rocky or hilly region such as during the later battles in Tunisia.
Below : Described as the 'trump card of the African desert' — the 88mm Flak gun 18 in its AT form. When the base dug-in to the level of the armour shield, the gun presented a very small target to advancing tanks and could penetrate 99mm of armour at 2,200 yards.

many of the German anti-tank guns look ineffective. The only answers were either a heavier gun than the 50mm PAK 38 or the liberal provision of tungsten-cored ammunition. This could withstand higher striking velocities and ensure penetration where steel shot might fail, but the supply of tungsten to Germany from its dwindling sources in Eastern Europe was precarious and eventually was reserved for machine-tool production alone.

Krupp were asked to produce a solely anti-tank version of the '88', known as the 88mm PAK 43. Instead of the two-wheeled split-trail carriage, considered necessary for quickness into action, the Krupp design was a four-legged platform based on the normal anti-aircraft gun pattern, but enabling the gun to fire while still on its wheels in an

emergency. The cruciform platform gave the new 88 a 360° traverse and since this design was not intended for anti-aircraft work the gun was not so high, barely 5ft (1.5m) to the top of the shield.

The gun's performance was improved by enlarging the chamber and developing a bigger cartridge. The advanced carriage design led to manufacturing problems and delays, and in an attempt to get the guns into action quickly a two-wheel carriage was improvised, using stock components from other weapons. The result, which was clumsy and heavy, was officially known as the 88mm PAK 43/41. The troops who had to push it through the Russian mud nicknamed it 'Barndoor'. Even so, there was nothing wrong with its performance: it could defeat

Below : This model of the 88mm, the PAK 43 (an improvement on the PAK 41) is mounted on a travelling chassis. When the wheels were detached a turntable allowed the gun a 360° traverse, a much lower silhouette, and gave a flatter trajectory to the armour-piercing shells. A similar version of the 88, on the standard two-wheeled artillery gun-carriage, was known as the 'Barndoor'.

168mm (6.6in) of armour at 30° at 1100 yards (1005m) range, and even at 3300 yards the shell still had more power than the original 88 had had at 1100 yards, but there were drawbacks. The new cartridge developed an intense smoke cloud which, in calm weather, tended to hang around the muzzle for about 20 seconds and obscured the gunlayer's vision. The long barrel tended to vibrate under high rates of fire, and accuracy went seriously astray. But provided the rate of fire was kept down to 15 rounds a minute or less — and with one shell weighing 51lb (23kg), this rate would be unlikely to be kept up for long – the accuracy was good.

When the Allies landed in Normandy in 1944 the 88s were waiting: not only the Flak 18 and PAK 43 but a third version, the 88m Schiffskanone C/35 in Unterseebootlafette C/35. This 88, a naval gun used in coast defence, was unrelated to the other two weapons and had an inferior performance; it is interesting only to exemplify how 88s came in a variety of shapes and sizes.

By this time, too, the 88 was a standard tank gun but by this time also, the Allies were in a better position; their tank armour was thicker and their tank and anti-tank guns were of equal or greater power.

The anti-tank 88 no longer had the built-in advantage of range. The superior penetration of the tungsten-cored ammunition of the British 17-pounder and US 90mm brought the contest down to more level terms. The '88' was a powerful weapon, but it was no longer a 'super-gun', although much of the myth remained until the war ended.

Anti-aircraft gun

Anti-aircraft (AA) guns were first used in World War I (1914–1918) when they were adapted from equipment designed for other roles. Their job was to prevent enemy aircraft flying at such a height that they could observe, photograph, range artillery, bomb with accuracy or attack troops at low level; and they had to prevent hostile aircraft from flying in formation which allowed them to use the power of their combined defensive armament against counter-attacking aircraft. These requirements persisted until the end of World War II, by which time the great speed of jet aircraft made AA gunnery impractical against high flying targets.

The air forces of the warring nations turned, in 1915, from being mere information-gatherers to more aggressive roles and, as a result, the arms manufacturers found a new outlet for their products. For the lighter aircraft, the machine-gun became the standard weapon, but for heavier machines something bigger was needed. This led to the development of a number of cannon and heavy machine-guns. Most failed to live up to their promise. But one, the Oerlikon, did. The Oerlikon company was not slow to point out that their weapon fired at 550 rounds a minute and used a 60-round magazine. Until this time the anti-aircraft gun was usually something in the order of a 3in artillery piece firing a 12lb (5.4kg) shell some 10 to 15 times a minute and demanding a great number of men with technical expertise to do it.

As early anti-aircraft pieces were highly inaccurate, it was clearly much better to fire 45 third-of-a-pound shells

Below: With aircraft becoming an ever-increasing threat to the armoured fighting vehicle throughout World War II, it became clear that such vehicles would have to provide their own air cover. The Germans converted a wide variety of tanks and half-tracked vehicles to carry AA guns. An early type of conversion was the 1 ton semi-tracked vehicle Sdkfz 10 shown below. This carried a 2cm Flak 38. Later vehicles, such as the Flakpanzer IV, mounted quadruple versions of this gun.

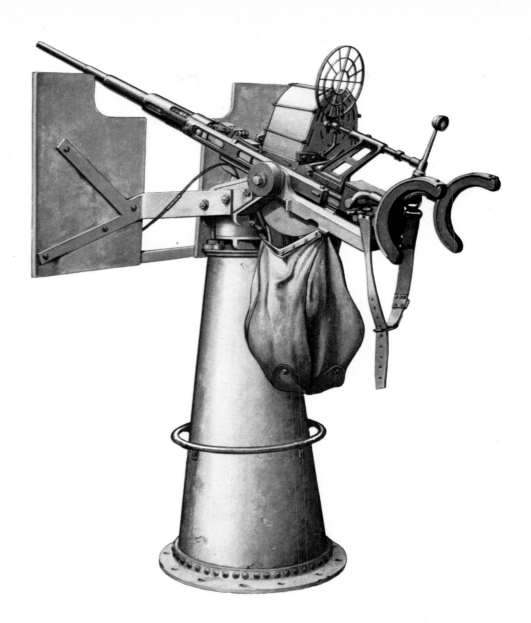

Left : Oerlikon Mk II : Overall length 8ft ; Weight (gun only) 150lb ; Weight of Mk IIA mounting 1,146lb ; Calibre 20mm ; Rate of fire 465 to 480 rounds per minute ; Muzzle velocity 2,725fps ; Magazine capacity 60 rounds ; Maximum range at 45° elevation 6,250 yards ; Effective range 1,000 to 1,200 yards.

Below : MkII's firing mechanism :
  1. *Ejector*
  2. *Magazine interlock lever*
  3. *Magazine catch lever*
  4. *Magazine interlock rod*
  5. *Magazine interlock fork*
  6. *Trigger box cover*
  7. *Parallelogram lever arrangement*
  8. *Safety cam*
  9. *Trigger*
  10. *Trigger hook*
  11. *Catch retaining grips*
  12. *Sear*
  13. *Trigger casing buffer springs*
  14. *Breech Block*
  15. *Striker*
  16. *Lip on breech face piece*

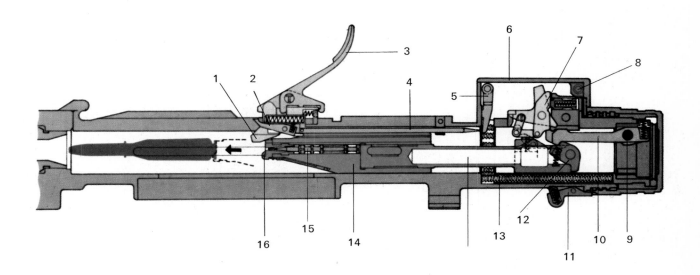

The United States 'Skysweeper' 75mm anti-aircraft gun represents the final stage of development of the heavy gun before it was superseded by the missile. It was used during the last part of World War II and in Korea. The gun aimed itself automatically by radar and a computer. Loading was also mechanized, the automatic loader (shown on the right) taking rounds alternately from the left and right ammunition cylinders. Power was provided by an electric motor mounted above the barrel. The gun's recoil was reduced to a manageable level by the muzzle brake at the end of the barrel, a set of 'fingers' ridged on their inner surface so that they caught the slipstream of the shell and pulled the barrel forward. If the computer failed, the gun could still be aimed by eye from the seat. If the electric power failed too, it could be loaded manually and aimed by means of handwheels and the emergency sighting mechanism on the far side of the barrel.

1. Ammunition cylinders
2. Emergency manual sighting mechanism
3. Transmission box
4. Motor to drive loading mechanism
5. Muzzle brake to control recoil
6. Optical rangefinder
7. Predictor computer
8. Firing platform
9. Seat for optical rangefinding
10. Case ejection chute
11. Rammer tray
12. Magazine
13. Ramming rolls
14. Round
15. Fuse
16. Fuse jaws
17. Round is fired
18. Breechblock closes
19. Case is ejected

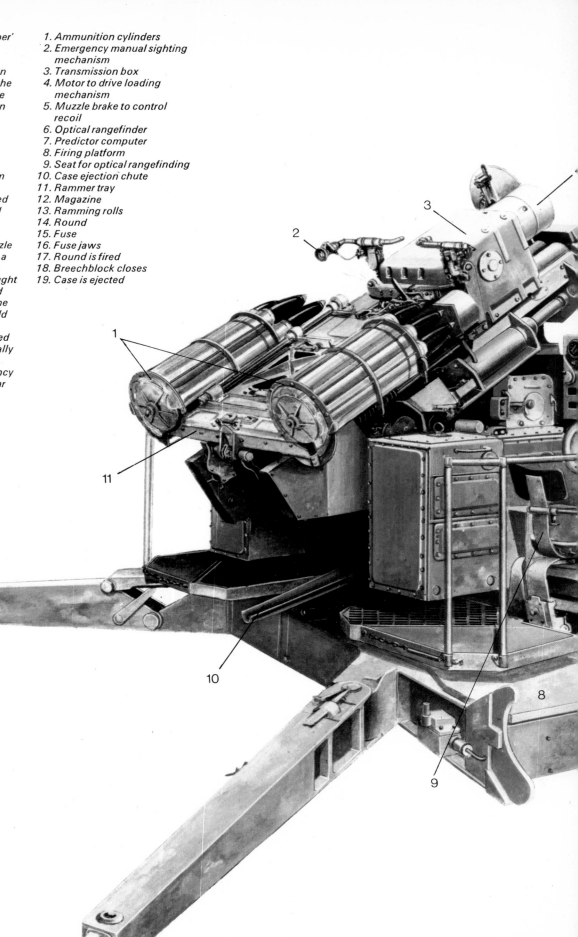

80

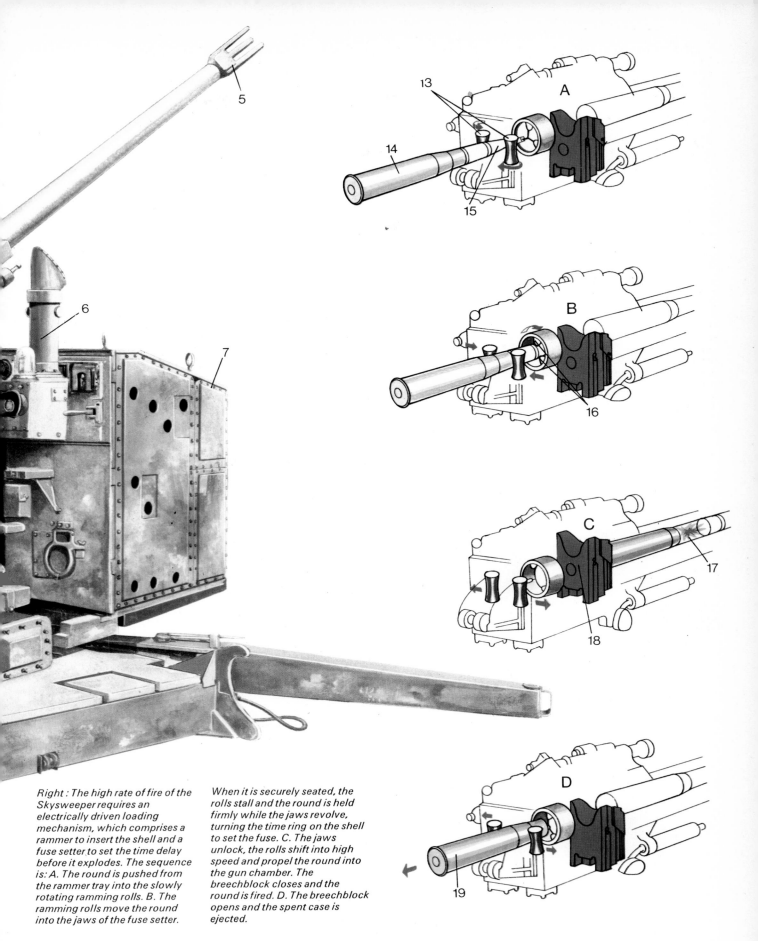

5

6

7

13

14

A

15

B

16

C

17

18

D

19

Right : The high rate of fire of the Skysweeper requires an electrically driven loading mechanism, which comprises a rammer to insert the shell and a fuse setter to set the time delay before it explodes. The sequence is: A. The round is pushed from the rammer tray into the slowly rotating ramming rolls. B. The ramming rolls move the round into the jaws of the fuse setter.

When it is securely seated, the rolls stall and the round is held firmly while the jaws revolve, turning the time ring on the shell to set the fuse. C. The jaws unlock, the rolls shift into high speed and propel the round into the gun chamber. The breechblock closes and the round is fired. D. The breechblock opens and the spent case is ejected.

in five seconds than a single 12lb shell in the same time. By dispersing the shells, the possibilities of hitting an aircraft were greatly increased. Thus the idea of putting the maximum amount of metal and explosive into the air in the shortest possible time became the accepted way of dealing with low-flying, fast-moving aircraft.

While the AA shell is travelling upwards towards the target aircraft, that target is itself travelling through the sky. For example, a target travelling at the now modest speed of 200 mph (320km/h) would travel almost 1¾ miles (2.8km) during the 30 second time of flight of a 3.7 inch AA shell. The position of the target is known at the moment the gun fires but once the shell starts on its way no further control can be exercised over it, and so certain assumptions must be made about the behaviour of the target during the time of flight for the projectile to meet it. These assumptions are that the target will maintain a constant course, height and speed shortly before and during the flight of the shell or, if any of these are changing, it will be at a constant rate. The higher and faster the aircraft is flying, the longer the time of flight of the shell and the less likely are the assumptions to be justified.

The apparatus that was developed to pinpoint the future position of the target was called a predictor. Although extremely complex in design, it was simple in principle. The predictor followed the path of the target and measured the bearing (direction) and elevation. The change in bearing and elevation in a short period of time enabled the course and speed to be calculated and this, with the height supplied by a modified range finder, gave all the target data. Initially an optical range finder was employed, but this could not be used at night and later was replaced by radar. The trajectory of the shell depended on its initial velocity, the retardation due to its shape and diameter, its weight and stability in flight, together with the meteorological conditions at various altitudes through which it passed. All these factors were fed into the predictor.

The likelihood of a direct hit was obviously very low so the high explosive filling of the shell was detonated by a time fuse set to function after the calculated time of flight for the shell to reach the target. The lethal radius of the bursting shell was sufficient to allow for some error in

Right : Early models of the Mk VIII 2pdr pom-pom did not carry flashguards on the barrels, although the basic design did not change. Ships, yards and store installations were all issued with this popular weapon. For army use the base was modified in order that it could be bolted to a mobile transporter.
Far right: A blowpipe missile being launched. To protect the user from injury by flame or blast, the first stage burns for only a fraction of a second, the main stage being ignited when the missile is at a safe distance.

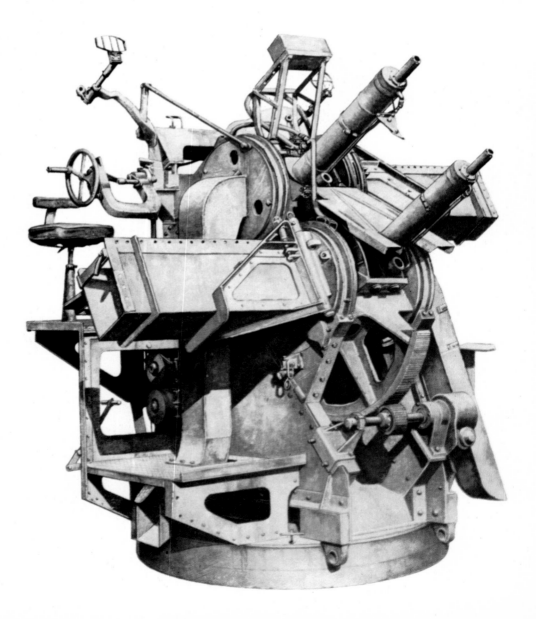

prediction. The automatic fuse setter received data from the predictor and set the fuse of the shell immediately before the automatic loader placed it in the chamber of the gun. If all was correct, the shell was sent on its way to intercept the target and either hit it or exploded sufficiently closely to destroy it.

An improvement on the time fuse was the proximity fuse, which enabled the fuse setting procedure to be omitted. The proximity fuse works by using a radio device built into the shell, to detect when it is near the target. The strength of the signal determines when the fuse should detonate the shell.

Types of anti-aircraft gun The light anti-aircraft (LAA) gun was extremely mobile and capable of very rapid deployment. A high rate of traverse and elevation was essential because at close ranges the angular rate of change of the target was very fast. The most popular calibres were 20mm and 40mm. The 20mm guns were used singly, in pairs or on quadruple mountings, and fired fused high explosive shells at the rate of 500–700 rounds per minute. These guns were aimed by hand with open 'cartwheel' type sights and engaged targets flying up to 400 mph (640km/h) at ranges of 1000 yards (900m) or less. Both sides in World War II used similar kinds of guns designed almost entirely by the firms of Oerlikon and Hispano-Suiza. The 40mm guns were less mobile than those of 20mm but the greater high explosive content of their shell ensured that a hit was virtually certain to bring an aircraft down. They generally fired at about 120 rounds a minute at targets up to 5000 feet (1500m) and although the great majority used relatively simple open sights, predictors were

sometimes used to calculate the future position of the target and aim the gun accurately.

The heavy anti-aircraft (HAA) guns varied from 3 inch calibre through 3.7in and 4.5in up to 5.25in and could engage targets up to 60,000 feet (18,300m). Owing to the great height and speed of the targets the fire control equipment was complicated and the need to fire the largest shell made automatic loading mandatory. The high muzzle velocity required to cut down the time of flight, and the rapid rate of fire needed to give the greatest chance of a hit, led to excessive barrel wear and short accuracy life for these guns.

The future of the AA gun The invention of the jet engine gave aircraft the ability to reach greater heights and to fly at higher speeds and the HAA gun is now obsolete. The chance of a hit has so diminished that they have passed out of service in all modern forces and have been replaced by ground to air missiles which can change course in flight, fly to great heights and automatically seek out and destroy the target before it can reach the point at which it can release its bomb load.

The increased use of very high speed jet fighter-bombers in the battle zone has led to the retention of 20 and 30mm LAA guns firing at very high rates of fire and often fitted with complex controlling gear frequently linked to early warning and control radars.

Missiles operated by one man, such as the British 'Blowpipe', are being developed to seek out the low level attacking aircraft and may become commonplace although the relative cheapness of the LAA gun and its ammunition may enable it to remain in service for many years to come.

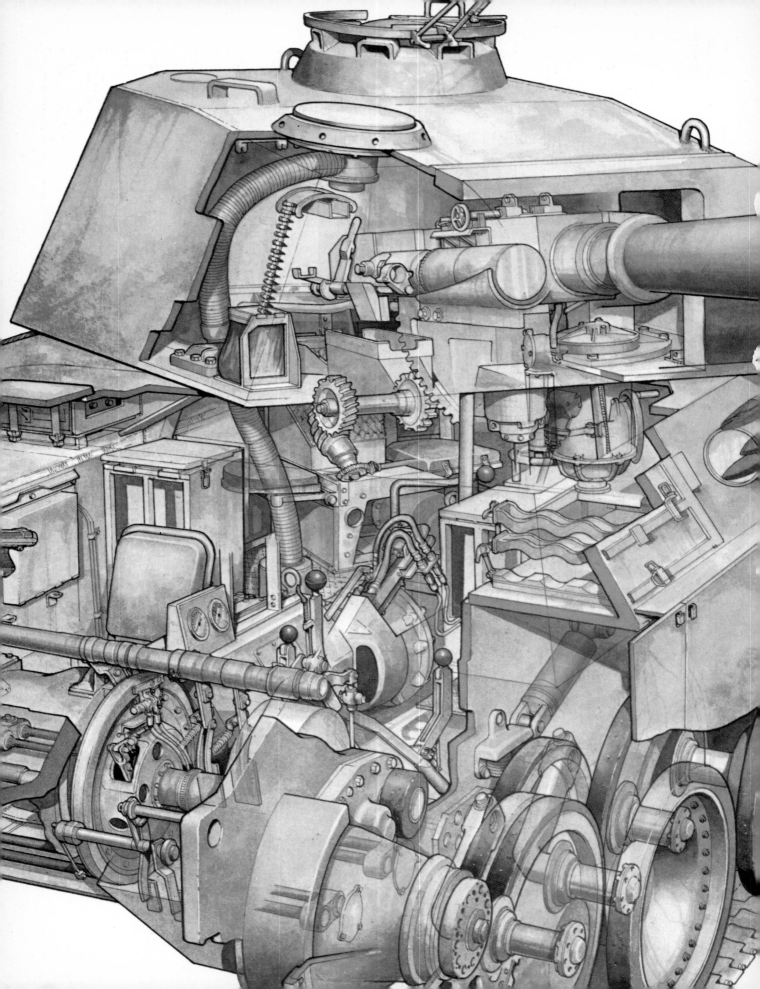

TANKS

For reasons of secrecy, during World War I, 'tank' was the name given to what, by definition, remains to this day, an armoured fighting vehicle (AFV) with good cross-country performance. Its modern purpose differs only slightly from that of the original. The initial concept was of a mechanically driven machine which, with relative immunity, could cross terrain that was made almost impassable by enemy weapons and fortifications such as trenches and barbed-wire entanglements. Once close to the enemy lines the tank was intended to destroy the machine-guns which were holding up the advance of the less well protected elements of the army, the infantry and horse cavalry.

Left : Detail of the PzKpfw VG Panther tank.
Above : The lethal '88'-armed PAK 43/3 Jagdpanther, Germany's successful tank destroyer. Hitler watched the first demonstration on 20 October 1943. By the end of the war, 382 had been made for heavy AT gun battalions. It was an ideal defensive weapon.

Genesis

When the idea was first suggested in the autumn of 1914, and rapidly developed in the months and years to come, the pattern of war on land had reached a state of stalemate. Defences founded upon trenches and barbed wire barricades, and protected by intense barrages of bullets and shells from massed machine-guns and artillery, could no longer be carried by the existing means of assault without appalling outlay in lives and *matériel*. Moreover, even after a successful attack had been made, the assaillants were so exhausted that the defenders had little difficulty in re-establishing fresh, strong positions close in the rear of the original ones lost.

Tanks were developed almost simultaneously by Britain

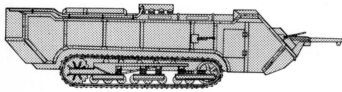

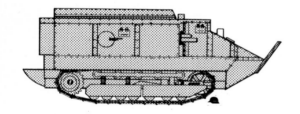

Top: 'Little Willie'. The first AFV, described (for security reasons) as a 'tank'. No more than a 18-ton armour-plated box on tracks, it was planned to put a 6pdr gun in a rotating turret. The resulting high centre of gravity prohibited this.

Above : The two heavy French tanks of World War I. The Char St. Chamond top, and the Schneider Char d'Assault below. Both tanks carried the French 75mm gun as their main armament and used the Holt tractor as the basis of the vehicle. The cross-country performance was poor, however, due to the excessive overhang, and high centre of gravity of both vehicles.

and France, their leading proponents among the British being the First Lord of the Admiralty, Mr. Winston Churchill, and Colonel Ernest Swinton, and on the French side, Colonel Jean-Baptiste Estienne. The British were the first, on 15 September 1916, to send a few tanks into action — monsters weighing 30 tons (30,482kg), with armour only 8mm thick, armed with two 6pdr guns and several machine-guns and driven by a 105hp petrol engine at a speed which rarely exceeded 5mph (8kph). Their capability of crossing broken ground was made possible by caterpillar tracks — the one element in their construction which was original in form if not in concept. Their main purpose was to dominate the enemy (German) trenches so that infantry and horsed cavalry might move through the 'gap' thus created and advance deep into enemy territory.

Neither in 1916, nor on the first occasion when the French tried their machines in April 1917, was this object achieved, but the essential need for armoured warfare and mobility, both latent in soldiers' minds, reasserted itself. Before the war ended in November 1918, tanks had grown to be an essential weapon in eliminating trench stalemate. Moreover, during the final stages of the war, tanks had also demonstrated their improved reliability, increased speed and longer range of action, giving them the ability to carry the war deep into enemy territory. Consequently it was suggested that they might perform the role previously taken by the cavalry as the arm of mobile decision, and since their guns could be fired direct at enemy targets while the gunners remained comparatively safe behind armour, tanks also tended to assume the role of the other decisive arm in war — the artillery.

Between the two world wars, from 1919 to 1939, the opinions of those who saw tanks purely as assistants to the infantry, cavalry and artillery, clashed with a minority of

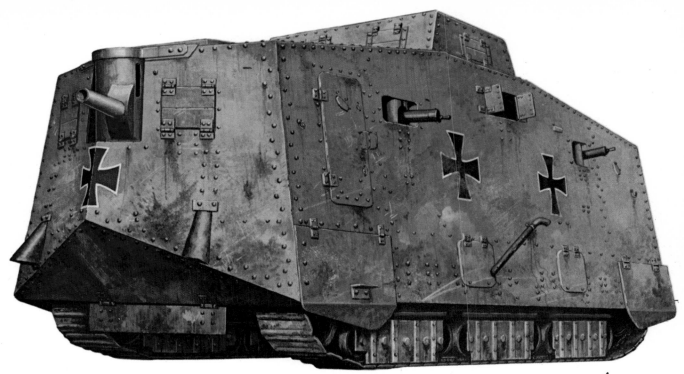

dedicated thinkers and practitioners who insisted that armoured fighting vehicles represented the core of a new weapon system that would revolutionize the art of war. They said that machines of such mobility, protection and firepower would be decisive in overcoming more than enemy front-line positions and claimed that, by being able to move deep into the enemy rear, they could destroy an entire nation's will to fight. In essence, they envisaged tanks as a means of striking against morale in addition to causing physical destruction: they promoted a terror weapon. They preferred the tank as an economical way of waging war, not only because armoured warfare had been positively demonstrated as being far less costly in lives in relation to the results achieved, but because a vehicle could easily carry the rather cumbersome radio sets of the day. The control of armoured formations of many men and vehicles could be implemented more efficiently by speeding up the passage of orders by radio-telephony, so achieving the utmost economy of effort along with relative ease of co-operation among fighting men in action.

By 1939 the tank, in the shape that we know it today, had taken form, although the differing emphasis applied by the general staffs of various nations created machines that were widely disparate in construction. For example, the Germans tended to produce Main Battle Tanks with armour only 30mm thick, a 37- or 75mm gun and a speed of about 20mph (32kph), while the French opted for tanks with armour up to 60mm, a 37-, 47-, or 75mm gun and a speed of 25mph (40kph). But while the Germans designed a much more efficient fighting compartment for their crews and fitted radio in all tanks with a view to conducting long range, fast-moving operations, the French tended much more to restrict their tanks to infantry pace and had little declared intention of conducting far-ranging movements. For this reason they fitted thick armour in

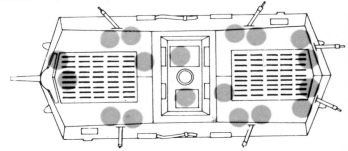

Top : The A7V Sturmpanzerwagen (1918). Above : The 240 sq. ft. armour interior of the A7V, which had to house two officers and 16 men.

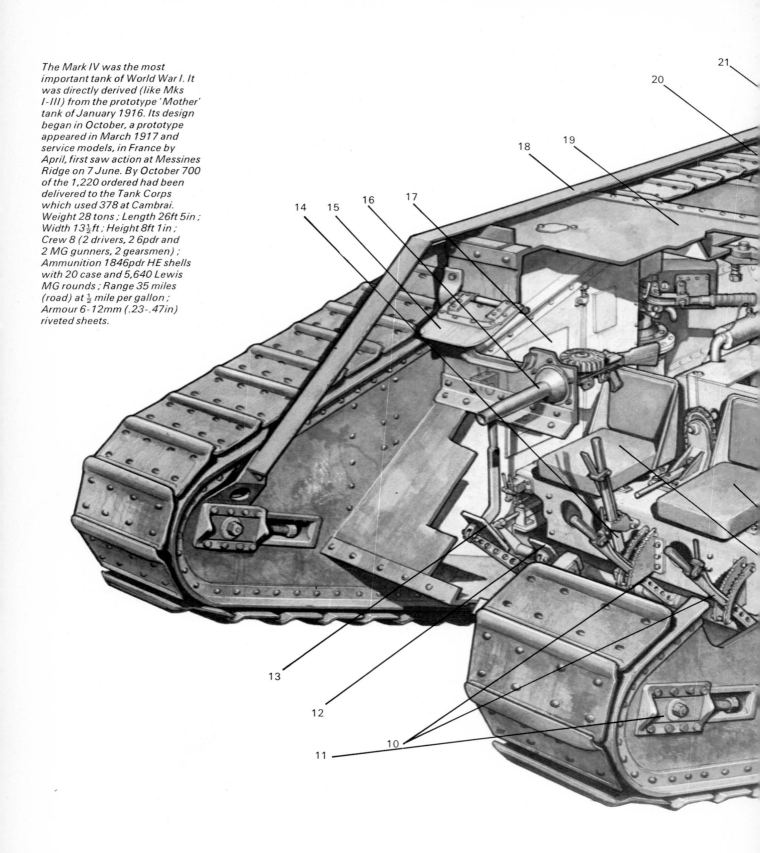

The Mark IV was the most important tank of World War I. It was directly derived (like Mks I-III) from the prototype 'Mother' tank of January 1916. Its design began in October, a prototype appeared in March 1917 and service models, in France by April, first saw action at Messines Ridge on 7 June. By October 700 of the 1,220 ordered had been delivered to the Tank Corps which used 378 at Cambrai. Weight 28 tons ; Length 26ft 5in ; Width 13½ft ; Height 8ft 1in ; Crew 8 (2 drivers, 2 6pdr and 2 MG gunners, 2 gearsmen) ; Ammunition 184 6pdr HE shells with 20 case and 5,640 Lewis MG rounds ; Range 35 miles (road) at ½ mile per gallon ; Armour 6-12mm (.23-.47in) riveted sheets.

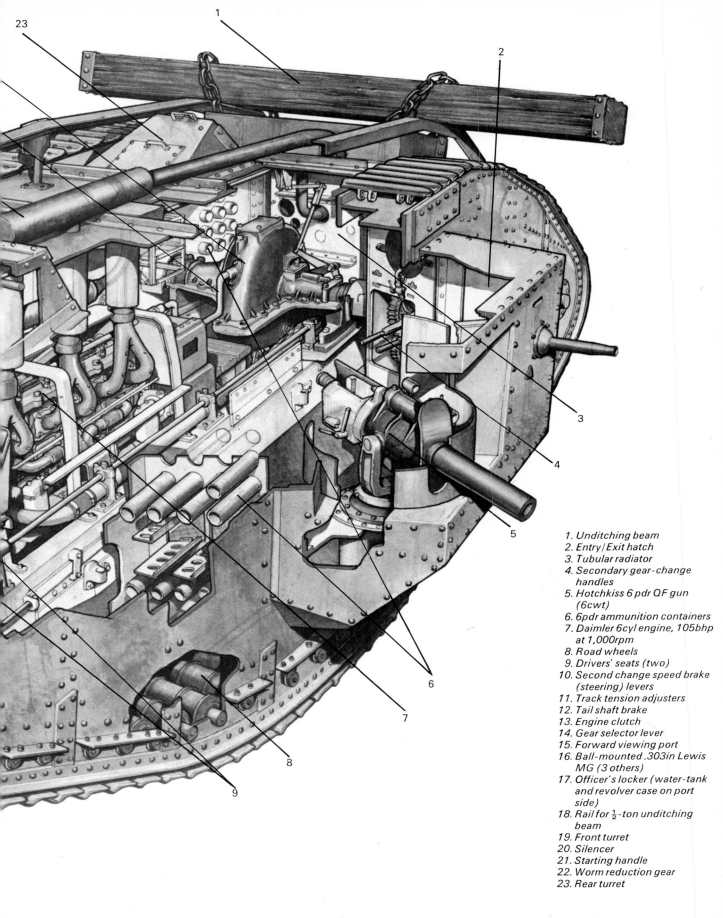

1. Unditching beam
2. Entry/Exit hatch
3. Tubular radiator
4. Secondary gear-change handles
5. Hotchkiss 6 pdr QF gun (6cwt)
6. 6pdr ammunition containers
7. Daimler 6cyl engine, 105bhp at 1,000rpm
8. Road wheels
9. Drivers' seats (two)
10. Second change speed brake (steering) levers
11. Track tension adjusters
12. Tail shaft brake
13. Engine clutch
14. Gear selector lever
15. Forward viewing port
16. Ball-mounted .303in Lewis MG (3 others)
17. Officer's locker (water-tank and revolver case on port side)
18. Rail for ½-ton unditching beam
19. Front turret
20. Silencer
21. Starting handle
22. Worm reduction gear
23. Rear turret

Top: The tank's debut in battle, 15 September 1916. This example is a 'Male', with a 6pdr gun either side. During World War I the tank was used primarily to support infantry.
Above: The wheels which were fitted at the rear of early Mark Is as an aid to steering. These were later removed as they were easily damaged. The tanks were actually steered by braking and varying the speed of each track.

order to compensate for slowness of movement.

The opening campaigns of World War II demonstrated beyond doubt that the German concept (which had been adapted from that of the more far-seeing British) was a war-winning method. High priority was then given by all nations to the creation of armoured, mechanized forces. At the same time, ways to destroy tanks were constantly under development through the progressive introduction of much more powerful anti-tank guns and mines. Against these threats the tanks themselves underwent steady improvements in armour protection and striking power, besides benefiting from the steady sophistication of tactical techniques that allowed them to outwit the enemy. Bigger guns (up to 120mm) and heavier armour (up to 150mm) inevitably raised weight so that, while speeds of Main Battle Tanks remained constant at a little above 20mph (32kph), powerplants had to be significantly enlarged — from about the 250hp mark in 1939 to 650hp or more in 1945, in the case of German machines, for example. By 1945 Main Battle Tank weights were close to the 40 ton (40,642kg) mark and there were some heavies in action (the German Tiger IIs) of over 60 tons (60,963kg).

The war came to an end at a time when the future of the tank was again uncertain. Nobody seriously doubted the continuing need for armoured protection. Such doubts as existed centred on the ability of tanks to survive against the latest anti-tank weapons, notably the small hand-held infantry weapon ('bazooka' types), with their 'hollow-charge' warhead, which could penetrate the thickest armour. On the other hand, the advent of the atom bomb and the knowledge that, in due course, tactical versions of this powerful weapon would be used on the battlefield, gave a boost to the tank's prospects. Armour gives good protection against atomic effects, including radiation, and the vehicle's mobility can quickly take it away from heavily irradiated areas. Moreover, it was soon discovered that, even though modern anti-tank weapons did cause quite heavy casualties, they were by no means fatal to the tank's ultimate chances of victory. Time and again, particularly in the confrontations between Israel and the Arab States, the tank has proved the dominant battle-winning weapon. Furthermore it is now realised that, not only can conventionally armoured tanks of about 50 tons (50,803kg) be given an excellent chance of survival, particularly if they are handled with tactical skill, but that the latest arrangements of armour are giving so much higher a standard of protection against even the most powerful guns and missiles that the tank stands a better chance of survival today than ever before. Therefore the tank has every prospect of remaining a dominant weapon for many years to come — a point strongly underlined by the many nations with effective armies which continue to buy more and more tanks of the latest design. An educated estimate in 1975 put the number, worldwide, at 100,000 (of which 60,000 were of Russian design). But these machines, although retaining the essential features of their predecessors, are immensely complex and often extremely expensive. The Americans hope to produce their latest tank at $508,000 (at 1972 values) — and may be considered fortunate if they succeed. It is certainty that, within the specifications applied by the general staffs, tanks will continue to raise their automotive power and effectiveness, will improve their level of protection proportionate to weight and will increase their striking power so that they are always able to destroy the enemy no matter what he may do in return. At the same time a variety of devices will be fitted to enhance the general combat ability of fighting machines, and a whole series of variations, such as those which have been introduced from the beginning, will continue to appear.

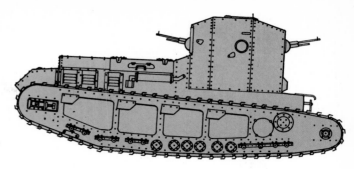

Above : The British Medium A Whippet. This was powered by two Tylor 45bhp engines which gave it a speed of 8mph (13kph). Each engine drove one track, which made control of its 14 tons difficult. The crew of three had four Hotchkiss .303 machine guns, for which 5,400 rounds of ammunition were provided.

Below : Renault FT 17 Light Tank. Weight 6.7 tons ; Crew 2 (driver and gunner) ; Gun 37mm Puteaux (237 rnds).

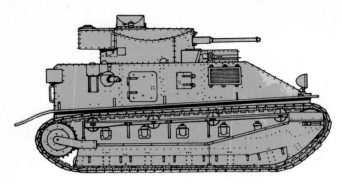

Above: Vickers Medium Mk IIA an improved Mk II, which included an armoured housing for the radio.

Tank layout

The modern tank consists of the hull, on top of which is mounted a rotating turret. The hull is carried on a bogey suspension running on linked tracks and contains the driver, ammunition stowage, powerplant, fuel and the transmission. The turret houses armament, some of the ammunition, night-fighting equipment, usually the communications systems and a crew normally composed of the commander, the gunner and the loader who also acts as radio operator. In some light tanks, however, the turret crew is only two, the commander assuming the duties of loader while the gunner works the radio. Every effort is made by designers to reduce weight and silhouette. An important factor in achieving this has been to make the driver adopt a semi-reclining position in order to lower the overall height of the hull. This was first introduced in the British Chieftain tank in the late 1950s.

Automotive components

Powerplants

A major influence in the selection of powerplant is the type of fuel to be used. Setting aside nuclear fuels, which so far have proved impractical, the vital desire to reduce the risk of fire has made diesel fuels the most attractive. Russian tanks run on diesel and so does the British Chieftain, but the American Main Battle Tank (the M60 series) uses petrol, although it must be pointed out that petrol is not so great a fire hazard as unprotected ammunition. It is, of course, highly desirable, for logistic reasons, that the engine should be made to run on almost any kind of fuel and with this in mind a NATO specification of the 1950s asked that all future battle tanks should have multi-fuel engines. British attempts to meet this specification in the

Below : British Mark VIB. Weight 5.5 tons. Crew 3. Armament one .5in Vickers MG (main), one .303in Vickers MG (secondary). Armour varying from 4-14mm. This vehicle was developed from the Carden-Loyd tankette.

Chieftain led to a one ton (1,016kg) increase in weight, and prolonged and troublesome development. Eventually the aim was achieved but the Chieftain finally went into service as a diesel-fueled tank, its capability of using other fuels ignored as a result of the complexities involved.

The automotive performance of tanks depends in the main on two criteria — the ratio of power-to-weight and the tank's weight as applied to the ground through its tracks. The higher the power-to-weight ratio and the lower the ground pressure the better the tank will perform, particularly in crossing soft ground. For example, the 50 ton (52,835kg) Chieftain with its 720hp engine (power-to-weight ratio 12:1) and a ground pressure of 13psi (0.97kg/cm^2), is at an automotive disadvantage to a 40 ton (40,642kg) German Leopard with its 830hp engine (18:1) and a ground pressure of about 12.2psi (0.86kg/cm^2) a difference which makes itself apparent in the far greater agility of the German machine.

Power, of course, can only be obtained at a price and there have to be compomises so that, in its pursuit, fuel consumption does not become so excessive that insufficient can be carried to give the tank an acceptable radius of action. The present day aim is to give Main Battle Tanks about 200 gallons (909 litres) of diesel fuel to enable them to cover about 350 miles (563km) on roads (far less across country). Size, too, is critical, if the tank's overall dimensions and weight are to be kept within limits such as are imposed by the permissible weight, width and height over bridges and on normal transport systems. Few tanks weigh much more than 50 tons (50,803kg) today and not many are more than 13ft (3.96m) wide and 11ft (3.36m) high. Most service tank engines produce about 800hp, but the latest generation of engines, developed in the USA and Germany, are giving about 1,500hp without a significant increase in bulk over their predecessors.

Transmissions

Enormous quantities of energy can be wasted in transferring power from the engine to the tracks. The output goes through a clutch to the gearbox where it is usual for something in addition to the traditional function of a gearbox to take place: tank gearboxes, be they manually, semi-automatically or fully automatically operated, also incorporate the steering mechanism since tracked vehicles cannot be steered like wheeled vehicles. It is necessary to slow down or to stop one track while speeding up or allowing the other to run. In the early tanks great wastage of power was caused by actually braking one track, but the more sophisticated systems subsequently devised incorporated what is known as regenerative steering. In this system, the power subtracted from one track is transferred, usually through a differential, to the other so that both tracks are driven, though at different speeds, in order to slew the tank. Many gearboxes of this type can also provide a neutral turn so that, when steering is actuated by the driver, the tank rotates on a point.

From the gearbox power is usually transmitted via additional reduction gears in a so-called final drive, to a toothed sprocket driving the tracks.

Tracks

Tracks are made up of 100 or more pin-jointed links so designed as to give sufficient flexibility and also to enable each link to be man-handled with relative ease during maintenance. Adjustments to track tension have to be made quite frequently since stretching takes place as a result of wear and strain, a point eventually being reached in which the track has to be completely replaced after it has stretched to the limit. Tensioning is normally effected by adjustments to the idling roller over which the track passes at the other end of its journey from the sprocket. Track links are usually made of steel in order to impart the longest

Below: Russian BT7 Medium Tank. Along with the earlier but similar BT5 this type made up the bulk of the 500 Soviet tanks at Khalkhin-Gol. Weight 13.8 tons; Crew 3; Armament 45mm M1932 gun (172 rnds) and two 7.62mm MGs (2,394 rnds); Armour 6-22mm.

Panzer PzKfw II

1. Armoured fuel-tank, right-hand side only
2. Tank commander's seat
3. Maybach H1 Tr 6-cylinder 140bhp engine, turning at 2,600rpm
4. Radiators (two)
5. Tray for aerial when lowered
6. Hand-operated mechanism for elevating 20mm cannon
7. Drive sprocket
8. Steering levers
9. Driver's seat
10. Gear box: synchromesh six-speed and reverse
11. 20mm cannon. 180 rounds in 10-round magazines
12. Hand traverse for turret

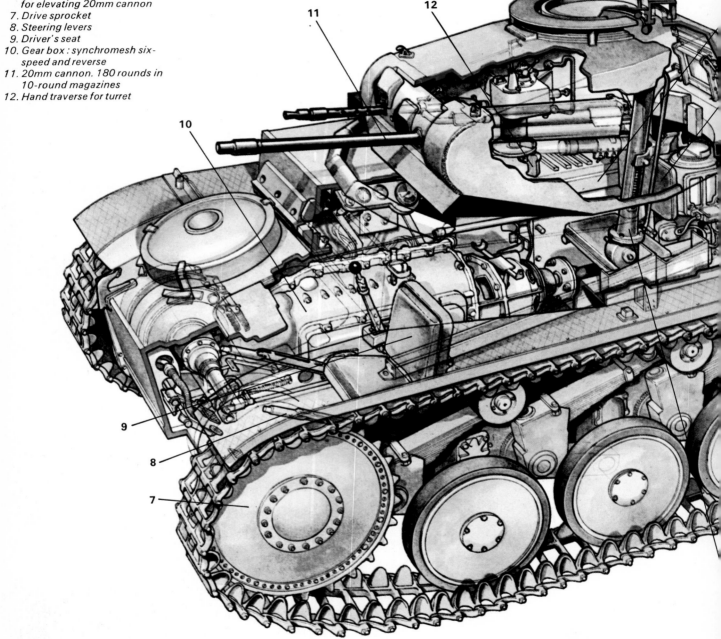

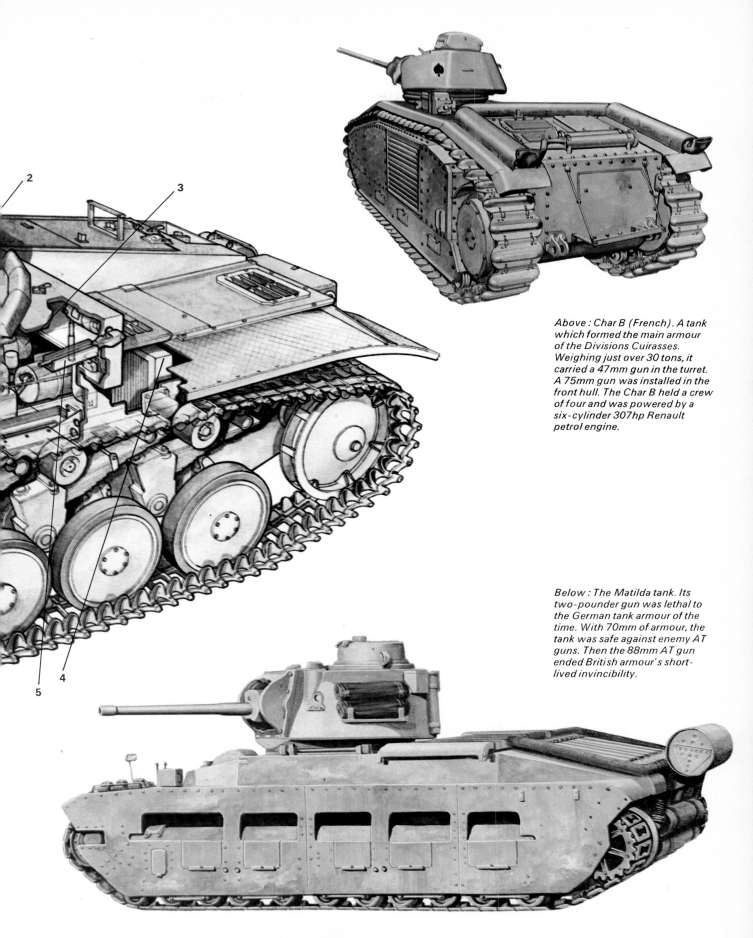

2

3

4

5

Above : Char B (French). A tank which formed the main armour of the Divisions Cuirasses. Weighing just over 30 tons, it carried a 47mm gun in the turret. A 75mm gun was installed in the front hull. The Char B held a crew of four and was powered by a six-cylinder 307hp Renault petrol engine.

Below : The Matilda tank. Its two-pounder gun was lethal to the German tank armour of the time. With 70mm of armour, the tank was safe against enemy AT guns. Then the 88mm AT gun ended British armour's short-lived invincibility.

possible life, and because steel links give better traction than those with rubber pads, the other most commonly employed type. Rubber tracks have the advantage of quieter operation, a facility which is often in tactical demand for stealthy approach near the enemy. Despite their lower tractive efficiency they are in increasing use because they inflict less harm to roads which, during peacetime training, receive, quite unwarrantedly, costly damage from steel tracks.

Suspension

The tracks themselves have to be carried on what is known as the suspension, an arrangement of road wheels and, sometimes, jockey rollers, allied to sprocket and idler, around which the track is passed. The weight of the tank is transferred to the tracks and hence to the ground. It follows that the greater the track surface that can be laid on the ground, the lower the ground pressure. This, like everything else, is arrived at by a design compromise : not only must track length be governed by the length of the tank, but its width is critically related to the maximum width of the vehicle. Suspensions, which today consist of four to seven rubber-tyred wheels, do more, however, than attach the track to the tank. They are meant to provide as smooth a ride as possible for the crew of the tank whose demand is for a steady platform from which to execute their task while on the move over the roughest terrain. Generally each road wheel is independently sprung by torsion bars mounted transversely within the hull, although on some types wheels are mounted in pairs and sprung by coil springs. Hydropneumatic systems have also been made, at extra outlay, to adjust the tank's posture by raising or lowering the hull on the tracks. It is the suspension's principal task to minimize pitching and bouncing, for it is of no use if a tank can advance at high speed, but only with

Below : PzKpfw III Ausf. E. Along with the PzKpfw IV this was the standard German medium tank of World War II and saw action in almost every theatre.

Above : General Heinz Guderian (right) in an SdKfz 251 armoured half-track during the invasion of France 1940. The vehicle is topped by a frame antenna aerial. Such vehicles enabled officers like Guderian and Rommel to be at the forefront of their battles.

the crew inside being thrown about so much that they are injured, let alone being prevented from getting on with their proper tasks. There is a limit to the efficiency of suspensions compatible with the overall design of the tank. The speed at which it is tactically desirable to move is open to debate. While maximum cross-country speeds of up to 40mph (64.4kph) have long been possible, most suspension units limit this to an average of 20mph (32.2kph) and even less over badly broken terrain.

Protection

It has sometimes been argued that speed of movement provides good protection for a tank. But, as shown above, a limit is placed on speed. Moreover, a good shot will nearly always hit a fast moving bird. A tank cannot constantly be on the move. It must often stand still to allow its crew to study the ground or lie in wait for the enemy and, above all, to shoot with the greatest possible accuracy. Time and again tanks will have to indulge in a stand-up fight with the enemy and under these circumstances the best protection (apart from destroying the enemy before he has opened fire himself) is some form of armoured skin, an essential component which absorbs, on average, 45% of a tank's total weight.

The most common type of armour is made of nickel-chrome steel, which has the best chance of resisting enemy shot without cracking. To save weight, armour is usually thickest on a tank's front (particularly the turret) where experience shows that most hits are received. Greater protection is obtained by sloping the armour, although the slope as well as thickness naturally tends to reduce the inner dimensions of the hull and turret: there is clearly a criterion of space needed inside by which armour

Below : The British Infantry Tank Mk III Valentine. Built as an Infantry type it was outclassed by German armour, but gave valuable service in battle until 1943.

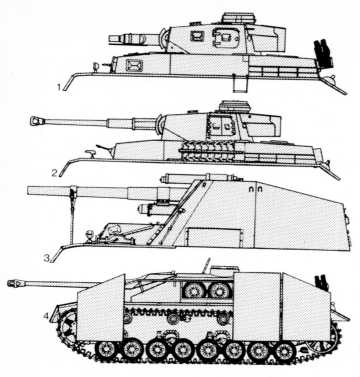

Above : One of the main German tanks of World War II was the PzKpfw IV, the chassis of which formed the basis for a variety of armoured fighting vehicles, such as those illustrated above.
1. *A PzKpfw IV with the short 75mm gun.*
2. *A PzKpfw IV with the long 75mm gun and single muzzle brake.*
3. *A SdKfw 'Hummel' 15cm self-propelled gun. Another variant, similar in appearance, was the 'Nashorn' mounting the 88mm PAK 43 anti-tank gun.*
4. *A StuG IV 75mm assault gun. Like the StuG III, this tank was developed to provide close infantry support. It is shown with added side armour to protect it from bazooka fire.*

arrangement is governed. Likewise the type and quality of armour is affected by the kind of attack that may be expected. Armour-piercing shot which arrives at high velocity and a flat trajectory is more easily defeated by a well sloped steel plate, but a chemical-energy warhead (see below) that arrives at a steep angle is the more likely to penetrate by its explosive effect. Special means to defeat chemical-energy warheads have long absorbed designers' attentions since this type of attack allows immense thicknesses of armour to be penetrated by a relatively small projectile. By spacing armour, to allow an air gap between the two plates, the explosive effect can be dissipated to a certain extent. It has also been discovered that some materials, such as plastics which are not much use against steel shot, have properties which defeat chemical-energy rounds. Hence composite armour of two complementary resistant materials provide an answer which will be found on many tanks in the future.

The history of the development of tank armour is long and complex and has been closely controlled by industrial feasibility. Many promising ideas have failed on the grounds of manufacturing difficulty. Today most tank hulls are made of welded plates or from several castings joined together, the need to make the hull watertight to facilitate wading through streams being important. Turrets, on the other hand, are often cast in one piece. The less armour components there are, and the fewer the holes that have to be made in them for taking hatches, gun ports and so on, the stronger the overall fabric. By no means least, must come considerations of expense: few operations in the construction of a tank can be as costly as the fabrication of its armoured skin. At times a lower level of protection has to be accepted in deference to expense, bearing in mind that the tank which is invulnerable has yet to be built.

Striking power

The first attempts at knocking out tanks were by the employment of ordinary field artillery, a method which gradually changed to include the development of specialized guns with high muzzle velocities in the anti-tank role. But while every effort was made to give the artillery and infantry arms a strong anti-tank capability, inescapably the tank itself assumed an anti-tank role since it usually mounted a good anti-tank gun and was best suited by its characteristics to combat similar vehicles.

Warheads
Essential to the capability of an anti-tank weapon system is the effectiveness of its warhead. Against the thin plating of the original tanks a conventional 75mm high-explosive shell was quite effective if a hit was obtained. But scoring a hit was the main problem, particularly at the longer ranges with inaccurate guns of low velocity that had an extensive zone of dispersion for their shots. Higher velocity guns produced far greater accuracy, while the problems of judging range were also reduced when the line of shot of a flat trajectory more closely coincided with the line of sight. Increases in armour thickness also raised demands for something more powerful than a normal high-explosive round in order to achieve disruption or penetration of the target. The original solution to this problem was provided by the adoption of solid shot which, by a combination of

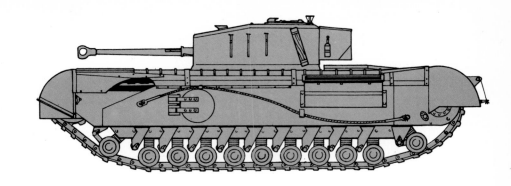

Right : The Churchill Infantry Tank Mark VII was one of the most successful British tanks of World War II. Late models mounted a 75mm gun. Its chassis formed the basis of numerous special-purpose vehicles, such as bridge-layers and flame-throwers.
Below : The British Crusader III, used extensively in the western desert.

Below : The American Grant Mark I, forerunner of the famous Sherman tank. Its superior armament made it a welcome addition to the British 8th Army.

mass and velocity, could more easily penetrate thicker plates or castings. Throughout the history of the attack on armour, therefore, much effort has been devoted to the development of kinetic energy methods and continues to be a prime activity to this day.

The calibre of guns can now be as large as 122mm and the weight of projectile as much as 56lbs (25.4kg). Muzzle velocity, which was a mere 2,800fps (853.44mps) for the British 40mm (2-pounder) gun of 1939, can now be as much as 5,200fps (1584.96mps) with the latest Russian 115mm gun. These increases in velocity have been achieved, in the main, by manipulation of the projectile — either by squeezing it through a tapering barrel or barrel attachment, or by reducing the diameter of the shot (thus lessening its resistance to air pressure in flight) while applying greatly increased force to its propulsion. Squeezing soon fell out of use because of the scarcity and cost of the special tungsten steels required. The second method is today in common use, based upon the Discarding Sabot. With this type of projectile a smaller diameter shot is carried as a core by an outer casing which falls away from the shot after it has left the gun barrel. The Russians have developed this further by stabilising the shot with fins and raising velocity by making what amounts to a 'dart'. At the same time they have introduced a special long tip to the projectile which is 'consumed' as it penetrates armour, thus enabling the 'dart' to go through thicker plates than the ordinary solid shot.

Somewhat similar in action to this latest Russian projectile is that of chemical-energy warheads, which exploit the Munroe Effect of exploding a charge within optimum range of the armour and directing the resultant jet of high-velocity gases at high temperature to a very considerable depth until they emerge at the other side carrying molten debris with them — to the peril of everything standing in the way. A second type, the thin-walled warhead High Explosive Squash Head (HESH), achieves its purpose by being exploded against the armour with a slightly delayed action fuse so that a shock wave disrupts the armour and causes a scab to be detached from the other side at high velocity. Chemical-energy rounds have their limitations, as was partly shown in the section on protection. In addition to being prone to defeat by special armour arrangements, they are only really effective when fired at relatively low velocity and this makes it all the more difficult to hit the target as a result of range estimation difficulties. On the other hand, the HESH type has the advantage of being multi-purpose in that it is also an effective conventional round for use against unprotected targets in the open.

The tank's main armament, although its main purpose is to fire high-explosive and anti-armour projectiles, also can be used for smoke rounds, 'canister' (a sort of spread shot device for use against men in the open) and flares for night illumination. Tanks, however, have only limited storage space for ammunition and rarely carry more than 60 rounds each. Therefore, since the majority must be of the HE and AP natures, there can be little room left for the other kinds which are only carried for emergencies or special pre-planned tasks.

Guns

Over the years, advances in technology have produced guns that are capable of withstanding enormous pressures,

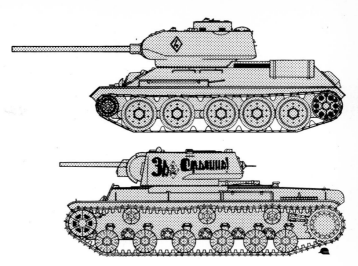

Top: The T-34/85, an upgunned version of the T-34/76 with an 85mm gun in an enlarged turret.
Above: The Russian KV-1 which was the heavy companion to the T-34/76 mounting the same 76mm gun and utilizing the same engine and transmission.
Opposite page, top: The famous Russian T-34/76 tank, which made its first appearance in 1941. This illustration shows German infantry resting against a disabled T-34. Note the additional fuel tanks carried at the rear, and the large forward hinging commander's hatch. This was later re-designed as it exposed the commander to flanking fire. The T-34 was the most advanced tank of its day and was superior to any of the tanks possessed by the Germans. It consequently prompted the Germans to make a rapid re-evaluation of their own tank design.
Centre: The German answer to the T-34 was the excellent Panther tank which utilized many of the Russian tank's design features, such as sloping armour, a high velocity anti-tank gun and an excellent power-to-weight ratio.
Bottom: This diagram illustrates the advantage of sloping over vertical armour. In simplified terms this is because a piece of plate with a thickness T, when set at an angle of 60°, will achieve the same degree of protection from penetration as a piece of plate twice as thick, T2, set vertically.

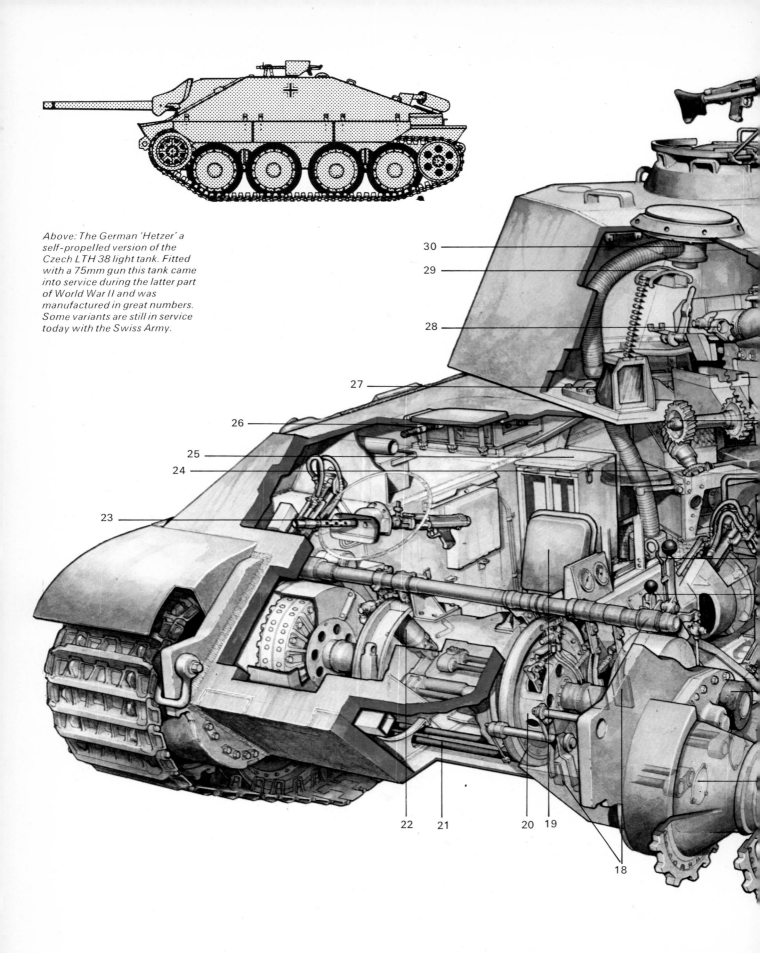

Above: The German 'Hetzer' a self-propelled version of the Czech LTH 38 light tank. Fitted with a 75mm gun this tank came into service during the latter part of World War II and was manufactured in great numbers. Some variants are still in service today with the Swiss Army.

30

29

28

27

26

25

24

23

22 21

20 19

18

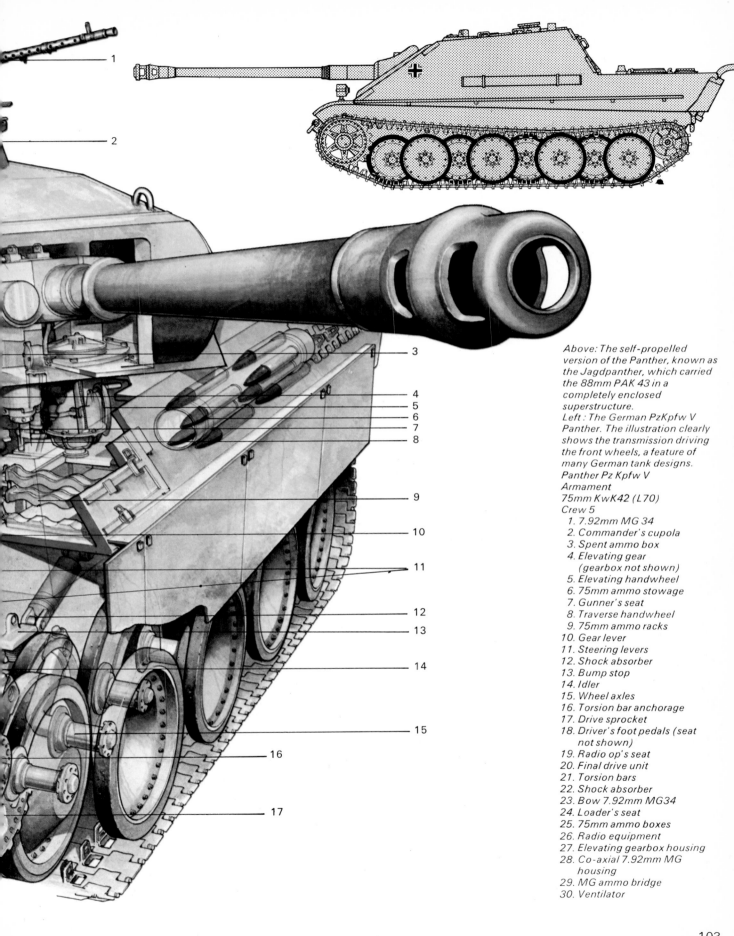

Above: The self-propelled
version of the Panther, known as
the Jagdpanther, which carried
the 88mm PAK 43 in a
completely enclosed
superstructure.
Left : The German PzKpfw V
Panther. The illustration clearly
shows the transmission driving
the front wheels, a feature of
many German tank designs.
Panther Pz Kpfw V
Armament
75mm KwK42 (L70)
Crew 5

1. 7.92mm MG 34
2. Commander's cupola
3. Spent ammo box
4. Elevating gear
   (gearbox not shown)
5. Elevating handwheel
6. 75mm ammo stowage
7. Gunner's seat
8. Traverse handwheel
9. 75mm ammo racks
10. Gear lever
11. Steering levers
12. Shock absorber
13. Bump stop
14. Idler
15. Wheel axles
16. Torsion bar anchorage
17. Drive sprocket
18. Driver's foot pedals (seat
    not shown)
19. Radio op's seat
20. Final drive unit
21. Torsion bars
22. Shock absorber
23. Bow 7.92mm MG34
24. Loader's seat
25. 75mm ammo boxes
26. Radio equipment
27. Elevating gearbox housing
28. Co-axial 7.92mm MG
    housing
29. MG ammo bridge
30. Ventilator

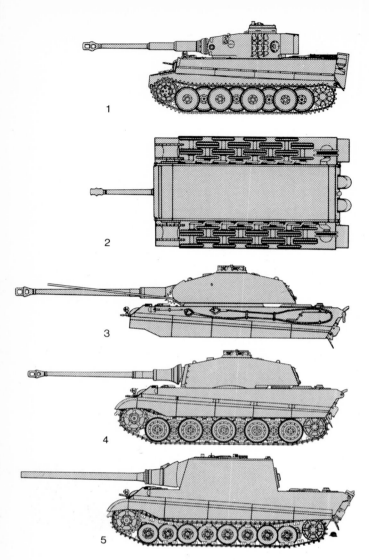

Above : Development of the
German Tiger tank during
World War II.

1. Tiger I. Perhaps the most
   famous tank of World War II,
   designed to carry the equally
   famous 88mm gun.
2. A view from beneath a Tiger I
   minus the tracks showing the
   large overlapping bogie
   wheels. This type of
   suspension was used on
   many German AFV's and gave
   a more even load distribution.
3. One of only 50 Tiger IIs to be
   equipped with a Porsche
   turret, showing the bad shot-
   trap under the mantlet.
4. A Tiger II with the Henschel
   turret. The design of the
   Tiger II was modified to
   incorporate such features of
   the Panther as sloping
   armour.

5. The Jagdtiger, mounting the
   largest gun installed on any
   AFV during the war, a 128mm
   PAK 44L/55.
   Opposite page, top : M10 Tank
   Destroyer (French Army).
   Weight 29 tons ; Crew 5.
   Armament 3in (76mm) AT gun
   and two .5in machine guns.
   This was a 1942 US design of a
   3in (76mm) gun on an M4
   chassis with an open-topped
   turret.
   Centre : The M4 Sherman, the
   standard Allied tank during
   World War II. On the left is the
   earlier M4A1 version with
   a cast hull and 75mm gun.
   On the right the M4A3E8 with
   modified suspension and a long
   76mm gun. This tank is still in
   service with the Israeli Army.
   Bottom : A US Army truck speeds
   past an upturned Tiger I.

thus making it possible to fire high-velocity projectiles.
Nevertheless, these very costly barrels soon wear out. For
example, a 105mm gun barrel may fire only 120 rounds of
high-velocity armour piercing shot before it becomes so
worn and wildly inaccurate that it has to be replaced.
Moreover, the same forces which propel the round towards
the enemy also hurl the gun backwards, a reaction which
has to be absorbed and arrested by a recoil mechanism
inside the turret, usually a combination of springs and
hydraulics. Space within the turret is at a premium. So
while the recoil has to be contained as much as possible,
the mechanism must also be designed within bounds. At
the same time sufficient distance must be allowed to the
rear of the breech for the loader to insert the round without
jamming it at the back of the turret or against the roof. The
height of the roof is also governed by the need to depress
the gun, thus raising its breech, such depression being
essential if the gun is to be fired from a hill top into a valley
below without exposing the entire tank to view. To the
problems of finding space for ammunition must also be
added those of its safety, accessibility and weight. Since
ammunition easily catches fire, it is best kept in water
jackets which flood if penetrated by enemy shot. Not only
must ammunition stowage be such that as many rounds as
possible come easily to the hand of the loader, but the size
and weight of each round cannot be allowed to become so
excessively big as to be cumbersome, a situation which
begins to arise with ammunition much bigger than 105mm.
Most tank-gun rounds come in one piece with the projectile fixed to the propellant case. For the British 120mm
gun, in the Chieftain, the round is separated, with the
loader compelled to load the projectile followed by the
charge which is bagged and not, as is usual, in a metal
case. Automatic loaders have been employed but they
take up additional space and raise problems of ammunition
selection among other complexities.

Because the gun is so heavy (one ton or more) it has to
be finely balanced in its cradle and the turret also balanced,
so that stresses and strain are reduced, and so that the
power- or manually-operated elevating and traversing
machinery needs a minimum of power to do its work.
Tactically it is felt desirable by several nations that the
turret and gun should be stabilized by gyro and electronic
means so that the gun can be kept pointing in the same
direction unless the gunner chooses to alter his lay. Within
certain limits this enables him to fire quite accurately on
the move, although it in no way performs as a device for
exact target tracking.

The acquisition of targets by members of the crew,
particularly the commander and gunner, are vital and
frequently have to be undertaken when all hatches are
fully closed. So the commander is provided with a rotating
cupola, fitted with episcopes, that gives him all round vision
as well as facilities for sighting, and periscopic binoculars.
Having acquired his target through the binoculars, the
commander can line up his own sights and then super-
impose the alignment of the gun by overriding the
gunner's controls. The gunner himself usually has a peri-
telescope and an ordinary telescope, both of which give
magnification and are provided with appropriate graticules
and scales to enable accurate fire to be aimed according to
the nature of ammunition demanded.

Above : An M26 Pershing heavy tank which saw service in Europe in 1945. Weight 41 tons ; Crew 5 ; Armament 90mm high velocity gun (70 rnds) and 3 machine guns (two .3in in hull and .5in in turret).

Right : By 1945 British tanks were designed with larger calibre guns. The Comet illustrated here, based on the Cromwell chassis, had a 17pdr (77mm) gun.

Opposite page: Israeli Centurions fitted with the Vickers 105mm gun. This gun was so successful that the Israelis fitted it to the Russian-built T-54s and T-62s that they captured from the Egyptians.

As already implied, the problem of range-finding is crucial to obtaining a hit. Visual estimation or guess work is no longer good enough to satisfy the sheer necessity for a hit with the second if not the first round fired. In American tanks there has been a strong tendency to use optical rangefinders while the British have adopted a 'ranging gun' of sub-calibre to the main armament which, by firing short bursts at the target, establishes the range and enables the gunner to transfer this information to the appropriate scale for the main armament. In the course of widespread introduction today, however, is range-finding by laser beam. This gives very precise readings at greater distances to those of other devices, acquiring information which can be fed to a computer in the tank, which makes all the calculations and helps lay the gun accurately.

Missiles

Prior to the introduction of laser range-finding, the chances of scoring a hit from a gun on an enemy tank above 1,860 yards (1,700 metres) was too low for satisfaction. As a result, armoured targets at the longer ranges enjoyed a useful measure of immunity. To overcome this disadvantage a weapon system was sought that did not depend upon an exact knowledge of range to make it effective. Attack from aircraft was one such method, but not always easy to arrange nor quick enough in response. Guided, rocket-propelled weapons were the most generally acceptable solution. Missiles of up to 4,375 yards (4,000 metres) range were produced that were 'flown' to the target either from signals sent by the operator through manual control along a wire dispensed by the missile in flight, or semi-automatically so that, by influence of its internal mechanisms, the missile was made to follow the line of sight established by the operator between himself and the target (See the chapter on missiles.) At quite slow velocities (for anti-tank missiles usually about 900 feet per second), chemical-effect warheads are ideally suited to

this kind of system, although the advent of new combinations of armour mentioned above may well down-grade their effect. The Americans have gone one stage further by mounting the 152mm Shillelagh gun/missile system in the M551 and M60A2 tanks. This is a weapon which launches a semi-automatically guided missile, but which can also fire conventional rounds of ammunition, although at relatively low velocity.

Missiles have characteristics, however, which mitigate against their combat effectiveness. Since their time of flight is prolonged, there is ample opportunity for the enemy to take evasive or preventive measures. Furthermore, rate of fire and response is much, and at times unacceptably, lower than desirable. Tanks survive by being 'quick on the draw' and these costly missiles are not slick enough in a split-second close-range engagement. They remain, as yet, a complementary, special weapon for particular occasions even though, by eliminating recoil problems, they do allow a hard hitting projectile to be launched from a small and inconspicuous vehicle, such as the British FV438.

Secondary weapons

It is over-expensive and, at times, tactically inexpedient to fire the main armament, and yet the tank must be able to defend itself economically against close range targets such as enemy infantry. Indeed it is one of the tank's weaknesses that the crew inside are often unable to manage their local protection without calling upon infantry escorts. To rectify this, machine-guns are carried, one co-axially mounted with the main armament, another on the turret roof — usually on the commander's cupola to be aimed and fired by him from inside, either against ground targets or, in desperation, low-flying aircraft. Grenade-launchers are also fitted either to provide a quick, local smokescreen when under attack or to ward off an enemy who may have

crept close to launch short-range hand-held projectiles.

Each member of the crew also carries a personal weapon, of course, such as a pistol or sub-machine gun and within the turret can be found hand grenades and coloured signal flares.

Ancillary equipment

It is possible and often desirable to carry an extensive array of useful, though frequently complex and expensive, items of ancillary equipment on a tank such as internal fire-fighting apparatus, detectors to announce when enemy surveillance is being made by radar or infra-red scanners, gadgets which say when an enemy shot has passed too close for comfort and, above all, those devices which greatly enhance the vehicle's fighting capacity. Unfortunately the cumulative cost of these appendages can become almost equal to that of the basic vehicle and therefore they may often only be fitted in small numbers. Moreover, there simply is not sufficient room inside the average tank to house everything available if certain basic requirements are to be retained, and it can happen that, with so many warning lights flashing or audible signals being heard, the crew becomes confused and the original intention of providing extra information counter-productive.

Communications equipment

It is rare for fighting vehicles to be without radio today and for the sets not to be rugged, simple to operate and capable of a high performance commensurate with their task. Tank formations' leaders require sets with a range up to about 50 miles (80.47km) for communication with higher formations, plus sets with good speech facilities at 20 miles (32.19km) range to the lower levels, down to the individual tank. At the lower levels a range in excess of 10

Right : The British Centurion tank, designed and built during the latter stages of World War II, but too late to see action. It was the first tank in the world to have its main armament stabilized in both lateral and vertical planes to facilitate firing on the move. This feature is illustrated in the diagram above. Once the gun is locked on to target, its position remains constant regardless of of any pitching movement on the part of the vehicle. The schematic diagram, above centre, illustrates the basic principles of gun stabilization.

Above right : A drawing of a typical bore evacuator. As the shell passes the cylinder it builds up pressure. When it has passed the pressure is released and in the process sucks the power fumes towards the muzzle, and away from the interior of the tank.

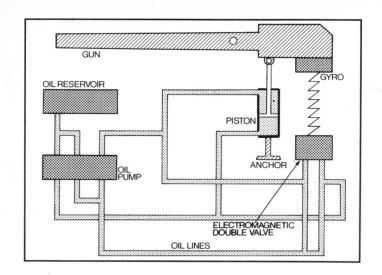

GUN

OIL RESERVOIR

GYRO

PISTON

OIL PUMP

ANCHOR

ELECTROMAGNETIC
DOUBLE VALVE

OIL LINES

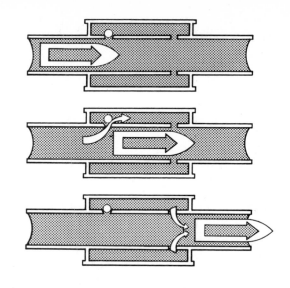

Above : Three basic tank suspension systems.
Top : Horizontal volute spring suspension as used on the American M3 Grant and M4 Sherman.
Centre : Torsion bar as used on many German tanks, in this case a PzKpw III. The bars take up space inside the tank and therefore increase the tank's height.
Bottom : Coiled springs as used on the British Black Prince tank.

miles (16.1km) is rarely needed and not provided, but a separate set from the 'command set' is needed for communication at the lowest levels of all between individual tanks within line of sight and with local infantry and artillery controllers. Finally, to enable the crew members to talk among themselves, an inter-communication set is usually incorporated with the main radio, each crewman wearing a headset so as to hear orders above the noise in excess of 100 decibels frequently generated when a tank has all its machinery in operation.

Target Acquisition

In addition to the optics described above, far more sophisticated means are available to detect camouflaged targets and targets made invisible by darkness, fog or smoke. Doppler radar mounted on a tank will pick up moving machines and men out to a considerable range and thus give warning of an enemy's approach. Closer in, the presence of the enemy may be revealed by illuminating him with white or infra-red light (the latter having the advantage of being visible only to special receivers). Most tanks are fitted with searchlights that have a dual-capability in this respect, and with infra-red viewing optics. Better still can be the 'passive' viewing devices such as low light image-intensifiers and for Isocon television cameras since they make use of ambient light and require no artificial source for illumination. Yet another way of 'seeing' is through heat-sensing of objects which have a different local temperature to that of its surroundings. Many viewing devices do far more than enable the tank crew to watch their target : they also provide the capability to shoot in the dark and so enable combat to continue on a 24-hour basis, that is until everybody collapses with fatigue. Indeed, it is now one of the accepted requirements that a tank crew should be provided with a modicum of comfort and, certainly, the means to survive inside the tank when fully closed down in an air-conditioned environment for many hours and, possibly, several days without remittance. Drinking water, food and cooking equipment have to be provided and comfortable seats in which the men can take a nap — one more advantage enjoyed by the driver in his reclining seat if not by the turret crew who are cramped and seated upright.

Navigation

The commander's problems of knowing his exact position at any one moment, by juggling with a map, and carrying out all his other duties has always been a sensitive one, since to be mistaken in this respect, can have fatal consequences. Navigation devices are now fitted to some tanks and can either be calibrated to show merely the location of the tank in relation to the map grid, or can actually be provided with a 'moving map display' which plots the tank's exact position on the map. These machines work to quite high factors of accuracy dependent upon their relation to the tank's movements and the quirks of gyroscopic, mechanical and electronic components.

Aids to mobility

The most common hindrances to a tank's mobility, apart from artificial obstacles, are streams, rivers and soft ground. The latter (as previously mentioned) can be overcome more easily if the tank has high power-to-weight ratio and low ground pressure : the British Scorpion (with a 5psi (0.35kg/cm²) ground pressure) can cross ground

An Israeli Centurion tank mounting the Vickers 105mm gun. An American Browning machine gun is mounted on the turret.

Above : A Chieftain tank,
weighing about 52 tons, fords a
shallow river. It is capable of
crossing water up to 15ft (4.6m)
deep. Its running gear consists
of a set of tracks 24in (61cm)
wide, weighing 9,640lb
(4,363kg), and 12 pairs of twin
wheels.
Right : A gunner in a Chieftain
tank with his hand on the
elevating handle looks through a
periscopic gunsight. He will
also obtain information from a
machine gun test burst to
ensure that he is on target before
firing the main gun. Later a laser
rangefinder is to be fitted.

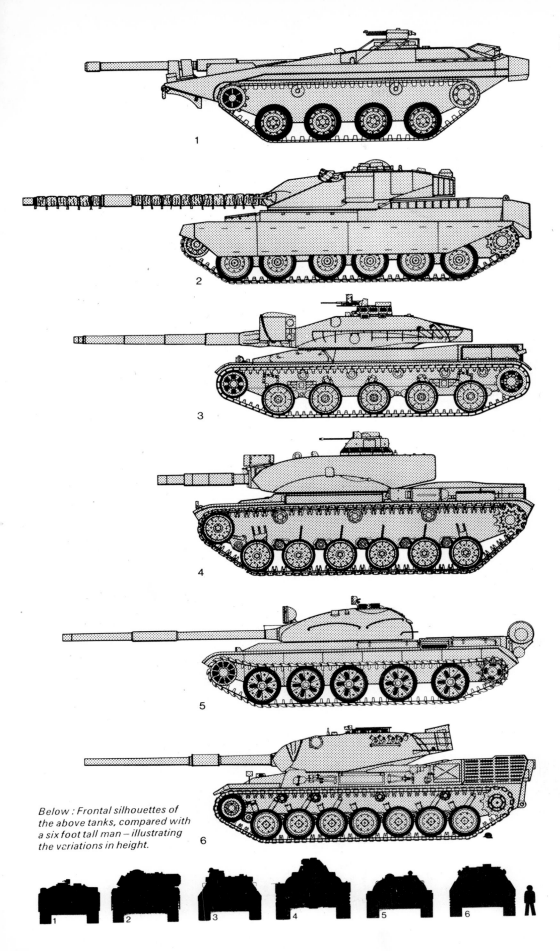

A comparison of the main battle tanks in service today.

1. Swedish S tank. A revolutionary design in that the 105mm gun is fixed in the hull. The gunsight is linked directly to the sophisticated hydro-pneumatic suspension system. Both the commander and the driver-cum-gunner have duplicate controls enabling either of them to drive and aim the gun simultaneously by altering the alignment of the hull. The gun is loaded automatically and the suspension locked at the moment of firing to give stability. Another innovation is the use of a Rolls Royce diesel motor for cruising and a small Boeing gas turbine for moving at high speed. Weight 37 tons, range 225 miles.

2. British Chieftain. At present the most heavily armed and armoured tank (weighing 52 tons) in the world. The 120mm gun is ranged by a co-axial ranging machine-gun or a laser range-finder. Range 310 miles. Crew 4.

3. The AMX30, the French main battle tank. A controversial design in that the maximum armour is only 50mm thick (that of the Chieftain is 150mm), the French favouring mobility and firepower before protection. Fitted with a gyro-stabilized 105mm gun firing anti-tank shells. Weight 36 tons. Crew 4.

4. The American M60 A2, fitted with a low-velocity 152mm gun capable of firing Shillelagh missiles. The Americans are at present developing a gun tank to replace the M60 series following the cancellation of the German/American MBT70. Weight 46 tons. Crew 4. Maximum armour 110mm.

5. The Russian T-62, is a direct descendant of the T-34, the T-62 uses Christie-type suspension giving it excellent mobility. It has a 115mm gun and an extremely low silhouette. Weight 40 tons. Crew 4. Maximum armour 100mm.

6. The German Leopard tank is in service with many NATO countries. It uses the same Vickers 105mm gun as the Centurion and M60. Weight 39.6 tons. Crew 4. It has excellent cross-country performance.

Below: Frontal silhouettes of the above tanks, compared with a six foot tall man – illustrating the variations in height.

113

Above: Illustrations of crew positions in a British Chieftain tank.
Insets: Infra-red searchlights.
Left: The Centurion's light is exposed on top of the turret.
Right: That of the Chieftain is enclosed in a box on the side of the turret.

Right: A Chieftain tank fitted with a 'Simfire', that is a machine which simulates the action of firing and registers the accuracy of the gunner without the expense of using live shells. A laser pulse projector (A), is positioned on top of the gun barrel. The gunner aims at the target and fires the gun trigger. This activates the projector which fires a beam of light. As the trigger is pressed, the flash and bang generator (B) fires small charges to make the action of firing more realistic. If a hit is registered by the laser beam the laser detector units (C) register the information on the commander's interior control box. In the case of a hit on the operator's tank, the same control box cuts out the engine and radio and ignites a smoke generator on the back of the turret.

Left: The latest Russian T-64 (T-70) tank armed with a 122mm gun.

B

A

C

115

in which a man on his feet might sink. Deep and wide water courses demand special equipment, however. For the shallower kind it is sufficient that the tank should wade across on its tracks, the depth to which it can do so depending upon the level at which waterproofing is inherently provided. Since most tanks can instantly be made watertight at the turret ring, while their welded hulls, hatches and automotive compartments are either sealed or unaffected by flooding, it is possible for them to wade almost to the top of the turret. But if the water is deeper than that, two alternatives are available: either the tank can be fitted with a schnorkel tower atop the turret to allow air to be drawn in while the vehicle is totally submerged, or it can be made to swim by fitting a canvas screen which displaces sufficient water to provide flotation. For fairly obvious reasons of bulk, no Main Battle Tank is an inherent swimmer.

Schnorkelling presents various problems in the preparation of the vehicles prior to entry into the water and the training of the crews, not all of whom take kindly to a claustrophobic experience. Swimming is much easier to practise since the canvas screens are quickly and easily erected and the tracks act as paddles. Moreover, should anything go wrong, the crews can more readily escape. But while it is fairly simple to enter the water via a river bank, climbing out at the other side presents difficulties since traction is lost when, with the nose up, so little track is laid on the ground while the rest is still in the water. Therefore special arrangements often have to be made at the far bank to complete the operation, be it by deep wading or swimming.

Below: A notable exception to conventional tank design is the Swedish turretless S-tank, whose gun is fixed in the hull. The gun is elevated (1) or depressed by altering the pitch of the hull, which has adjustable hydro-pneumatic suspension, and traversed by turning the whole vehicle. This has the disadvantage that the gun cannot be fired while on the move. However, the lack of a turret and the S-tank's ability to dig itself into the ground with its bulldozer attachment (2 and 3) make it an excellent defensive weapon ideally suited to Swedish requirements.

Other types of AFV

So far, for the most part, the main consideration has been given to the Main Battle Tank because it is the 'Capital Vehicle' of any armoured army, usually the most heavily armed and armoured and certainly possessing the greatest versatility. Main Battle Tanks in themselves are not, of course, sufficient to satisfy the demands of every task thrust upon armies since it is impossible and undesirable to incorporate every capability into one vehicle. Apart from the cost of an 'universal' machine, there are some battle-field tasks which occur relatively infrequently. For example, if vehicles have a relatively good wading or swimming capability there is less need for assault bridging. There is a demand, then, for specialized vehicles in support of the Main Battle Tank, the number provided depending upon the expected need and the money available for their purchase. It is perhaps unnecessary to add that specialized vehicles are best founded on the chassis's employed for the principal tanks of an armoured force.

Bridging tanks

About 90% of all obstacles that require bridging in normal terrain are less than 30 feet (9.14m) across and therefore the provision of a 40 foot (12.19m) bridge which can be laid by mechanical means from a vehicle whose crew is protected by armour can overcome almost every such difficulty when the enemy is using a stream or deep trench to hold up an advance. Usually a tank, with its turret removed, is fitted with hydraulic lifting apparatus which raises the bridge from its rests on top of the hull and pushes

Above : A tank in a 'hull-down' position. While retaining full visibility the tank is well protected by the hill or obstacle, giving a very small target to an opposing gunner.

Below : A Scorpion tank weighing about 8 tons and mounting a 76mm gun, a 7.62mm machine-gun and two three-barrelled smoke projectors.

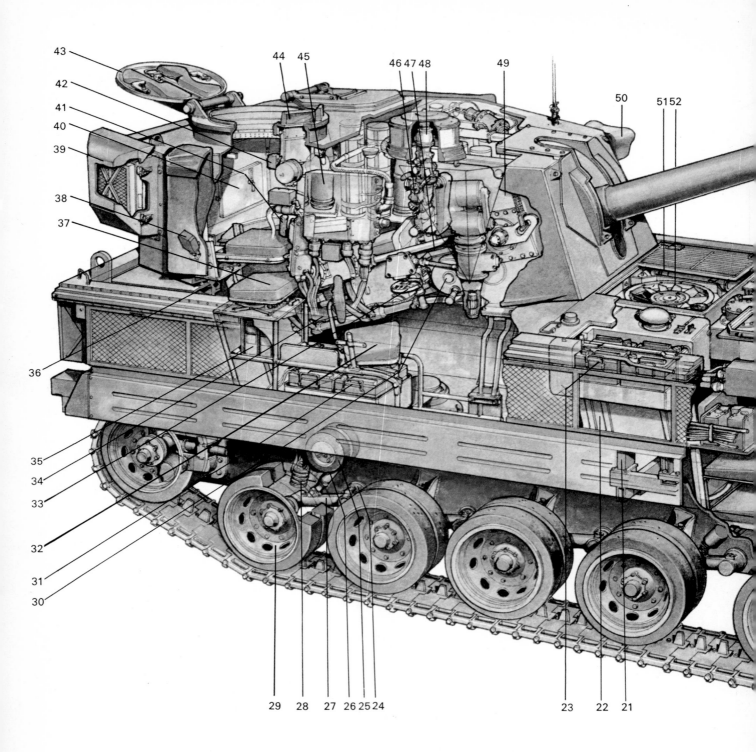

43
42
41
40
39
38
37
36
35
34
33
32
31
30

44 45

46 47 48

49

50

51 52

29 28 27 26 25 24

23 22 21

ABBOT QF 105mm SPG
1. 105mm QF gun
2. Muzzle recoil brake
3. Air inlet louvres
4. Firewire support frame
5. Lifting 'eye'
6. Flotation screen storage
   bracket
7. Flotation screen
8. Headlights (1 pr i/r)

9. Steering unit oil tank
10. Steering unit
11. Fuel pipes
12. Brake operating levers
13. Half-shaft
14. Final drive gears
15. Final drive sprocket
16. Accelerator pedal
17. Gear lever
18. Steering lever

19. Instrument panel
20. Gear-box
21. Engine support frame
22. Fuel tank
23. Hull batteries
24. Torsion bar anchorage
25. Guide roller
26. Shock absorber
27. Axle arm
28. Bump stop

1

2

54   55

3

4

5

6

7

8

9

10

11 12 13 14 15 16 17 18 9

ABBOT DATA

Crew *No. 1, layer, loader, driver*
Weight laden *17.4 tons (17,527kg)*
Weight unladen *14.5 tons (14,878kg)*
Ground pressure *12.3lb/sq in (0.856kg/sq cm)*
Length *(inc gun) 18ft 11in (5.77m)*
Height *8ft 9½in (2.68m)*
Width *8ft 9in (2.67m)*
Track width *1ft 1½in (343mm)*
Ground clearance *1ft 0½in (317mm)*
Engine *Rolls-Royce K60 MK 4G multi-fuel in-line, 6-cylinder, vertically opposed piston two-stroke compression-ignition giving 240bhp at 3,750rpm*
Fuel *85 gallons (386 litres)*
Fuel type *Diesel, gas turbine, MT80 petrol, or a mixture of these fuels*
Armour:
    Hull *Side/nose 0.47in (12mm)*
    Bottom *0.23in (6mm)*
    Top/rear *0.39in (10mm)*
Turret *Front/Sides .39in (10mm)*
    Top *.47in (12mm)*
    Rear *.39in (10mm)*
Armament *QF 105mm L 13A1 7.62mm Bren L4A4, on No. 4, Mk1 mount*
Performance *Max speed on level road 30mph (48kh) In water 3 knots Maximum gradient 30 deg*
Abbot ammunition
HE *(High Explosive) Weight 35lb 6 oz (16.05kg) Fused percussion Direct Action (FPDA); Air burst time; mechanical or proximity (CVT)*
Smoke, *base-ejection, fused time mechanical target indicating, fused timer mechanical direct action, or CVT (12 rounds carried)*
Illuminating, *fused time mechanical*
HESH *(High Explosive Squash Head)*
SH *(Squash Head—practice)*
    The cartridge system has eight different charges, based on two separate cartridges: super-charge, and the normal cartridge containing charges 1 to 5. Additionally sub-zone charges A and B are available, fired from a normal cartridge case emptied of its original charge bags.
    The gun is loaded with two elements, the projectile and the cartridge. The projectile is pushed home by an electrically operated rammer; the cartridge is put in by hand. The cartridges are brass-based, with electrically fired primers.

29. Road wheels
30. Gun elevator
31. Turret batteries
32. Layer's seat
33. Hand-traverse wheel
34. Rammer
35. MG ammunition
36. Turret ring
37. Commander's seat
38. Commander's radio
39. Filter housing
40. Loading door
41. Traverse controller
42. Smoke-discharger firing box
43. Hatch cover
44. Commander's periscopes
45. 105mm ammunition stowage round fighting compartment
46. Dial-sight mounting
47. Telescopic sight
48. Dial sight
49. Gun cradle
50. Smoke discharger (each side)
51. Oil filters
52. Cooling fans (2)
53. Fume extractor
54. Driver's access hatch
55. Second-stage air-cleaner element (lifted from unit)

the bridge forward to lay it in position across the gap. The vehicle then disengages from its bridge and makes way for the other vehicles that follow. Some bridges are 70 feet (21.34m) long and are designed to unfold as they are launched into position, and most are so equipped that they can carry wheeled as well as tracked vehicles.

Self-propelled artillery

It is a well-known (but occasionally overlooked) principle that the most effective armies win their battles by the co-operation of all arms. Artillery (see Chapter 00) provides the highest proportion of sustained fire-support within battle groups and therefore must be enabled to keep pace with its most mobile components. Hence it has become common practice to mount field-artillery on tank chassis, sometimes even enclosing the gun crew within an armoured turret so that the machine looks not unlike an ordinary tank. With the larger pieces, those bigger than 105mm, it is normally practical only to enclose the crew behind partial cover or perhaps leave them totally exposed, trusting to concealment, the vehicle's mobility or luck to provide a measure of protection.

Guns which are designated mainly for anti-tank purposes have often, in the past, been given only a limited traverse, pointing forwards from the hull of a tank from which the turret has been removed. The Germans and Russians were the main exponents of this method. The outcome was an effective fighting vehicle which lacked the tactical flexibility of a turretted tank, a shortcoming which still relegates the SP Anti-tank gun to a subsidiary role in battle.

APCs and MICVs

From its earliest days the tank has been, in the minds of

Below : US M7 self-propelled howitzer. Weight 22 tons ; Crew 7 ; Armament 105mm M2 howitzer with 45 traverse and 69 rnds, .5in MG in pulpit mount.
Right, top : Abbot SPG in close-up.
Right, centre : The Russian SU-100. A self-propelled 100mm gun is mounted on the T-34 chassis.
Right, bottom : The Russian SU-152 heavy assault gun. Weight 50 tons ; Armament 152mm howitzer.

many, little more than an armoured personnel carrier (APC) – that is a machine to carry men in relative safety through enemy fire to the point at which dismounted action began. By the end of World War II there were many such machines, some, such as the armoured half-tracked vehicles made by the Germans before 1939, being purpose built, others, such as the fully tracked type converted by the British from tanks with their turrets removed, being improvised. Well before the war was over, however, there was strong impetus to give APCs the capability to fight if only in their own defence – a single machine-gun in a sub-turret or on an external mounting might suffice, although the Germans were mounting their armament behind shields.

After the war, work began on purpose-built APCs – most on tracks but some on wheels, many with a strong swimming capability aided by screens, few with a pronounced combat ability. Designs were largely subservient to the philosophy that the APC should act as an armoured taxi on the periphery of the battle by transporting the infantry to within assault distance of the objective, the men's final charge to be made on foot. Little more than lip-service was paid to the principle that the APC should have the same cross-country performance as the tanks they were meant to support. By the mid-1960s specifications for a vehicle which carried both infantry and a good main armament – gun or missile or a combination of both – were abroad and appeared for the first time when the Russians displayed their BMP-76 in 1967. This AFV can carry eight infantry-men plus a crew of three and is armed with a 73mm gun and a small anti-tank missile ('Sagger'). Many more nations are developing their own Mechanized Infantry

Above : A German SdKfz 251 armoured half track in France 1940. Another photograph showing the occupants more clearly and taken at the same time is on pages 96/7.

Below: The West German GEPARD self-propelled AA system equipped with two Oerlikon KDA 35/90mm automatic machine guns

Combat Vehicles (MICVs), as this type of vehicle is now called, with the German Marder, with the agility of a Main Battle Tank, weighing 14 tons (14,225kg), armed with a 20mm cannon and carrying a complement of 10 men, providing a typical example of the breed. Unfortunately the MICV is proving as expensive as a Main Battle Tank, so the debate is by no means resolved. A trend is, nevertheless discernible. In any future war, while Main Battle Tanks, dominate the battlefield, subsidiary actions may well take place with MICV *versus* MICV.

Missile carriers

Since the anti-tank guided missile needs only a small vehicle as its launcher, the opportunity to mount these weapons on light AFVs, unarmoured vehicles and helicopters, has been seized upon. Often missiles are mounted, unprotected by armour, atop an APC, though in the case of the British FV 438 a special housing has been made for its Swingfire missiles and their controller within a conventional tracked APC called FV 432. Vehicles such as these have the advantage that they can engage their targets while partially or even totally out of sight, giving them a useful ambush capability in defence. In attack, however, they are extremely difficult to deploy. Furthermore, of course, they have hardly any other role other than as an anti-tank vehicle.

Anti-aircraft tanks

While a number of tank hulls fitted with rapid fire weapons in a special turret were introduced during World War II, it is only in recent years that they have reappeared in some quantity, led by the Russians. The air threat against armies is increasing and dangerous, though not perhaps as dangerous as sometimes claimed. Helicopters armed with anti-tank missiles have certainly accentuated the threat, but the surface-to-air missile has been shown in recent

122

Left : Austin armoured car. It weighed 4.5 tons and was in service between 1917 and 1925.

Below : Commonly referred to as the 'Greyhound', the most common American armoured car of World War II was designed and produced by Ford. Armed with a 37mm gun and a .30in machine gun, its top speed was 56mph.

123

A British Saladin armoured car shown on exercises in West Germany. It mounts a 76mm gun and its six wheels give it a good cross-country performance.

wars to have its limitations. On the other hand, extremely rapid-fire anti-aircraft tanks, with their target acquisition improved by radar, have enjoyed notable successes in shooting down low-flying strike aircraft. Hence the renewed popularity of armoured, mobile anti-aircraft guns which are increasingly to be found as guardians of battle-groups at the front, with their weapons reaching out into enemy territory should an air attack start from there. It follows that they have a useful role in a ground action, if pressed, although a major problem is that of ammunition supply. So high is the rate of fire of their guns that the logistic problem is immense since many such vehicles carry barely enough ammunition for a 30-second engagement.

Minesweepers

Mines which could cut a tank's track or even disrupt its hull were laid in huge quantities during World War II and today, with improved and larger mines, can be sown quickly in even larger numbers by mechanical means. So the need for minesweeping armoured vehicles is as necessary as ever. It is all the more surprising, therefore, to find that the most effective type is still the flail, such as was used so successfully during World War II, although 'ploughs' and explosive effect measures also play a part in minesweeping. Mines thus remain a potent threat of one of the tank's principal characteristics – its mobility.

Armoured cars

On occasions the wheeled armoured fighting vehicle, generally known as the Armoured Car, has been called a Wheeled Tank—which in many respects, except for its suspension, it is. The disadvantages in terms of mobility of a wheeled vehicle compared with a tracked one need no elucidation. The advantages of the wheeled fighting vehicle may not be quite so obvious. In essence they score over the tracked machine because of their greater economy in action, their higher speeds and their longer range. They also have the gift of silence which, in the reconnaissance role in which they are chiefly employed, can be crucial to success. They possess one other advantage when employed in helping to keep the peace in a situation of civil unrest: armoured cars do not have the same evocative effect as tanks and can sometimes be employed quite offensively without arousing the ire of propagandists and people to whom the very word 'tank' is the epitome of blatant provocation and aggression.

Amphibious vehicles

Most famous of all military amphibians, and still one of the most versatile vehicles in use, is the American built General Motors Corporation DUKW ('Duplex Universal Karrier, Wheeled'), first built in 1942 and primarily used for ship-to-shore transport. Based on a truck chassis, it has a six cylinder 4.4 litre engine. All six wheels, which have rubber tyres, are driven.

The wheels all steer on land, and on water they assist a rudder. A single propeller is driven through a transfer case — a gearbox which enables it to be switched in and out. The six and a half ton amphibian can achieve 50 mph (80 kph) on land and 6 mph (10 kph) on water. Production ceased in 1945, but 'ducks' are still in use with armed forces all over the world.

Another major class of amphibian is known in the US as the LVT, short for Landing Vehicle, Tracked. The LVT, nicknamed the 'Buffalo', starred as a rescue vehicle. It was designed in 1932 by Donald Roebling for use in the Florida swamplands and later developed as a military vehicle for carrying men and materials over rivers or on sea-borne landings.

The LVT is driven on both land and water by tracks equipped with W-shaped protruberances (grousers) to give greater thrust. Buffers set between the driving wheels support the tracks and prevent them from being forced inwards by water pressure. This gives a greater effective driving surface.

Later models were fitted with Cadillac engines and automatic gearboxes. Current LVTs have side screens along the top run of the tracks and a cowl over the front of them, so that water carried forward by the top of the tracks is directed towards the rear again and so contributes to the

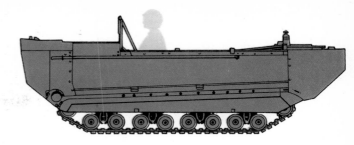

Above: The UK M29C 'Weasel' amphibious light carrier, variant of a 1942 ½-ton cargo winter-warfare tracked vehicle. Its feather tread pressure of 2lb/sq. in, less than a man's foot, meant that it was the ideal vehicle for muddy ground.

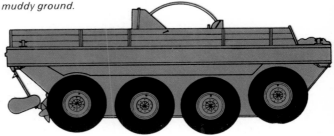

Above: The British 'Terrapin I' wheeled amphibian lorry. UK equivalent of the US DUKW, had a 4-ton cargo capacity.

Below: The DUKW, an amphibious six-wheeled 2½-ton 'sea lorry', first used in March 1943, for short-haul delivery of men and equipment from ship to shore.
Manufacturer's code:
D – 1942
U – Utility
K – Twin rear axles
W – All-wheel drive

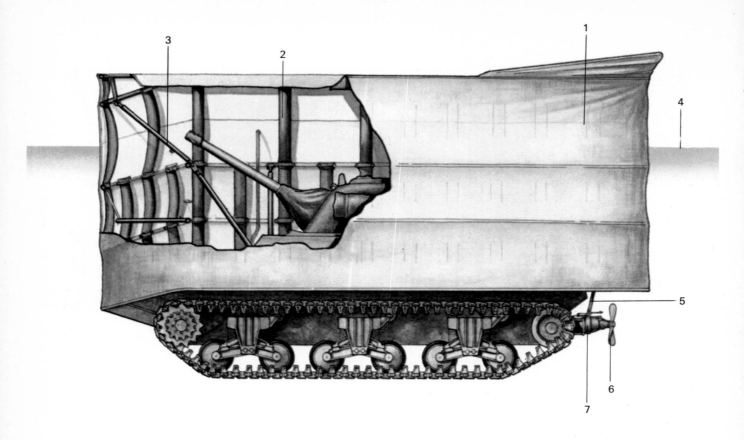

Above: The Sherman Duplex-Drive (DD) tank. A basic Sherman, with five crew, a 75mm M3 gun and two MGs, fitted with a collapsible canvas screen and twin propellers linked to the tank's track. In calm water, a speed of 4 knots was attainable. (1) Canvas screen. (2) Tubular rubber air pillars. (3) Bow frames. (4) 3ft water-level, inadequate in anything but calm seas. (5) Rod link to tiller. (6) Twin 3-bladed screws. (7) Drive from idler wheel.

Opposite page:
Top: An amphibious LVT Mk 4 Buffalo tractor. The LVT 4 carried 20 Marines, or 4.5 tons of cargo and vehicles. Its tracks gave it a water-speed of 6 knots. Land speed was 25mph, which enabled the LVT to surmount coral reefs and other obstacles. The 26ft, 14-ton Buffalo carried several .5in and .3in MGs. The Buffalo shown here has a hull-mounted MG.
Centre: Tracked landing vehicle (LVTs) coming ashore during Operation 'Deep Furrow', Mediterranean 1971. These vehicles, about 30ft (10m) long (12ft (4m) wide) and 10ft (3m) high can carry between 25 and 30 people and weigh about 38 tons (38,500kg) when fully loaded.
Bottom: Control centre of the amphibious command ship USS Mount Shitney. Amphibious assault ships within its command can carry up to 1500 troops plus amphibious vehicles, aircraft, helicopters and missiles.

forward thrust. Another gain in thrust comes from grilles at the back which channel the wash straight behind the vehicle. LVTs can cope with rocky beaches and heavy surf with equal ease.

During World War II, it was often necesary to convert a military vehicle into an amphibian, and Duplex Drive was devised by Nicholas Straussler to allow tanks to float into battle. The DD Sherman was so used on D Day in 1944. A platform of mild steel is welded round the water-proofed tank's hull and a raised canvas or plastic screen is erected round it to give buoyancy. This is generally supported by a series of rubber tubes inflated from cylinders of compressed air carried on the tank's superstructure.

Small propellers were originally driven by the tracks on early models, but the vulnerability of propellers on land led to the increasingly widespread use of water jet propulsion. A ducted propeller sucks in water from under the body and squirts it through steering valves at the back. Russia leads in this field, but the armies of many nations now have troop carriers and reconnaissance vehicles driven by water jets.

Flotation screens are used on many military vehicles such as the US Vickers 37 ton tank, the Scorpion light tank and APC, but most modern designers prefer either to forget all about temporary amphibious qualities or to build their tanks as true amphibians.

The Russian PT-76 amphibious tank is powered by a water-jet which allows the vehicle to cross rivers submerged. This type of amphibian was pioneered before World War II by the British and then by the Germans whose submersible tanks were to have been used in Hitler's

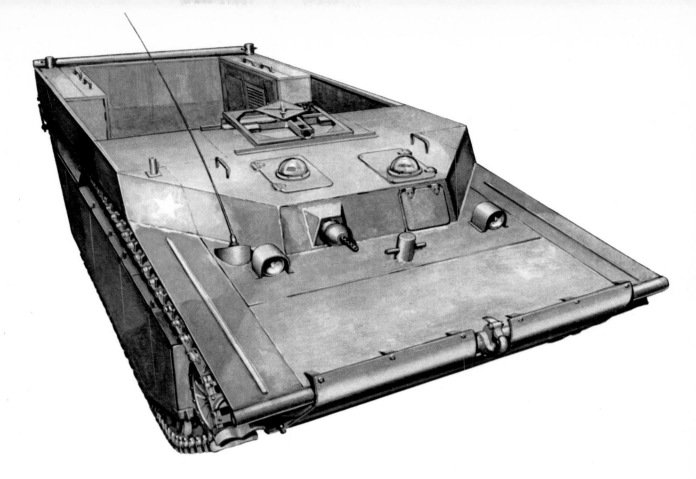

abortive invasion of Britain.

They have schnorkels (air tubes) extending to the surface, bringing air to both crew and engine. The French AMX30 tank, for example, has a 15ft (4.6m) long tube, wide enough to allow the commander to stand in the top and relay instructions to his submerged crew.

The main problem in converting standard battle tanks for amphibious operation is the problem of sealing the vehicle against water, a problem especially difficult where the turret meets the hull.

The air tube principle was also used on the British Austin Champ jeep. It had an extendable air pipe leading to the carburettor on the waterproofed engine. True amphibious jeeps were the World War II Volkswagen Schwimmwagen and the GPA ('General Purpose Amphibious') version of the American Jeep, which is still popular.

On the GPA Jeep, the watertight hull was constructed separately from the basic chassis to make replacement easy. The propeller was countersunk for protection, and was driven by a separate shaft mounted alongside the main drive to the rear wheels. It weighed more than a conventional Jeep, but could still reach 50 mph (80 kph) on the road.

The armoured fighting vehicle, and especially the tank, has revolutionized land warfare in this century. Whether or not they will continue to dominate the battlefield remains to be seen. However, as long as the objective of an army is to occupy and secure the territory of the enemy, then the tank will continue to be the centrepiece of any future conflict.

Salt water covers some 70% of the surface of the globe. Most of the world's resources, communications and political power border or traverse those seas. Island peoples depend almost entirely upon what they can get from the ocean or carry across it. It is to protect their own nations' trades and interests, while influencing or preventing the maritime activities of other countries, that warships exist.

Merchant vessels and warships are alike in that both have to survive the hazards of the sea, while carrying complete life support systems for their crews. Nothing can be obtained from their surroundings except fresh air — and even that is denied in submarines and enclosed compartments.

The merchant ship is designed to move large quantities of cargo with little effort and a small crew, thus making a profit for the owner. The warship needs a higher speed for action, and a big crew to absorb casualties and still function efficiently. But not even the state has unlimited funds, so warships must be cheap to build and to maintain. Every warship is therefore a compromise between the basic requirements of seaworthiness, speed, accommodation and cost, and the ever-changing problems of weapons, protection and tactics.

Development

Physical contact was the dominant characteristic of the earliest combats on water. Any canoe, raft or boat could leave off fishing or trading to carry a party of warriors to raid a neighbouring village. Clubs, knives, arrows and spears dealt with the opposing tribesmen on shore or in their own little craft. Captives and stolen goods were brought back in triumph and the boatmen returned to more peaceful occupations. Even when coastal vessels grew larger, most early warships were essentially merchantmen, carrying soldiers with hand weapons for service afloat or ashore.

Classical galley
However, the Mediterranean empires of classical times developed a specialized type of warship known as the galley. Although this slim vessel carried a square sail for

WARSHIPS

use in a following wind, manoeuvrability and high speed in action were provided by oars. Banking and staggering them in two tiers (a bireme) or three tiers (a trireme), added power without appreciably increasing the length or the beam.

Desperate hand-to-hand struggles were common, but the galley's chief weapon was the ram. This was originally a projection of the keel, probably first continued forward of the stempost to provide added buoyancy and a clean cutwater. Later rams may have been special structures nailed to the bow.

As the tactical aim was to sink an opponent by ramming him amidships or in the stern, while keeping one's own hull intact, galleys maintained a tight line-abreast formation. Sometimes they met the enemy bow to bow, with serious results to both vessels. At other times a skilful captain and well-trained crew shipped their oars at the last moment, their galley smashing along the adversary's oars and immobilizing him ready for the final ramming. Frequently, the line which had started to open out, or had been outflanked, backed water until it regained cohesion or reached the security of narrow waters. Battles often ended with the losing side's surviving vessels being hauled up on to the beach to be defended by soldiers.

Co-ordination with the army's movements was also necessary for daily replenishment and repair. Galleys were too narrow to permit the stowage of much food and water, nor was there adequate room for sleep. Also, early Greek galleys were built of short-lived fir for lightness and economy. So until they became too large and heavy, these warships were customarily beached every night.

From 700 BC until the Battle of Lepanto in 1571 AD, galleys remained the arbiter of Mediterranean sea-power. They varied in length from 60 to 180 feet (18m to 55m) and from 8 to 20 feet (2.4m to 6m) in width. There were improvements in construction and rig, and some galleys were widened to carry small amounts of valuable cargo. There were changes in the disposition of oars and rowers, resulting in some types of galleys being designated quadriremes and quinquiremes. The number of oarsmen varied from 20 to 300, with a few officers and soldiers manning the catwalk above the rowing benches. Some

Above: The 64,000 ton bulk of the Japanese battleship Yamato can be gauged by comparison with the Aichi floatplane on the stern of the ship.

Below: Third Warspite shown damaged at the Battle of Lagos, 18 August 1759.
Opposite page, below: The second Warspite – launched in June 1666.

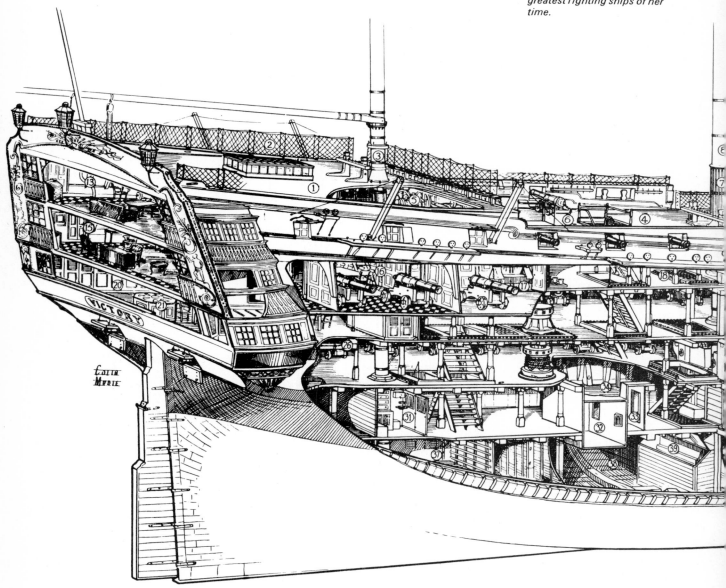

big Roman galleys were completely decked and fitted with fighting castles to carry 120 heavily armed marines who rushed across a special boarding bridge on to the enemy ship. The armament of fast Byzantine galleys called dromons (or runners) included the much-feared Greek fire, while the very last type of galley (the galeass) was equipped with cannon.

In spite of these fairly late innovations, galleys controlled the Mediterranean by ramming and boarding, the latter tactic being similarly employed by men-at-arms in the warships of northern Europe until the 16th century. The oared longships and sailing cogs and carracks were merely merchantmen whose later forecastles, aftercastles and

fighting tops gave a height advantage to soldiers directing crossbow bolts, spears and rocks upon their antagonists below.

Ironclad ram

Ramming never completely disappeared from naval history. The introduction of steam power in the 19th century gave rise to the idea of ironclad rams, which enjoyed a certain respect in the world's navies for some 30 years. The increasing range of naval gunnery rendered such close-quarter work less likely, although P-boats (patrol boats) were built with hardened steel bows to ram submarines during World War I. However, accidental collisions and operational experience demonstrated that ramming, even

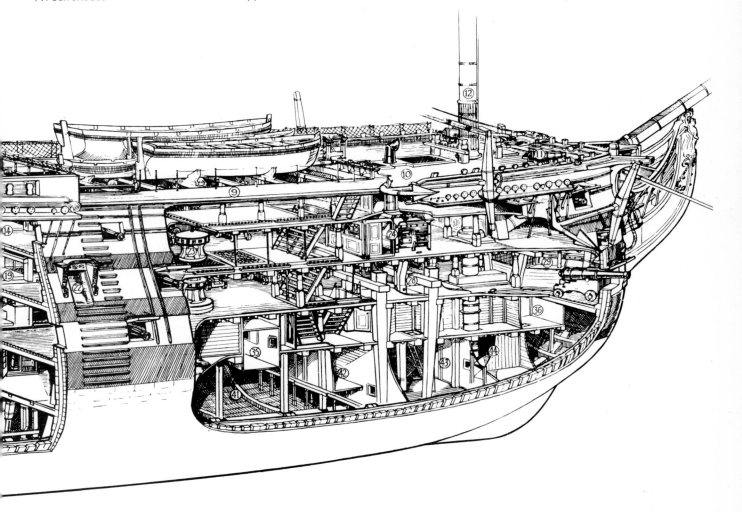

by purpose-built vessels, could easily result in serious – if not fatal – damage to the attacking warship. Yet, as the so-called 'Cod War' has shown, just the threat of collision is still something of a tactical manoeuvre, while the trawl-cutting equipment used by Icelandic gunboats is certainly a close-contact weapon.

There will always be the possibility that an unflinching captain might hazard his own ship to prevent the enemy's escape, although it now seems incredible that any future warship would ever be built specially for ramming. But it could happen that a desperate nation might hurriedly complete a number of cheap craft (with or without explosive devices) whose crews would sacrifice them-

selves in an attempt to stave off defeat, as did the Japanese in the closing stages of World War II.

Boarding also lingered on in naval warfare. The capture of an enemy warship, rather than its destruction, was still regarded as an obvious sign of success in Nelson's day, and boarding has been occasionally used during the wars of the 20th century. The release of British prisoners from the German Altmark and the capture of the German submarine U-505 are two of the best known incidents, while one of the most recent was the taking of the USS Pueblo by North Korea in 1968.

Warships of all nations send boarding parties across to merchant ships to search for contraband and if necessary seize or scuttle them. Although rarely opposed, such parties are armed and ready to use force. The examination of merchantmen will inevitably continue to be a traditional task performed by future warships. Their armament will have to include small arms, bayonets, hand grenades and demolition charges for issue to the boarding party, who would probably be ferried across by helicopter or by boat.

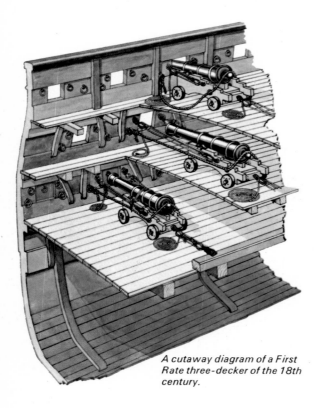

A cutaway diagram of a First Rate three-decker of the 18th century.

'Great gun' ship

For about 2,000 years, battles fought by warships and pirate vessels, built for ramming and boarding, had decided which ruler could move his army across the sea in safety, and which merchantmen and coastal peoples could trade and live in peace. Then, from the time of the Spanish Armada in 1588 until the middle of the 19th century, the sail-driven 'great gun' ship dominated the world's oceans. These vessels changed little in appearance. The Swedish Wasa of 1628 had two gun-decks carrying 48 24pounder (10.87kg) muzzle-loading cannon with an effective range of 765 yards (700m). She had three masts and an overall length of 204 feet (62m) with a tonnage of 1,300 tons (1,320 tonnes).

HMS Queen, launched in 1839, had three gun-decks carrying 100 32pounder (14.5kg) cannon with an extreme range of 3,000 yards (2,745m). She had three masts and her wooden hull was 204.5 feet (62.3m) long, with a tonnage of 3,104 tons (3,153 tonnes). There were improvements in rig, hull design and navigation equipment during the two centuries separating these two vessels. Some attention was paid to living conditions. There were variations in ammunition, but this was basically still solid shot relying upon impact for its effect. Gun sights remained

A British 64-gun Third Rate Line of Battleship. This class was the smallest considered fit for the line of battle and was the largest warship type built outside the Royal Dockyards. They replaced the 70-gun ships built since the seventeenth century but were similar in size and design. Forty-five '64s' were constructed between 1748 and 1787, but thereafter the roomier '74' having 30 per cent more firepower, predominated.

Seven '64s' fought at Camperdown—the last fleet action that saw them in any numbers. *Ardent* took the heaviest loss and had 98 round-shot embedded in her hull. Captain Bligh commanded *Director*, built in 1784.
Tonnage: between 1,370 and 1,440 tons
Length of lower gun-deck: 160ft
Complement: 485 men
Cost, minus guns: £40,000

Conjectural armament at Camperdown:
Upper (Main) Deck: 26 x 18-pounders
Lower (Gun) Deck: 26 x 24-pounders
Quarter-Deck: 10 x 9-pounders
     ,,   ,,   : 6 x 18-pdr carronades
Forecastle: 2 x 24-pdr carronades
Total: 70 guns
Carronades boosted a 600!b-broadside to 669!b.

SMS ('Seiner Majestat Schiff') Goeben, wearing the Ensign of His Imperial Majesty's German Navy, and with her officers and crew crowding her decks, leaves port.

primitive, victory going to the gun's crew who, through hard discipline, held most steady in action.

Because these cannon were mounted in the sides of the ship, every captain desired to present his broadside to the enemy's bow or stern, while protecting his own ends. So line ahead became the typical battle formation, and crossing the enemy's 'T' (so that the whole of one's fleet could fire while the enemy's guns were impotent) was the tactical aim of every engagement. Some battles were inconclusive and others ended in general confusion, but the important thing was the line of battle, and the warship built to receive hard pounding and hand it out was the ship of the line (or line-of-battle ship).

Smaller vessels (frigates, sloops, corvettes and cutters) were only lighter versions of the sailing battleship, used for patrol and escort work. When they encountered rivals of similar build, they fought the same way battleships did – a certain amount of manoeuvring, followed by battering each other with cannon-balls, chain-shot and grapeshot until one sank or surrendered.

The one specialist warship of this period was the bomb. Her foremast removed, she carried one or more mortars throwing a round explosive shell which had to be ignited before being fired at an indirect shore target. This weapon was too slow and hazardous for use against moving ships at sea, which could close the range and hit back. General-purpose cannon still determined naval battles, although the future lay with the shell-firing gun. (A shell is a hollow round filled with explosive, compared with the cannon-ball, which is solid.)

'Dreadnought' battleship

As the 19th century bore on, shells became safer to handle and were designed with pointed noses to help them penetrate ships' sides before bursting between decks. Wooden battleships were then protected with iron plates, these ironclads themselves carrying rifled guns for greater range, accuracy and penetration. Steam engines ensured mobility and speed at all times.

By 1914 turbine-driven, oil-fired, dreadnought battleships (named after the first of their kind) were armed with six, ten or even fourteen breech-loading guns, whose armour-piercing shells could be hurled over $12\frac{1}{2}$ miles (20km). These high-explosive projectiles and their cordite propellant had to be brought from armour-protected magazines on revolving hoists suspended from the gun-turrets which traversed to give all-round fire. Rangefinders, directors and sights were developed to feed information to the transmitting station (a mechanical computer) which controlled the elevation and bearing of the guns.

Yet with turrets fore and aft, and sometimes amidships as well, battleships could direct most of their fire on the broadside. So the old line of battle was retained, and crossing the enemy's 'T' remained the tactical aim. On a few exceptional occasions, such as at Tsushima in 1905, Jutland in 1916 and Surigao Strait in 1944, the out-manoeuvred fleet was overwhelmed or forced to with-

draw. Dreadnoughts eventually became so expensive that they were not usually put at risk unless the gain was obvious — and so tough that only the French Bretagne was lost in direct combat with another dreadnought (and she was in harbour at Mers-el-Kébir). Those which blew up or sank had either been built as battlecruisers (which sacrificed armour for speed) or fell victim to the three-dimensional air/sea warfare. Although this type of warfare began earlier, it was most characteristic of World War II and is still prevalent today.

No longer did danger come from a parallel line on the surface, but from above and below the sea, and from all points of the compass. So a rough circle became the best tactical formation, with the surviving battleships in the middle for their own protection. The battlefleet had become a liability — and a target for an atomic bomb.

The great gun ships were scrapped, preserved as floating museums, or laid up in reserve. A reserved ship, the USS New Jersey, did see action during the Vietnam War. Fully loaded she displaced 59,000 tons (59,944 tonnes) on a length of 887.6 feet (270.5m). Her nine 16in (40.6cm) guns could fire 2,700pound (1.225kg) shells to a range of 24.25 miles (39km). Steel armour up to 19in (48.3cm) thick protected her own vital command, machinery, gunnery and magazine areas. But New Jersey did not fight in the line of battle in 1968–1969. Like a shallow-draught monitor or river gunboat, she was used for shore bombardment.

Aircraft carrier

Specialized warships are now needed to handle the different types of weapons employed in three-dimensional warfare. The most dramatic contender with the battleship as arbiter of the oceans (or capital ship) was the aircraft-carrier. As soon as aircraft showed some military potential, experiments began to prepare them for use at sea. At first, converted warships and merchantmen carried seaplanes which had to be hoisted out on to the sea and recovered by cranes, but subsequent vessels were constructed with flight decks. The original function of the naval air arm was to operate as an aerial observation platform for battleships, later machines carrying such weapons as would cripple an opposing fleet ready for destruction by surface ship gunnery. By the end of World World II, naval battles in the Pacific were being fought entirely in the air over the sea as propeller-driven aircraft reached out to a distance of 500 miles (800km) with bombs, rockets, torpedoes, depth-charges, mines and machine-guns.

Aircraft-carriers needed to be big ships for reasons which are still valid today. The long flight-deck must be well above the waterline so that aircraft can operate in bad weather. It must also be clear of superstructure, which involves locating the bridge, funnels and masts in an island on the starboard side. Fixed-wing aircraft are accelerated to flying speed by a steam catapult forward. Protection from hot jet blast is necessary at the after end

The British battleship Warspite shells German emplacements on the Normandy coast on D-Day. Each 15in gun produced eight times more firepower, pound for pound, than a broadside from the first Warspite built in 1596.

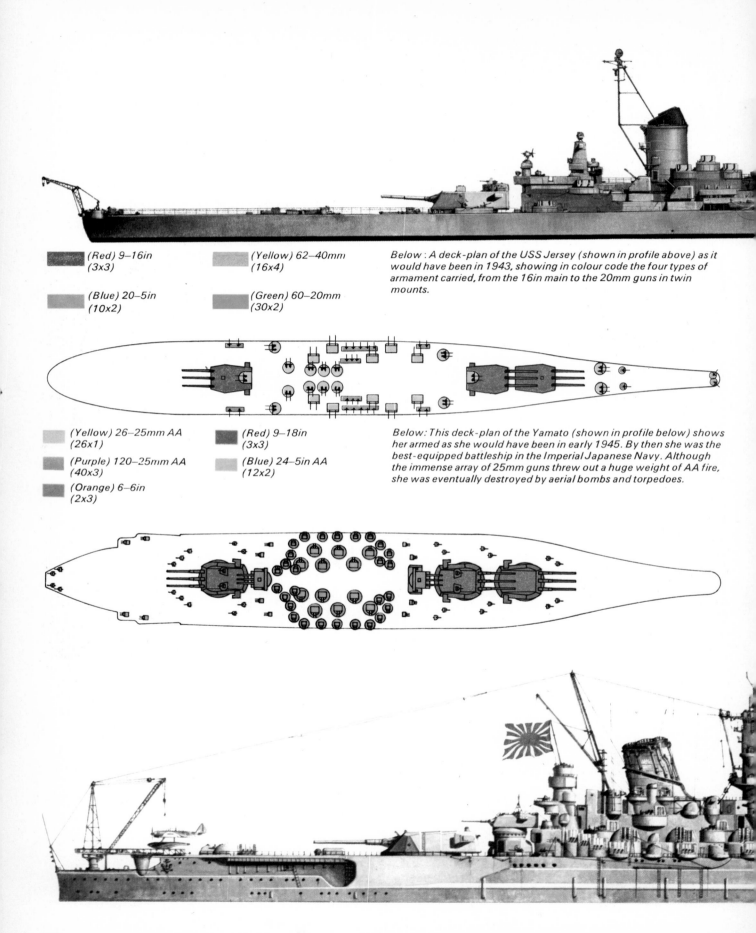

(Red) 9–16in
(3x3)

(Yellow) 62–40mm
(16x4)

(Blue) 20–5in
(10x2)

(Green) 60–20mm
(30x2)

Below : A deck-plan of the USS Jersey (shown in profile above) as it would have been in 1943, showing in colour code the four types of armament carried, from the 16in main to the 20mm guns in twin mounts.

(Yellow) 26–25mm AA
(26x1)

(Red) 9–18in
(3x3)

(Purple) 120–25mm AA
(40x3)

(Blue) 24–5in AA
(12x2)

(Orange) 6–6in
(2x3)

Below: This deck-plan of the Yamato (shown in profile below) shows her armed as she would have been in early 1945. By then she was the best-equipped battleship in the Imperial Japanese Navy. Although the immense array of 25mm guns threw out a huge weight of AA fire, she was eventually destroyed by aerial bombs and torpedoes.

Above: the USS New Jersey, the last battleship to see action, firing a full broadside.

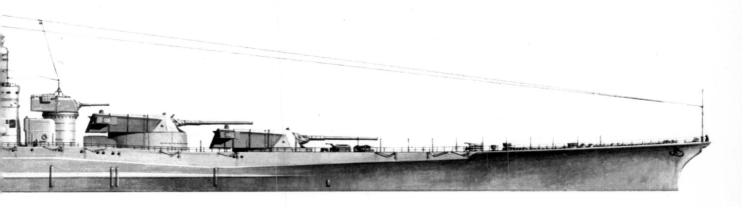

of the catapult to prevent damage to following aircraft, while the deck panels here must also be water-cooled. On return, the aircraft is guided on to the flight-deck by visual and audible landing aids. Once it has been arrested, the aircraft retracts its hook and moves to the starboard forward corner of the flight-deck. This allows any succeeding aircraft that misses the arrester wires to fly off the end of the angled deck and go round again. Below the flight-deck is the hangar, which must be a clear space two decks deep. Electric, chain-driven lifts transport aircraft between hangar- and flight-decks. Usually there are two lifts, serving both ends of the hangar, but some carriers have deck-edge lifts. Aircraft maintenance workshops are arranged along the sides of the hangar, which can be quickly drenched by a remotely-controlled sprinkler system in the event of a fire. Aircraft weapons and fuel are stored lower down, for maximum protection, and here too are the ship's own machinery spaces. Because of the unobstructed hangar above, the boiler uptakes have to be led across to the starboard side and then up to the funnel. (This is not necessary in nuclear-powered carriers.) Long-range radar, radio communications and computers are all needed for tracking and directing high-speed aircraft. Room must be found for all this equipment, workshops for its maintenance, and accommodation and office space

Left: Smoke and flame burst from the middle 16in guns of Nelson as she steams through seas in gale-force winds. Dazzle camouflage indicates a wartime photograph.

for all the necessary personnel. The result is a very big ship indeed. The USS Nimitz has a full-load displacement of 95,100 tons (96,622 tonnes) on an overall length of 1,092 feet (333m). She was designed to operate about 90 aircraft, although this number decreases as their size and complexity grow. Usually equipped with surface-to-air missiles, carriers generally rely upon their own fighters and fleet escorts for anti-aircraft defence.

Because the sea is so vast, it is difficult to locate even such a giant ship as this, but once found (perhaps by satellite observation), her squadron would be a prime target for nuclear attack. Partly for this reason, partly for economy, and partly due to the improved performance of helicopters and the introduction of V/STOL aircraft like the Hawker Siddeley Harrier, there has been a trend towards smaller carriers. The Russian helicopter cruiser Moskva, displacing 15,000 tons (15,240 tonnes) standard, has an after flight-deck only, with complete superstructure forward. The Royal Navy's proposed through-deck cruiser Invincible will have a complete angled deck and be 650 feet (198.1m) long with an estimated displacement of 20,000 tons (20,320 tonnes). Such ships can operate Harrier-type strike-fighters, with helicopers for anti-submarine or assault work. Missile-launchers provide anti-submarine, anti-ship and anti-aircraft capability, while the vessel herself is large enough to act as a command ship for squadron and amphibious operations. This hybrid vessel may also be finding favour in today's political climate because it is not so obviously committed to strike operations as the conventional aircraft-carrier.

Top: HMS Rodney in dock. Above: The same ship in the breaker's yard at Inverkeithing, Scotland, 1948. The great 16in barrels have been sawn off.

Submarine

The other great exponent of three-dimensional naval warfare is the submarine. By applying Archimedes' principle that a floating body displaces a quantity of water equal to its own weight, it is possible to build a craft into which water can be admitted. Its weight is thus increased sufficiently for it to submerge. The expulsion of the added water allows the craft to rise and float upon the surface again. One problem is how to control the amount of water admitted and expelled. The method Bourne had recommended in 1578 was followed by the Dutch mechanic Drebbel. He used an expanding leather bulkhead which could be screwed back into position to force out the ballast water. The craft was propelled by oars and a breathing tube led to the surface. Drebbel successfully demonstrated his boat in the River Thames in front of King James I.

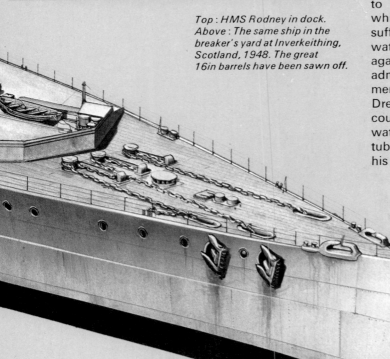

Left: The powerful lines of the '1921 unit' HMS Nelson, were identical to those of her sister-ship Rodney (see opposite page inset). During the years of World War II the AA armament was increased.

16in BREECH LOADER Mk 1 on Mk 1 TRIPLE MOUNTING
Longitudinal section—HMS NELSON

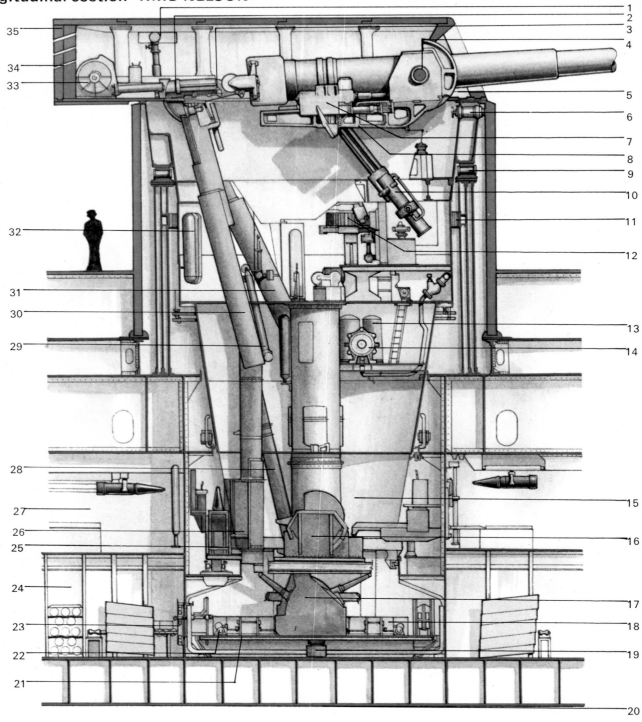

HMS Nelson
1. Rangefinder
2. Cordite tilting tray
3. Shell tilting tray
4. Trunnion
5. Blast excluder
6. Turret locking bolt
7. Rear cradle
8. Slide

9. Turret rollers
10. Elevating cylinder
11. Training rack
12. Training pinion
13. Gun washout water tanks
14. Hydraulic accumulator
15. Shell handling room
16. Shell loading bogie
17. Cordite tilting hopper

18. Swinging trays
19. Centre pivot
20. Ship's keel
21. Revolving pivot
22. Cordite rammer
23. Flash-proof door
24. Magazine
25. Shell loading bogie
26. Revolving scuttle

27. Shell room
28. Cordite hoist
29. Cordite lifting cylinder
30. Shell hoist (centre)
31. Shell hoist (side)
32. Air blast bottles
33. Rammer
34. Ventilating holes
35. Counter-balance weight

During the 17th and 18th centuries there were more experiments in propulsion and ballasting: a clockwork-driven paddle-wheel; leather bottles filled with water; and rocks carried externally and released from within.

The first submersible warship appeared during the War of American Independence. Built by David Bushnell, Turtle was a one-man, egg-shaped craft driven by a crank-operated propeller. A similar, but vertical, propeller controlled the depth, although the bilges could be flooded and pumped out as a means of ballasting. In her, in 1776, Sergeant Ezra Lee made an attack upon HMS Eagle, flagship of the British blockading fleet. Turtle carried a 150-pound (68kg) charge of gunpowder fitted with a clockwork detonator, which had to be attached to the target's hull. The screw securing the charge was not strong enough to penetrate Eagle's copper sheathing, Turtle was seen, and the attack abandoned although Lee and Turtle survived. About 1800, another American,

Above: The USS Nashville, an assault ship inspired by the original Royal Navy assault ships 'Fearless' and 'Intrepid', but on a larger scale. She carries several large landing craft which are released by flooding the stern until it is low enough for them to float inside the mother ship: they then leave through the stern door.

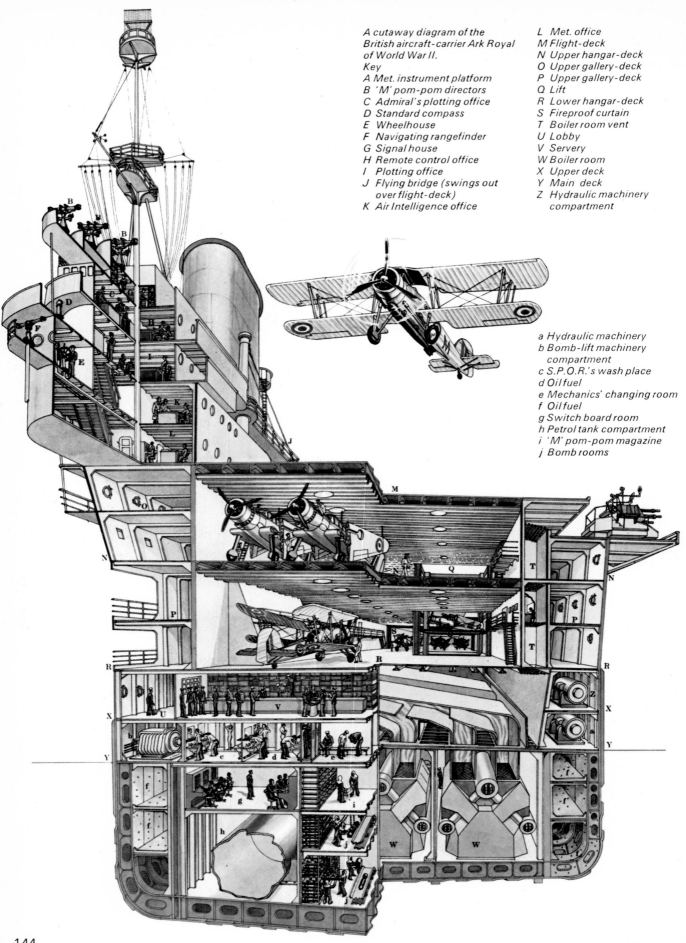

A cutaway diagram of the
British aircraft-carrier Ark Royal
of World War II.
Key
A Met. instrument platform
B 'M' pom-pom directors
C Admiral's plotting office
D Standard compass
E Wheelhouse
F Navigating rangefinder
G Signal house
H Remote control office
I Plotting office
J Flying bridge (swings out
   over flight-deck)
K Air Intelligence office

L Met. office
M Flight-deck
N Upper hangar-deck
O Upper gallery-deck
P Upper gallery-deck
Q Lift
R Lower hangar-deck
S Fireproof curtain
T Boiler room vent
U Lobby
V Servery
W Boiler room
X Upper deck
Y Main deck
Z Hydraulic machinery
   compartment

a Hydraulic machinery
b Bomb-lift machinery
   compartment
c S.P.O.R.'s wash place
d Oil fuel
e Mechanics' changing room
f Oil fuel
g Switch board room
h Petrol tank compartment
i 'M' pom-pom magazine
j Bomb rooms

144

Robert Fulton, built the larger submersible Nautilus, with a sail and a hand-operated stern propeller for surfaced and submerged mobility. Although a ballast tank was provided, she had no means of accurate depth control, and her explosive charge had to be fixed to the target. Nautilus sank two ships during successful trials, but was never used in action. In 1850 Wilhelm Bauer produced a boat with a cast-iron hull and a primitive trimming system in which weights were moved fore and aft. She was equipped with a hand-driven screw and sank at Kiel on her second dive, although her crew of three escaped. Compressed air stored in bottles was used in Le Plongeur to drive the engine and blow the ballast tanks. She was built in France in 1863 by Bougois and Brun. During the American Civil War, the Confederates improvised steam-driven craft trimmed to float with funnel and hatchways just above the surface. Some 50 feet (15.24m) in length and 7 feet (2.13m) in diameter, they carried an explosive charge at the end of a long pole. In 1864, one of these Davids, the CSS Hunley, drove her spar-torpedo into the side of the Federal warship Housatonic. The resulting explosion sank both the target and her attacker.

Torpedo

There is indeed a close association between submarines and torpedoes. Named after a genus of fish that stuns its prey by means of naturally produced electric shocks, the original torpedo was any explosive device which could sink ships by damaging their most vulnerable area below the waterline. Eventually the stationary sort which waited for a ship to set it off became known as a mine, while the original term was only used in reference to spar-torpedoes, the towed Harvey torpedo and self-propelled 'locomotive' or 'fish' torpedoes.

The first successful locomotive torpedo was developed by Robert Whitehead, a British engineer working in Austria. He demonstrated the weapon in 1867, and in 1872 the British government purchased the manufacturing rights. Compressed air drove a twin oscillating cylinder engine, giving a speed of 7 knots (13kph) for 700 yards (640m).

The Whitehead torpedo's introduction revolutionized naval warfare, for one small torpedo launched from an inexpensive boat could now sink the largest warship in the world's most powerful navy. To ward off fast torpedo-boats dashing in under cover of darkness (the 'swarms of mosquito craft' beloved of adventure writers), battleships were equipped with searchlights and quick-firing small-calibre guns. More attention had to be paid to internal watertight subdivision, while in harbour the big ships had to be protected by systems of net defences. Torpedo-rams and torpedo-gunboats were built to tackle torpedo-boats, which became bigger and faster, and were being armed with improved torpedoes.

When compressed air expands it absorbs heat and so loses energy. This was the reason for the Whitehead torpedo's limited performance until the introduction of the Fiume heater system in 1909, which is still in use today. Fuel oil was sprayed into a combustion chamber with compressed air and water. When ignited with a firing cartridge, the combination of hot gases and steam generated enough energy to drive a 350hp piston engine.

Before firing, a torpedo is pre-programmed to steer an

Top: Lt. Charles Rumney Samson, a pioneer of naval aviation, takes off from the Hibernia in a Short S.27 on 2 May 1912, with the ship under way. Earlier, on 10 January 1912, again in an S.27, Samson had taken off from the anchored cruiser Africa to become the first British pilot to take-off from a ship.
Above: A towed lighter transports a Sopwith Camel. Waterborne trailers that acted as one-aircraft carriers, towed lighters were seized upon by Lt. Samson as a possible means of launching fighters. Samson made the first attempt — his plane cartwheeled into the sea. Later operations were successful, resulting in the destruction of a Zeppelin.

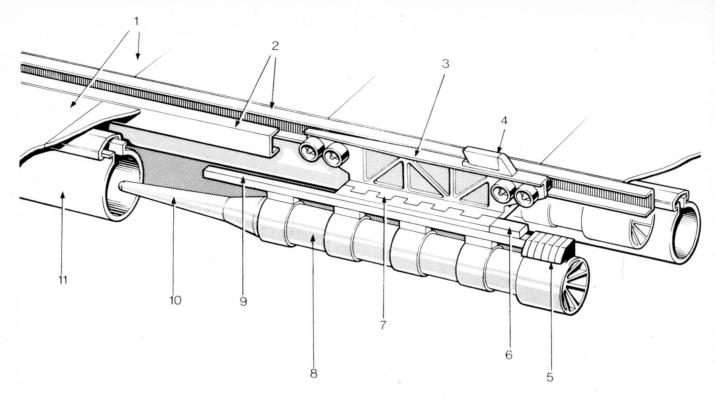

These diagrams show a typical modern steam catapult of the type used by the British and US navies. The details of the piston assembly and attached parts are shown above ; it moves from right to left. At the front is a pointed retardation probe, which slows the piston at the end of its travel by running into a water filled cylinder. The complete layout is shown below, though the cylinder tubes have been considerably shortened from their full length. The driving force is provided by high pressure steam from the ship's boilers. The piston is returned by a hydraulically operated grab which follows it catches it and pulls it back to the starting point.

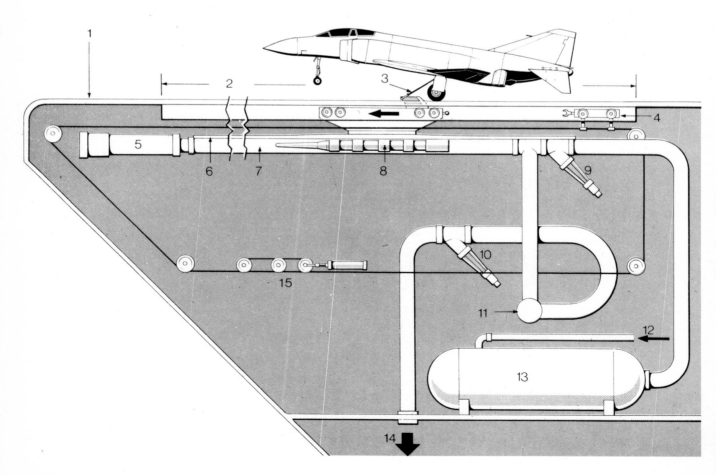

interception course while running at a suitable depth for causing maximum damage. Its course is controlled by a gyroscope which is run up to speed as part of the launching sequence and controls the vertical rudders via a small air motor. The depth mechanism is a combination of hydrostatic valve and pendulum, which senses depth variations and angles of rise and dive, and corrects them by means of a pair of horizontal rudders. It is important that the torpedo should remain level and not roll. This movement is largely reaction to the torque of the propeller, and is cancelled out by having two contra-rotating propellers. The warhead consists of 600-800 pounds (270-370kg) of high-explosive, inert to shocks, vibration and high temperatures, and called torpex. The exploder mechanism consists of a small inertia weight which is flung forward by the sudden deceleration of the torpedo hitting its target, striking the detonator. This explosion sets off a larger 2pound (0.9kg) charge called the primer, and it is the energy which this generates that detonates the warhead itself. Safety devices are fitted to make it impossible for the warhead to explode until it has been launched and has run for some distance. Correctly placed, a single hit is enough to sink a medium-sized merchantman or a small warship. A spread of torpedoes is fired at larger vessels at intervals of a second or so, the resulting time-lag in their arrival spacing them along the length of the moving target. A small cordite charge launches torpedoes from trainable multiple mountings on surface ships, while compressed air is used to fire torpedoes from the fixed, floodable bow and stern tubes in submarines. For by World War I, submarines had become practical ships of war, with their main weapon, which they have never forsaken, the torpedo.

Modern submarine

Significant advances in submarine development had been achieved by the American John P. Holland, who had begun experimenting in 1875. His design had horizontal rudders or hydroplanes, which enabled the boat to dive under control instead of sinking abruptly. His results so impressed the British Admiralty that in 1900 they decided to order a class of Holland-type submarines. Their general principles have continued to the present day.

The strength of the main pressure hull determines the depth to which the boat can dive. Of steel construction, its plates were originally riveted together, but this has now been replaced by welding. The pressure hull is circular in cross-section and is pierced by as few holes as possible: access hatches, torpedo tubes, periscope and mast sleeves, escape hatches (normally secured shut in wartime), engine exhaust and snort (schnorkel) mast leads, some trim tanks, and the log (speed indicator). Each opening is equipped with a method of closure which is tested to full diving-depth pressure.

Outside the pressure hull are the conning tower (or sail), the casing, and the ballast tanks. These are either saddle tanks (great bulges hung from the pressure hull) or the double hull type, in which a whole skin is wrapped about the pressure hull. Internal ballast tanks require additional penetration of the pressure hull, thus seriously reducing the diving depth. These are no longer employed.

Each ballast tank has two openings. The one at the bottom lets in the water required on diving and permits its expulsion by compressed air for surfacing. If this

Key to opposite page, top
1. Deck plates
2. Guide rails
3. Shuttle
4. Towing block projecting through deck
5. Seal closing block
6. Driving iron
7. Keyed joint between shuttle and piston assembly
8. Piston assembly
9. Sealing strip
10. Retardation probe
11. Cylinder

Key to opposite page, bottom
1. Flight-deck
2. Total stroke approx 200ft
3. Towing strop
4. Shuttle return grab
5. Retardation cylinder
6. Cylinder seal
7. Twin cylinder tubes
8. Piston and shuttle assembly
9. Launch valve
10. Exhaust valve
11. Exhaust collector box
12. High pressure steam supply
13. Steam receiver
14. Exhaust steam
15. Hydraulic jigger and pulley sheave assembly operates return grab via cables to retrieve shuttle and pistons after launch

Top: The first British Naval Phantom aircraft to be launched from HMS Ark Royal, shown at the moment of leaving the catapult. The towing strop is in the act of disengaging and falling away, while the aircraft continues under its own power.
Above: A US Navy Phantom before launching. The towing block projecting from its slot in the deck can be clearly seen.

Left: Occasionally an aircraft misses the arrester cables. If it cannot go round again, it is then stopped by a barrier of wire rope and webbing.

Key to top diagram
1. Approx. 6in (15cm) dia.
2. Landing aircraft picks up one cable with its own arresting hook
3. Six arresting cables strung across deck
4. Pulley sheaves guide cables up and across flight-deck
5. Braking cylinders (both sides of ship beneath flight-deck)
6. Cable resetting mechanism

Key to bottom diagram
1. Approx. 6in (15cm) dia.
2. Approx. 200ft (62m)

3. Cable resetting mechanism – multi-sheave pulley system with hydraulic jigger
4. Piston
5. As piston is pulled along cylinder fluid is forced out of small holes in cylinder wall at increasing pressure to provide braking effect
6. Spray containment tube
7. Cable drawn out by landing aircraft
8. Hydraulic cylinder absorbs energy of landing aircraft
9. Continuously cycling replenishing pump
10. Fluid return to reservoir
11. Hydraulic reservoir fluid-fresh water soluble oil and rust inhibitor

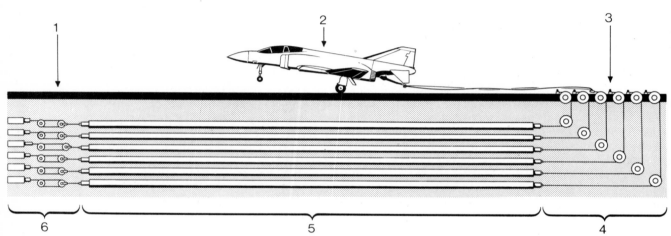

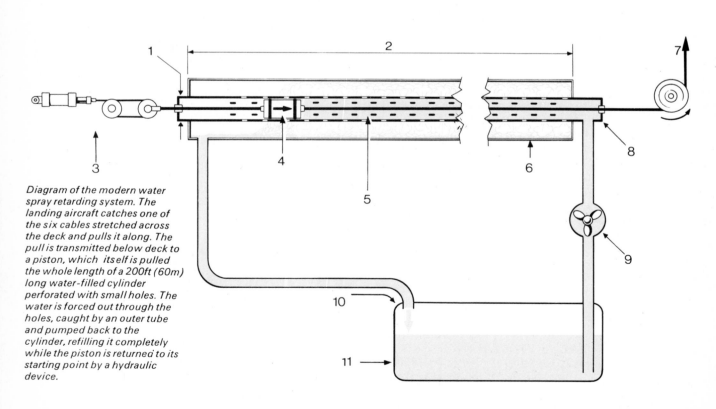

Diagram of the modern water spray retarding system. The landing aircraft catches one of the six cables stretched across the deck and pulls it along. The pull is transmitted below deck to a piston, which itself is pulled the whole length of a 200ft (60m) long water-filled cylinder perforated with small holes. The water is forced out through the holes, caught by an outer tube and pumped back to the cylinder, refilling it completely while the piston is returned to its starting point by a hydraulic device.

opening is merely a hole, the bank is known as free-flooding, but it may be fitted with a valve known as a Kingston valve. The valve at the top of the ballast tank which retains the air is called the main vent.

The submarine is dived by opening all the Kingston valves and then opening the main vents, thus releasing the air pressure and allowing the water to enter through the Kingston valves. The submarine is now in a state of neutral buoyancy and the slightest force will cause it to sink. This force is provided by the boat's forward motion and the angle of the hydroplanes, and directs it downward. Without this movement, the submarine would merely wallow on the surface. In effect, the submarine 'flies' in the water in the same way as an aircraft flies in the air. Once dived, the submarine must have the weights within it so adjusted that it can remain static and horizontal at the required depth. This state is achieved by transferring water into and out of the trim tanks situated at either end and amidships. The deeper a submarine goes, the greater the compression of its hull and the less the displacement, So, more water must be expelled from the trim tanks to ensure that the boat's displacement always equals its weight. Only then will the submarine be in stopped trim, when it can hover at the desired depth without mechanical assistance from propeller or hydroplanes.

Although steam propulsion was occasionally used for submarines, it presented major problems: a funnel; delay in shutting down the boilers before diving; and their subsequent latent heat after submerging. Petrol or gasoline engines produced fumes which were occasionally explosive, and presented the difficulty of storing a highly volatile fuel. The heavy oil engine, followed by the diesel, provided a means of propulsion using a low flash-point fuel, simpler and more dependable machinery, and an instant ability to dive. Of course, the engines had to be switched off quickly or else they would exhaust all the air in the boat. The diesel engines of modern patrol submarines provide the power required on the surface for propulsion and for charging the batteries. As the majority of such boats is now equipped with snort masts, both these functions can also be carried out at periscope depth, about 50 feet (15.2m) below the surface. The diesel can either be coupled through a clutch to the main electric motors and through a tail clutch to the screw (that is, direct drive) or it can drive a generator providing power for the main electric motors to turn the propeller. This system is called diesel-electric drive. Below periscope depth the submarine is driven by the main motors, drawing their power from large storage batteries below the main deck. These are charged when the diesels are running either by the main motors acting as generators in a direct-drive boat, or by the generators in a diesel-electric boat. Whenever pre-snort submarines dived, they relied entirely on their batteries and could only charge them by surfacing, usually at night.

Nuclear submarine

However, a diesel boat, with or without snort, is really only a submersible, because it is still dependent on the atmosphere for its support. The whole aspect of submarine operations was changed when the USS Nautilus got under way on nuclear power in January 1955. This was the first true submarine, able to operate for years without

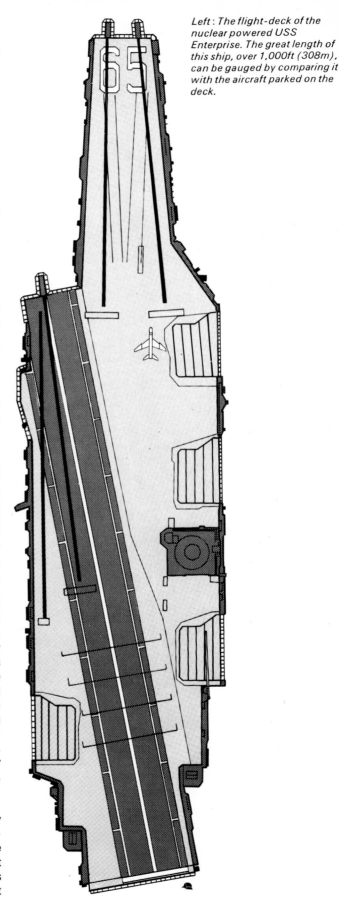

Left: The flight-deck of the nuclear powered USS Enterprise. The great length of this ship, over 1,000ft (308m), can be gauged by comparing it with the aircraft parked on the deck.

refuelling, to manufacture its own air and fresh water, to travel at high speed under water, and to remain totally submerged for periods impossible for diesel-driven boats. The British 'Swiftsure' class of nuclear-powered fleet submarines have a submerged displacement of 4,500 tons (4,572 tonnes) but can make up to 35 knots (65kph). However, the very size of nuclear submarines can limit their operations at periscope depth and over the continental shelf, so there is at present still a place for the smaller and cheaper diesel-powered boat in shallow-water service.

In nuclear submarines a coolant liquid is pumped in a closed circuit between a nuclear reactor, where it absorbs heat from the radioactive core, and a heat exchanger (virtually a boiler), where the coolant gives off the heat to a water feed, thereby generating steam. This is conducted through valves to the main propulsion turbines, connected either directly through a speed reduction gear or via turbo-electric drive, to the boat's propeller. Some steam is taken from the heat exchanger to the auxiliary turbines which power the many subsidiary systems. Hydraulic power is needed for operating the periscope, snort and other masts, opening and shutting torpedo tubes, main vent control and many other items. Few systems today are hand-operated and most systems are electronically controlled.

Early submarines had no periscopes, and even when they were introduced, some projected an inverted picture on a ground glass screen. Later improvements provided for ability to watch the sky as well as the sea, as well as radar-ranging, low light television scanning, and periscope sextants. SINS (Submarine Inertial Navigation System)

Above : An early submarine, the Turtle, built in the 1770s by the American David Bushnell. The craft carried a charge of gunpowder (S) designed to be attached to the wooden hull of an enemy warship. The first drawings of this vessel were not published until the 19th century, the operator is therefore portrayed wearing the clothes of this period.

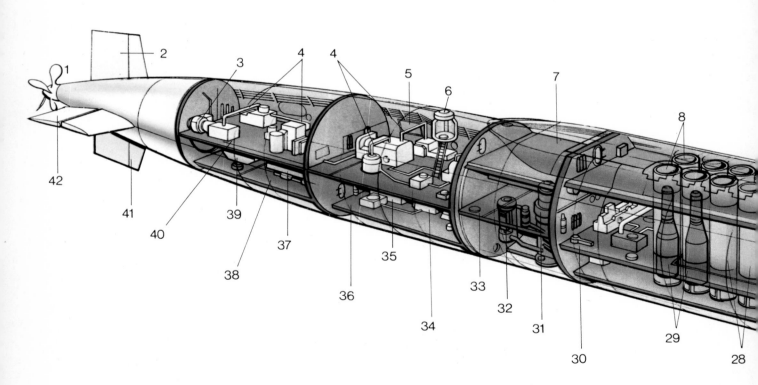

Left : USS Sam Rayburn, shown with all of its 16 missile hatches open.

Below : A cut-away view of a Polaris submarine. Because they are nuclear powered, these vessels can remain submerged for many months at a time. They are armed with 16 Polaris missiles each with a range of 2800 miles (4500km) as well as conventional torpedoes. The missiles can be launched from below the surface, and are equipped with nuclear warheads.

1. Propeller
2. Upper rudder
3. Turbine
4. Steam pipes
5. Forward engine-room upper deck
6. Aft escape hatch
7. Upper reactor deck
8. Missile hatches
9. SINS (submarine inertial navigation systems)
10. Snorkel exhaust
11. Radio antenna
12. Snorkel intake
13. Radar antenna
14. Periscopes
15. Port sail plane
16. Bridge
17. Sail decks
18. Bunks
19. Torpedo-room bunks
20. Forward escape hatches
21. Torpedoes on racks
22. Torpedo room
23. Mess deck (galley on port side)
24. Bunk deck
25. Control deck
26. Equipment deck
27. Missile decks
28. Missile tubes
29. Polaris missiles
30. Missile-room
31. Boiler
32. Reactor
33. Reactor deck
34. Carbon dioxide eliminator
35. Air compressor
36. Forward engine-room lower deck
37. Air conditioner
38. Aft engine-room lower deck
39. Condenser
40. Aft engine-room upper deck
41. Lower rudder
42. Starboard diving plane

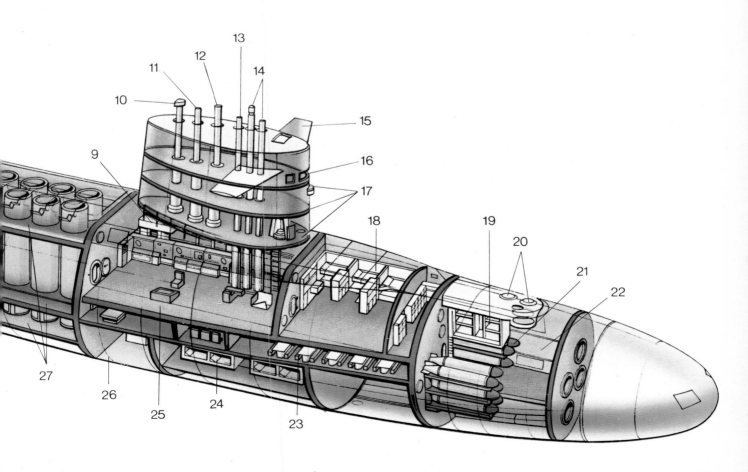

is a complex of gyroscopes which records every movement made after leaving a fixed position and produces an accurate dead-reckoning which only requires checking from external fixes every few days. The echo sounder is another submarine navigation aid.

Some of the first submarine torpedoes were released from collars on the outer casing, but even in early boats, torpedoes were ejected from tubes projecting from the pressure hull. Provided the tubes were fitted with efficient bow caps, the tubes could be reloaded. Methods of aiming torpedoes have progressed from eye-shooting to the modern computer-controlled system. The compressed air used in the Whitehead torpedo was 80% nitrogen, which is insoluble in water. Its expansion in the exhaust left a considerable trail of bubbles behind a running torpedo, a track which could be readily recognized by an alert lookout aboard the target and might give enough time for evasive action. This operational disadvantage was not

eliminated until battery-driven electric motors replaced the compressed air thermal system. The first of this type in action was the German G7E, the torpedo carried by the U-47 when she sank HMS Royal Oak in 1939. It was 20 feet (6m) long, 21 inches (53cm) in diameter and had a speed of 30 knots (55kph) and a range of 5,000 yards (4,500m) with a warhead weighing 672 pounds (307kg). It formed the basis of postwar torpedo design until the 1960s. World War II also saw the development of magnetic torpedoes (which are preset to pass below the target, where they are set off by the ship's magnetic field) and the acoustic torpedo, which homes on to the noise of the ship's propellers. Some close-range torpedoes can be guided by wire from the firing submarine. The 21 inch (53cm) Mark 48 torpedo issued to United States submarines since 1972 is 18.97 feet (5.8m) long and weighs 3,520 pounds (1,600kg). It has a speed of 50.4 knots (93kph), with a maximum range of 25 miles (46km) and

a depth of 3,000 feet (914m). If it misses its target, either through natural disturbance or because a decoy has been released – it can search and attack again. Like the Mark 46 in Royal Navy service (to be replaced by the Tigerfish) its engine burns liquid Otto monopropellant fuel. These torpedoes can now be used against submarines as well as surface ships, while Subroc is a missile which has been specially designed for the undersea war. Fired from a submerged torpedo-tube, it rises into the air until reaching the general locality of the target, where it dives into the sea again to search out and destroy the enemy. The widespread use of all these homing devices, and of the listening equipment carried by ships, aircraft, other submarines, or anchored to the seabed, emphasize the need for complete silence in submarine design and operation. Even the sound of machinery clatter or personnel movement may give away the submarine's position or attract a homing torpedo.

The gun was for many years a valuable weapon for use against independent merchantmen or lonely shore targets, but it was eventually defeated by the ability of radar to detect a submarine the moment she surfaced. An anti-aircraft missile to deal with helicopters that may have come too close is now entering service. Its launcher is at present situated in the sail or conning-tower, but a periscope mounting is envisaged so that the missile can be fired while the submarine is still submerged. It could also be used against small patrol vessels that might be able to evade a torpedo. Many of the larger missiles and torpedoes can be fitted with nuclear warheads. Some submarines have been specially designed to carry and fire ballistic missiles such as Polaris and Poseidon, the latter with a range of 3,000 miles (4,800km). Although these weapons are aimed at military and industrial targets far inland and are very much part of their nation's strategic strike force, missile-carrying boats also carry torpedoes for tactical use.

Below : USS Thresher, one of the US Navy's most sophisticated nuclear submarines, was especially designed to reach deeper-than-ever levels in the world's oceans. Unfortunately, while attempting to reach a depth of 1,000ft (308m) on 10 April 1963 the engine room flooded and the Thresher sank.

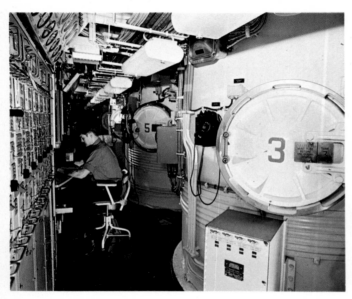

Assault ship

Another warship of strategic employment is the assault ship, a vessel used to transport and land men and heavy military equipment where there are no port facilities. It can carry several large landing craft for tanks and vehicles in a dock compartment at the stern. The dock floor is above the waterline and the space is dry during transit, but for a seaborne assault the ballast tanks along the length of the vessel are quickly flooded to bring it down to a deep draught and so flood the dock. Inside the dock there are batter boards to prevent damage to the landing craft and the ship. There is also a sloping apron of steel gratings up to the tank deck level, acting as a beach to reduce wave motion in the dock, and serving as a hard (loading ramp) for the landing craft. A hinged gate closes the dock at its after end. Troops are transferred to personnel landing craft when they have been lowered into the water and bowsed into (or held against) the ship's side to prevent relative motion. Assault troops can also be flown ashore from No 1 deck, which is kept clear aft to serve as a flight deck for helicopters. It must withstand the dynamic weight of these aircraft, and because it is over the dock, requires heavy deck beams for support as pillars cannot be used in this region. Indeed, the whole vessel of some 12,558 tons (12,760 tonnes) standard displacement is heavily stiffened to cope with the variations in loading due to ballast and cargo movements. Steam turbines are used for main propulsion and the engine room is below the vehicle deck, which has to be well ventilated to remove fuel vapour and exhaust gases. The flight-deck can also be used for extra vehicles if required. Orthodox landing craft could be replaced in the future by hovercraft.

General-purpose warships

In spite of the spectacular and costly development of aircraft-carriers, submarines and assault ships, general-purpose surface warships make up the bulk of every navy. They are used to escort big ships and merchantmen, or to hunt submarines and investigate other navies' activities; they can land a party of armed men to protect property during a riot, or a medical team after an earthquake; and if the situation becomes too delicate politically, they can sail away again. In all sorts of ways they can exert a more subtle influence than is possible by the overbearing appearance of aircraft-carrier, ballistic missile submarine or assault ship — which may well lose much of their effectiveness once their position is known.

Even these lesser surface warships are usually designed for a specific function, and they do perform most efficiently when complementary types operate together, although each one has some sort of anti-aircraft, anti-ship and anti-submarine armament. The different names applied to types in service indicate size rather than role, and are derived from traditional terms in general use earlier in the 20th century.

Cruiser

As its name implies, the cruiser was originally a warship for ocean patrol at an economic speed. Its gun armament and armour enabled it to deal with any hostile vessel

Top: The forward torpedo tube compartment of HMS Resolution. Torpedoes are still carried by modern submarines in case they have to engage enemy surface ships or submarines.
Above: The missile compartment of a Polaris submarine.
Opposite page: A cross-section of a Royal Navy fleet submarine hunter/killer. The role of this type of boat is to seek out and destroy other submarines and surface vessels using homing or subroc torpedoes.

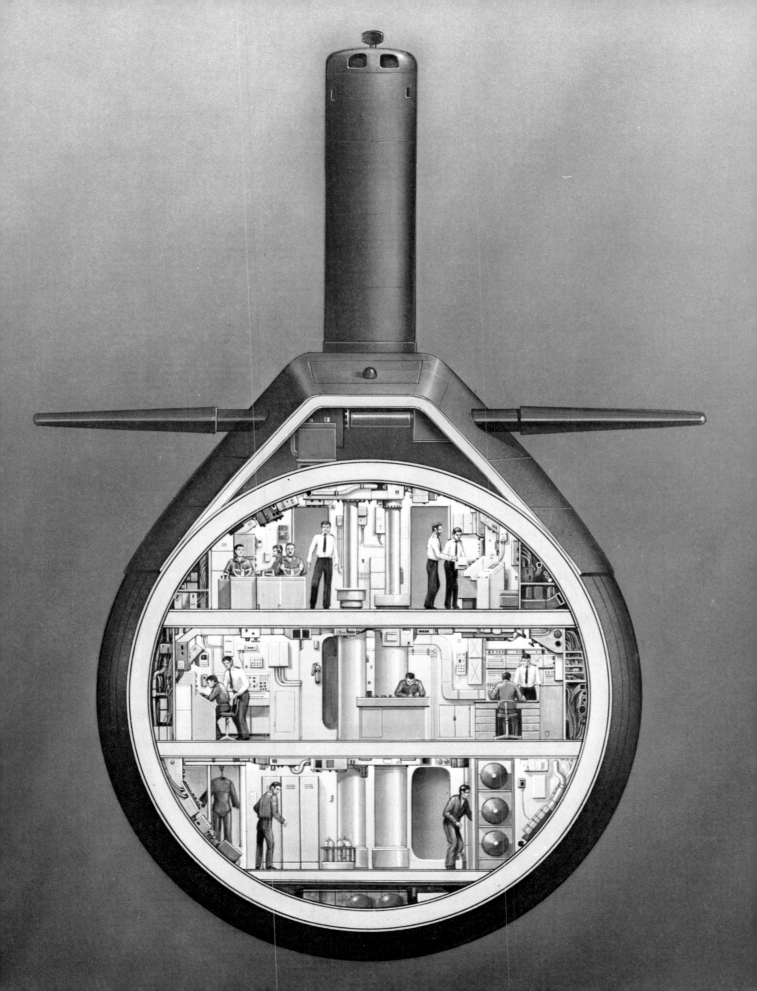

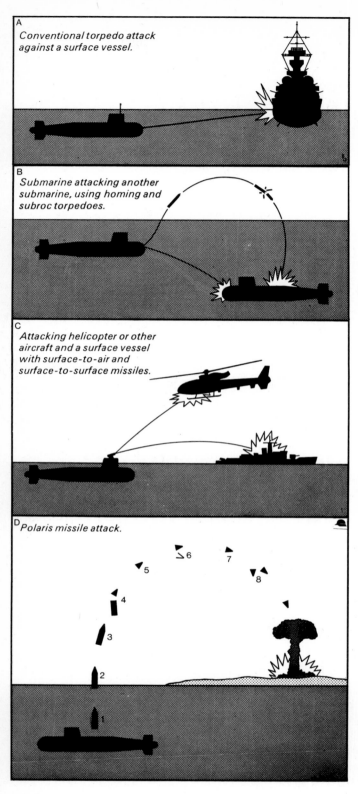

A Conventional torpedo attack against a surface vessel.

B Submarine attacking another submarine, using homing and subroc torpedoes.

C Attacking helicopter or other aircraft and a surface vessel with surface-to-air and surface-to-surface missiles.

D Polaris missile attack.

1. The missile is fired from the submarine by compressed gas. 2. On surfacing, the first stage of the missile ignites. 3. The guidance system directs the missile on to its preset trajectory. 4. The first stage is jettisoned. 5. The second stage motor is ignited. 6. The outer shell is jettisoned. 7. The guidance system 'arms' the warhead. 8. The warhead separates and free falls on to the target.

except a battleship. HMS Belfast, preserved near the Tower of London, is a typical example of the conventional cruiser.

The present-day cruiser is now a guided missile ship. In fact the Royal Navy's 'County' class were first designated guided missile destroyers (GMDs), but as most warships now carry guided missiles, and as the size of these ships approaches that of the conventional cruiser, it has seemed appropriate to reclassify them. Their main armament includes a twin Seaslug, beam-riding, anti-aircraft missile with a range of 28 miles (45km) at a height of 49,213 feet (15,000m). There are two quadruple Seacat anti-aircraft missiles for close-range work up to 5,195 yards (4,750m), which can be directed visually, by closed-circuit television, or by radar. These weapons can be employed against surface targets, but the Counties are now being equipped with the Exocet anti-shipping missile with a range of 23.6 miles (38km). The Exocet's flight path is kept at very low altitude by means of a radio altimeter, the problem of wave interference with the guidance system having been thoroughly investigated. Unlike the other missiles on board, no reloads are carried for the Exocet pack. Once fired, it can only be replaced in harbour, but this also applied to earlier warships' torpedoes (except those in the Imperial Japanese Navy). These cruisers usually carry a Wessex helicopter with dunking listening devices and homing torpedoes for anti-submarine duties. Helicopters can also employ missiles against fast attack craft. The Counties were built with two twin 4.5 inch (11.5cm) gun-turrets, and single 20mm Oerlikons have also been mounted.

The cruiser Bristol, of 5,650 tons (5,740 tonnes) standard displacement, has been designed around the Seadart surface-to-air missile which can also intercept other missiles at a range of 18.65 miles (30km) The Ikara missile, which is fired into the sea and homes on to a submarine, is another weapon fitted in this ship.

The Aegis system launchers on board the American 'Virginia' class, displacing 11,000 tons (11,176 tonnes) can be used for all types of missile. Ships can also carry special launchers for target drones (to attract incoming missiles), and chaff dispensers to confuse the enemy's radar. It seems likely that future design will concentrate on developing general-purpose missiles and launchers which can be used at high speed. The Americans have been testing a 100 ton (101 tonne) surface effect ship (hovercraft) with a speed of 60 knots (111kph), which fires a missile vertically to home on to the target up to a distance of 5.6 miles (9km).

Destroyer

The only counter to the threat posed by the torpedo-boat at the end of the 19th century proved to be an enlarged vessel of similar design called a torpedo-boat destroyer, later abbreviated to TBD or destroyer. Themselves armed with torpedoes, they increased in size and became one of the most useful general-purpose warships ever. There is probably no role performed by other warships which has not been carried out by a destroyer — except being a submarine. Some of the 2,050 ton (2,083 tonne) American 'Fletcher' class even carried a seaplane.

Modern destroyers perpetuate the type name and are next in size to cruisers. The German 'Lutjens' class displaces 3,370 tons (3,425 tonnes) while HMS Sheffield has a length of 410 feet (125m) and a displacement of 3,500 tons (3,556 tonnes). She is armed with missiles and guns, and also carries a helicopter.

Frigate

The most widely used type of operational warship is the frigate, named after the escort vessels of World War II. They carried adequate anti-aircraft and anti-submarine armament on a seaworthy hull, and were economical enough to accompany merchantmen right across the Atlantic, yet with sufficient speed to hunt and kill a submarine and then catch up the convoy again. Present-day frigates are directly descended from these ships and perform similar functions.

HMS Amazon of recent construction has a length of 384 feet (117.1m) and a displacement of 2,500 tons (2,540 tonnes). She has a speed of 34 knots (63kph), propulsion consisting of two Olympus gas turbines for high power and two Tyne gas turbines for economical cruising. Her armament comprises guns, missiles and a helicopter.

Apart from aircraft-carriers and submarines, which have to withstand the strains of operating aircraft or of diving to great depths, heavy plating is not fitted in modern warships. Armour will not resist nuclear weapons, and it increases the displacement so that more power is required to propel the vessel at speed. The hull is prefabricated and welded, T-bars being used for longitudinal stiffening. A grillage structure is best for coping with underwater explosions and shocks, while keeping the weight down. It is formed by passing the T-bars through the transverse framing, forming squares of stiffening to support the shell plates. Special quality steel is used where there are high stresses, corrosion being prevented by shot-blasting to remove mill scale and rust and then painting before use in construction. Some parts particularly susceptible to

corrosion are shot-blasted again and zinc-sprayed after building.

Weight can be further saved by using aluminium for the superstructure, but not in areas likely to be subjected to hot blast as it has a low melting-point. Abrupt changes in shape, such as the superstructure and the forecastle, cause a loss in strength, so these ends are sloped. Water-tight subdivision is achieved by transverse and longitudinal bulkheads, decks and watertight flats. Transverse bulk-heads are usually stiffened vertically, the plates being welded together horizontally. The T-bar longitudinals are connected to the bulkheads to help integrate the whole structure. Although watertight doors have to be fitted in bulkheads, they must be above the deep waterline level and all watertight compartments not normally occupied, are closed at sea.

Lattice masts were common in many vessels, but the

The Italian SSB two-man 'human torpedo' or 'chariot'. Like the British version above, it had to be conveyed to within striking distance by a parent ship as it had only a limited range. Both 'chariots' served in World War II.

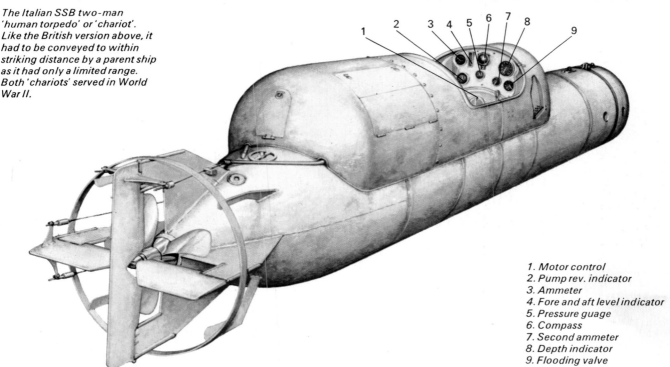

1. Motor control
2. Pump rev. indicator
3. Ammeter
4. Fore and aft level indicator
5. Pressure guage
6. Compass
7. Second ammeter
8. Depth indicator
9. Flooding valve

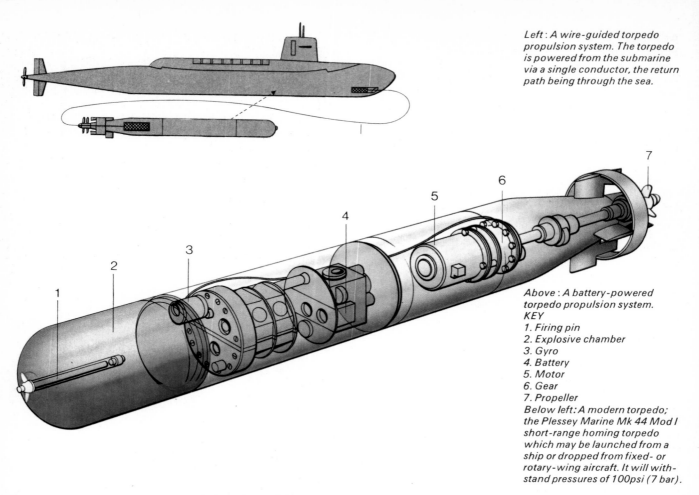

Left: A wire-guided torpedo propulsion system. The torpedo is powered from the submarine via a single conductor, the return path being through the sea.

Above: A battery-powered torpedo propulsion system.
KEY
1. Firing pin
2. Explosive chamber
3. Gyro
4. Battery
5. Motor
6. Gear
7. Propeller
Below left: A modern torpedo; the Plessey Marine Mk 44 Mod I short-range homing torpedo which may be launched from a ship or dropped from fixed- or rotary-wing aircraft. It will withstand pressures of 100psi (7 bar).

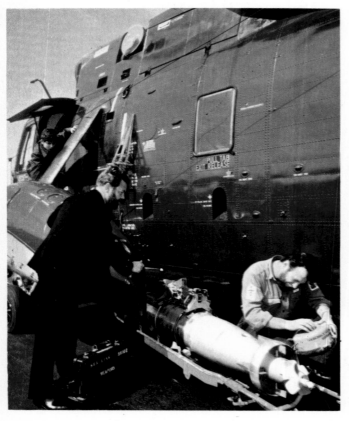

weight of modern equipment such as radar scanners, has led to the introduction of the plate mast which is stronger and less prone to vibration. The inside of the mast protects the cables and junction boxes which connect the aerial with their operating compartments. In some cases, mast and funnel are combined, being known as a mack. New forms of machinery layout below decks allow for a greater variety of funnel positions above deck.

A modern frigate is capable of running in a closed-down condition (like a submarine) in case of nuclear attack. Exposed decks are designed simply to allow washing down of fallout, while special precautions are necessary to prevent contamination through the ventilation system. The superstructure comprises an enclosed bridge, radar room, communications control room, electronic warfare office and computer rooms for action data automation, tactical information data evaluation, and a ship's inertial navigation system.

Below, accommodation includes the wardroom, officers' and petty officers' cabins, galley, recreation spaces and sickbay. There are gunbays, power rooms, gunners' stores, weapons stores, ratings' dining hall, galley, scullery, ship control centre, engineers' workshop and junior ratings' accommodation.

No 3 deck contains the sonar instrument room, junior ratings' mess, refrigeration stores and fuel stores. In the bottom of the vessel are the fuel tanks, tanks for helicopter fuel, lubricating oil and fresh water, the magazines and the sonar space.

Anti-submarine equipment

Sonar is the frigate's most important anti-submarine device. The word stands for sound navigation ranging, and this term has largely replaced the name asdic (derived from the Allied Submarine Detection Investigation Committee). A short pulse of sound (sometimes inaudible to the human ear) is transmitted by a transducer, usually mounted in the ship's bottom. (A transducer is any device that converts electric power into another form of energy, such as sound, and vice versa.) Variable depth sonar can be lowered over the stern to pick up echoes free from surface interference. The sound pulse travels downwards until it strikes the seabed or a submerged object, which reflects it back to the ship. It is picked up by another transducer and the time taken for the pulse to travel down and back is measured, approximately 4,800fps (1,460mps) being the speed of sound in water. The distance between the transducer and the echo-producing object can then be calculated. Both time interval and range can be measured on a rotating disc carrying a neon tube, which flashes when the reflected sound pulse (the echo) is picked up. The disc rotates at a constant speed, taking the neon tube past a fixed circular scale graduated in terms of distance. In some units, a permanent record is provided by a rotating stylus that darkens electrically sensitive paper when the echo is received. Other types have a cathode ray tube display similar to a television screen. In all cases the distance is read directly from a scale which may be calibrated in feet, fathoms or metres. Helicopters can also lower transducers while hovering above the sea (a process known as dunking) or lay sonobuoys which radio back returning impulses. During the 1960s extremely powerful transducers were laid permanently on the seabed

Above: Asdic operator on an Allied convoy escort ship in 1943, listening for echoes from enemy submarines.
Below: An anti-submarine craft equipped with sonar arrays for echo sounding and submarine detection. The flat transducer towards the stern is fixed, and its signals are beamed straight down to measure the depth of water beneath the ship. The depth in fathoms is indicated on the rotating disc display. The foward array, in the streamlined housing, scans through 360° to locate any submarines in the area. When one is detected it shows as a spot on the cathode ray display,

and its direction and distance are shown on the screen.
1. Submarine
2. Transmitted beam
3. Returning echo
4. Transducers
5. Sea bed

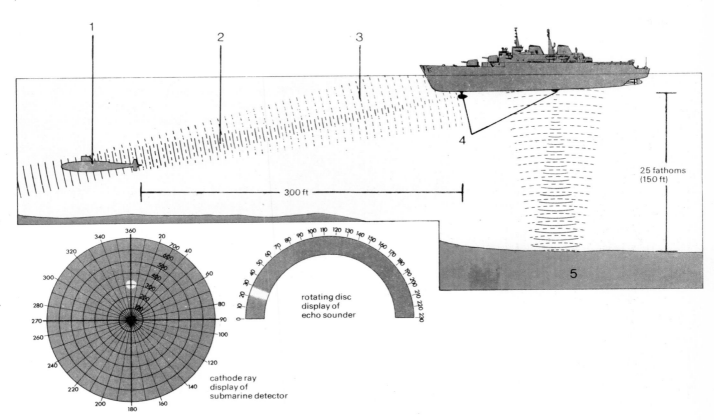

300 ft

25 fathoms (150 ft)

rotating disc display of echo sounder

cathode ray display of submarine detector

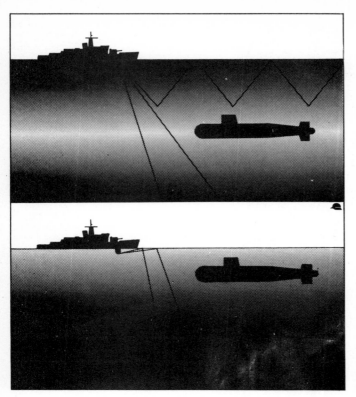

Above: Two diagrams showing how variations in water temperature can affect the performance of sonar waves. Layers of cold water can reflect sound waves back to the surface, creating blind zones within which the submarine can remain undetected. Conversely, warmer water can reflect the sound waves downwards into the depths. Today's submarines have hull-mounted sensors that can detect these rapidly changing zones and use them to advantage.

along the edge of the continental shelf bordering the United States' coastline. Transducers can also be of a passive type in which no sound is transmitted. Known as hydrophones, they listen for the noises made by submerged submarines.

Once the submarine has been located, the information is fed to the killing weapon. At one time this was the depth-charge, which was dropped over the stern after the attacker had passed over the submarine's last known position. This gave the enemy several seconds to evade the explosion. Later, Hedgehog was invented, which fired a shower of bombs ahead of the ship while still in sonar contact. This developed into Limbo, a three-barrelled mortar giving a three-dimensional pattern ahead of the frigate and crushing the submarine.

Surface warships, including frigates, have a variety of types of main engine: steam turbines; gas turbines; combined steam and gas turbines, enabling the ship to get under way from cold in a few minutes; a combination of two sorts of gas turbines for cruising and full power; diesels; and a combined gas turbine and diesel direct drive, reduction gearing or electric generators may interpose between the engines and the shafts, of which there may be one or more, for conventional or controllable pitch propellers. Many hulls are equipped with automated stabilizers, to provide a stable weapons platform.

Corvette and patrol craft

Next down the scale of warships is another deriving her name from a World War II escort — the corvette. The Russian 'Grisha' class, displacing 810 tons (822 tonnes) full load, has a speed of 30 knots (56kph) and is used for anti-submarine work.

Smaller corvettes can also fall into the next category which comes right down to 100 tons (101 tonnes) and less. These are not big enough to carry a varied armament and specialize in one or two weapons. This is apparent from their subdivisions into fast attack craft-missile, -gun, -torpedo, -patrol. Frequently built of wood and aluminium, they can do 40 knots (74kph) and are elusive targets. The missile-carrying ones pack a formidable punch, one of their most impressive successes being the sinking of the Israeli destroyer Eilat by an Egyptian 'Komar' class boat in 1967.

Several nations, including China, have built hydrofoils, which ride clear of the sea at speeds of up to 60 knots (111kph).

Patrol craft of less than 25 knots (46kph) are employed in a variety of coastal tasks, defending harbours, arresting smugglers and gathering intelligence. Often regarded as police or coastguard vessels, they are undoubtedly inshore warships, their single 20mm Oerlikon cannon or 0.5 inch (12.7mm) machine-gun being quite enough to deal with some small boat trying to approach the beach secretly.

Minesweeper

Minesweepers are also largely coastal in their operations, clearing shipping lanes into harbours. Their equipment must be capable of dealing with all the different types of mine. Contact mines have their moorings cut by a wire streamed from the minesweeper and kept clear of her hull by a paravane or float. The mine then bobs to the surface where it can be destroyed by gunfire. A magnetic influence mine is detonated by trailing a cable well astern, carrying a

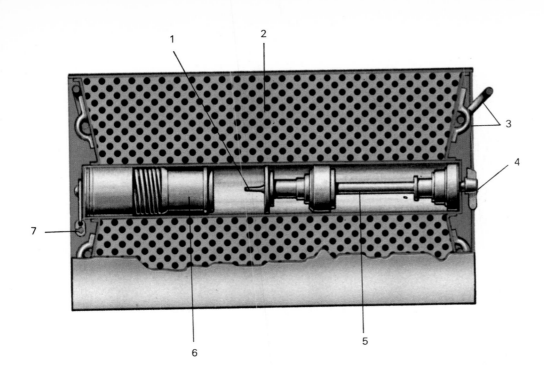

Below: The U-boat hunters' usual plan was to drop depth-charges in such a way that they fell round a diving U-boat. The pressure from all sides when the charges exploded would then tend to crush the submarine's hull or force her to the surface.
Bottom: A destroyer could throw patterns of depth-charges from the sides as well as dropping them off the stern. This enabled a large area of sea to be covered during an attack on a submarine.

pulsating electric current supplied by the minesweeper's generator. Also towed astern is a noise-making drum to set off acoustic mines.

But influence mines can be fitted with a delay device which allows the mine's mechanism to be tripped once, twice, several times by the minesweeper before being armed. Just because an area has been swept, it does not mean that it is safe. Mines never surrender, and pressure mines are the most difficult to deal with because they are triggered by the passage of a ship through the water. Some minesweepers, occasionally known as minehunters, therefore use high definition sonar to detect mines and assess their shape. Sometimes frogmen divers are sent down to defuse the mine underwater, but a special remotely-controlled mine-disposal weapon designated PAP-104 is entering service. Carrying a television camera, it is a miniature submarine 8.85 feet (2.7m) in length. Its weight of 1,543 pounds (700kg) includes a demolition charge which it places against the mine to destroy it. It can operate at a depth of 985 feet (300m).

The hull of a minesweeper must be made from non-magnetic materials such as wood and aluminium; HMS Wilton was the first large vessel to be built in glass reinforced plastic. Its lightness and non-magnetic properties make it ideal for minesweeper construction. It is believed that hull maintenance will also be reduced, as corrosion is no longer a problem. Wilton has a single skin about 1.26 inches (32mm) thick, built with moulded transverse framing which is constructed around blocks of rigid polyurethane foam. The joints of the frames are reinforced with bronze bolts, to ensure that they remain secure when subjected to underwater explosions. Bulkheads, fuel tanks, water tanks, partitions and sonar housing are all made from glass-reinforced plastic laminate bonded into the hull. The polyester resin reinforced with woven rovings used in Wilton is about one-fifth of the weight of

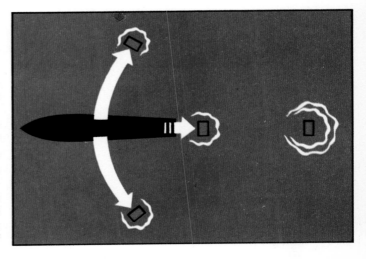

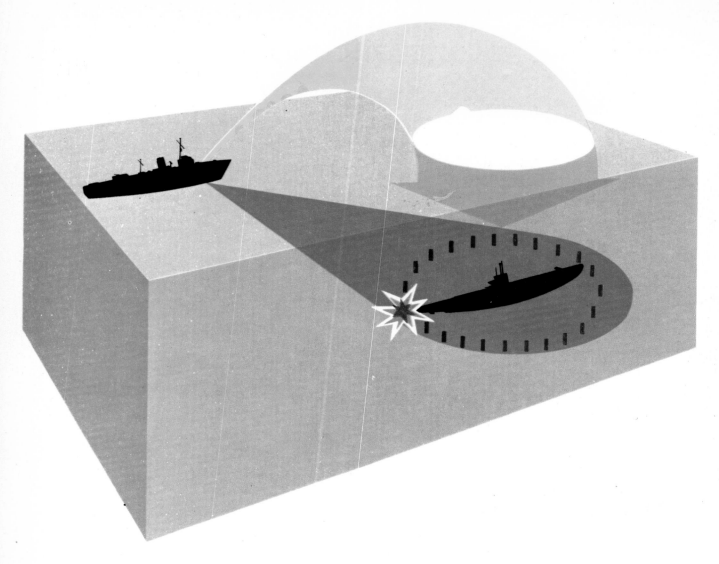

Above: The green area on this three-dimensional diagram is the sonar pulse. It pin-points a U-boat's position. Hedgehog bombs are launched to cover the same area. Here, one bomb has struck the U-boat's stern to explode on contact.

mild steel and has up to 64% of its tensile strength. Wilton was completed with equipment and machinery from HMS Derriton, which had been scrapped.

The depositing of mines, although sometimes done by specially constructed minelayers, is often carried out by all sorts of warships, as well as by aircraft.

Future development

Which of these types of modern warship will be the future arbiter of the ocean? Ballistic missiles can unleash tremendous destruction within minutes, but suppose there were no knockout blow? Aerial bombing was expected to lay waste whole nations in 1939, but World War II lasted six years, and there was action at sea for the whole of that period. Suppose a weak country harried the merchant ships of one of the nuclear powers. Would the latter be justified in dropping atomic bombs on the little country, or should they try to protect their merchantmen by conventional means? If the latter is adopted cruisers and frigates would seem to be the answer, with fast attack vessels (perhaps hovercraft) around oil rigs and in narrow

Left: A Hedgehog launcher on
the deck of HMS Spey – a 'River'
class frigate. The launcher fired
24 bombs at once surrounding
the U-boat's position with a
pattern. The bombs would
explode on contact and if the
pattern fell right it was probable
that one would score a hit.

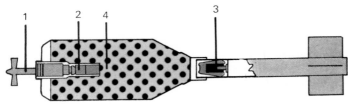

Left: The Hedgehog cutaway to
show the fuse detail and charges.
1. Percussion fuse
2. Exploder pellets
3. Explosive cartridge
4. Explosive charge

waters. And what of the oil pipelines, harbour installations
and underwater detection apparatus? These could all be
vulnerable to attack by midget submarines and frogmen.
Both have been used successfully in war. The Egyptians
have a two-man swimmer delivery vehicle with an endurance of about four hours at 3 to 4 knots (5.5 to 7.5kph).
A two-man, free-flooding, single-screw submarine built
of light aluminium is in service in the Yugoslav Navy.
while the United States of America has deep submergence
vehicles. These may be for research and rescue today, but
once any vessel proves its seaworthiness and military
potential, some naval task is found for her.

It is unlikely that the gun will entirely disappear. Most
are now radar-controlled and automatic in operation. As
a 'last ditch' defence against incoming missiles, the
United States Navy is equipping its ships with the
Vulcan/Phalanx unit – a 20mm six-barrelled Gatling gun.
In peacetime, a missile can be a disadvantage, for once
it has been fired, it homes on to its target. A couple of
rounds from an Oerlikon across hostile bows may well
have the desired effect without causing too serious an
international incident.

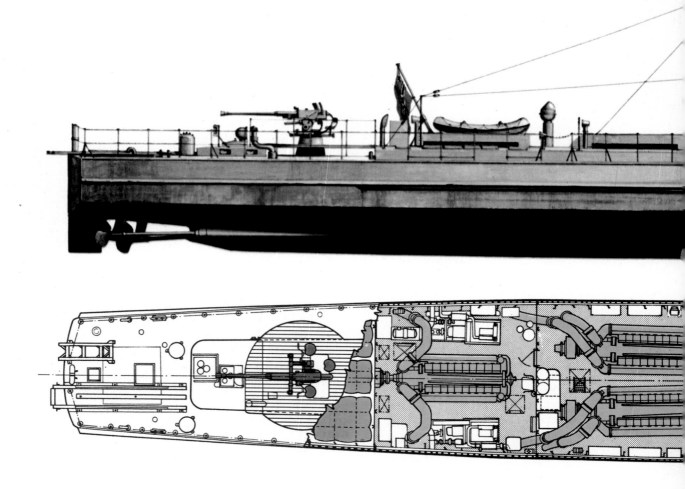

Left: The engine room of an
E-boat. A German engineer
checks one of the huge 4800bhp
diesels.
Right: A Royal Navy Vosper
Motor Torpedo Boat, which was
shorter and less well-armed
than the E-boat initially.

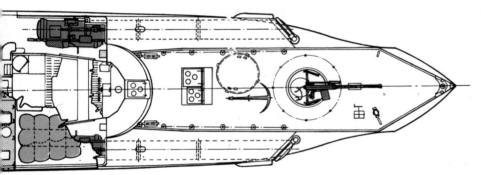

Left: The diagrams show side and deck plans of the E-boat S38. Built in 1942, each of her three Daimler-Benz diesel engines was capable of producing a remarkable 4800bhp – giving her a top speed of 35 knots. E-boats of this series were equipped with two enclosed torpedo tubes forward (shown in green on the deck plan). In this it differed from the British Vosper MTB which was fitted with exterior tubes. Fuel tanks were carried below deck (shown in yellow on the deck plan). Two tanks (not shown) carrying 200 litres each were situated in the stern. Three more tanks were positioned immediately abaft the engines (blue on the deck plan) and two more either side and below the bridge. The tank in use in the middle of the row had a capacity of 1450 litres, while the two on either side held 3150 litres of fuel. The S38 was armed with a 20mm cannon forward and a 40mm gun aft (green on the top plan). Eight mines could be carried at the stern.

1

2

3 4

5

6

7

8

9

10

Opposite page, top left: A comparison of modern warships showing their variety, size and complexity. The size can be gauged against the Enterprise (1) which is 1123ft (342m) long, and the Stenka (6) which is only 130ft (40m) long.

1. Aircraft-carrier Enterprise, nuclear powered, USA
2. 'River' class frigate, Australia.
3. 'Spica' class torpedo-boat, Sweden
4. Missile submarine Lafayette, USA
5. Cruiser, Long Beach, USA
6. 'Stenka' class fast corvette, USSR
7. 'Kresta' class cruiser, USSR
8. Class 'V' fleet submarine, USSR
9. 'County' class destroyer, UK
10. 'Krupny' class destroyer, USSR

Centre: An artist's impression showing many of the features of a modern, general purpose warship.

1. Variable depth sonar (VDS)
2. Anti-submarine mortar
3. Helicopter
4. Helicopter hangar
5. Seacat director
6. Seacat missile launcher
7. Long-range warning radar
8. HF/DF (high frequency direction finder) coil
9. Navigation radar
10. Gun director
11. Enclosed bridge
12. Gun turret
13. Stabilizer fin

Below: The modern HMS Sheffield (above) contrasted against the HMS Sheffield of 30 years (below). Today's Sheffield, although smaller, carries a far superior selection of armament and electronic equipment with a complement of 230 men compared to the 790 needed by the older ship.

HMS Sheffield 1975

HMS Sheffield 1945

Above: The large 'County' class guided missile destroyer, HMS Hampshire. Apart from two types of missile, her main armament is four 4.5 inch guns. This particular ship was taken out of service in 1976 to be de-equipped and scrapped.

Right: Two 'Spica' class fast patrol boats lie up in their cavernous underground shelter. Sweden's long coastline offers natural refuges, ideal for conversion, in which these short endurance, but high performance, craft can rearm and refuel in safety after Baltic sorties.

Obviously the missile has come to stay for the immediate future. The most likely tactical formation will be a circle or rectangle, each ship searching and firing three-dimensionally through her sector. This proved the most effective convoy and fleet defence against submarines and aircraft during World War II. In the Pacific, the screen of radar pickets did more than give early warning of *kamikaze* attack. They often suffered grievously from those suicide aircraft whose pilots were naturally so tense that they dived into the first enemy ship they saw. In the same way, a missile would home on to the nearest ship, which must defend herself and, if necessary, be expended in protecting the aircraft-carrier, transport or food ship within the circle.

Now that anti-submarine helicopters can operate from tiny decks, computerized missile packs are becoming smaller, and warships do not have heavy armour, there may be a tendency for merchant ships to carry their own weapons again; so that in the end specialized warships prove too costly and become armed merchantmen once more.

Three things at least seem certain. Training, efficiency, and speed of reaction will always matter. No navy will ever have enough ships — even the best ship cannot be in two places at once. And finally, whatever warships look like, whatever their function and classification, all the old individual names — Stuart, Godetia, Minas Gerais, Athabaskan, Peder Skram, Le Redoutable, Emden, Delhi, Vittorio Veneto, Mogami, Sleipner, Lepanto, Nuavenet, Resolution, Enterprise, Skory — will still be found in any future list of the world's navies.

AIRCRAFT

Above: The Japanese Aichi D3A1, one of the planes used to bomb Pearl Harbor in 1941, and designated 'Val' by the Americans.

If one includes lighter-than-air craft (aerostats) in the definition of aircraft, it can be said that the history of military aircraft goes back to the use of captive balloons as observation platforms by the French in the battle of Fleurus in 1794. But although such use by the French in the Napoleonic wars and by other nations in the subsequent century helped pave the way for the acceptance of aircraft as a useful adjunct to a nation's armed forces, the true future of aviation, both civilian and military, lay with the heavier-than-air craft (aerodyne), the first of which (the Wright brothers' Flyer I) flew in December 1903. Thus the practical age of flight has lasted only some seventy years; yet in this time there have been enormous strides made in the development of the aircraft's military potential, making it first the rival and now the master of the other armed services as the chief agent of destruction.

Acceptance of aircraft by the military as a useful weapon was slow, the first military aircraft being called for by the Americans in February 1908, and the various European nations gradually following in the next few years. This hesitancy was understandable, as the aircraft was as yet unreliable and capable of lifting only a small payload. Thus the role envisaged for these first service aircraft was that of reconnaissance. It should be noted, however, that a few brave spirits had started experimenting with the fitting of guns and bombs.

The importance of aircraft was amply demonstrated during World War I: aircraft soon brought back very useful information, and it was swiftly realized that it was worth preventing the flow of such information to the enemy. Thus were born the first fighters or scouts, as they were known at the time. Reconnaissance, both tactical and strategic, optical and photographic, and the allied task of artillery spotting remained the most important task of aircraft in World War I. But the need to destroy or protect such aircraft led to a see-saw battle in the development of fighting machines. It was soon realized, moreover, that if one could see a target from the air, then one could also profitably drop explosives, in the form of bombs, on such an objective. Thus there evolved three major types of fighting aircraft — scout or fighter, reconnaissance, and bomber. The scope of the last was considerably enlarged during World War I, the Germans, British, Italians and Russians in particular having ambitions in the field of large 'strategic' bombers.

Aircraft also found a role at sea: at first land- and sea-planes operated as patrol machines to watch for enemy surface and underwater craft, but soon offensive armament, including bombs and torpedoes, became quite common. The landplane also put to sea, in the form of small fighter aircraft operating from miniscule platforms fitted over the guns of the larger warships, and then from decks fitted to ships to form the aircraft-carrier, the type of warship that was to prove dominant in World War II.

Reliability and performance had increased steadily during World War I, and this progress was maintained in the first fifteen years after the end of that conflict 'to end all wars'. Biplanes, which had high structural integrity for a low airframe weight, were still in vogue, but design refinements and far more powerful engines gradually raised speeds from the 150 mph (240 kph) of 1918 to about 200 mph (320 kph) in 1930.

But now there came a revolution in the design of fighting aircraft, brought about by advances in aeronautical theory, metallurgy and engine design. Biplanes of wooden and mixed structure were phased out, and a new generation of metal, monoplane aircraft, with retractable undercarriages and enclosed cockpits began to enter the lists in the middle of the 1930's. The improvement over earlier types was marked, and proved in the Spanish Civil War (1936-9): fighter speeds, for example, quickly rose from 200 mph (320 kph) to over 300 mph (480 kph). At the same time both defensive and offensive armament also received considerable enhancement.

Aircraft thus played a more important part in World War II than they had in World War I. Medium bombers proved an essential adjunct to the ground forces, with fighter-bombers (single-engined types for the most part, with the capability of carrying bombs and rockets in addition to their gun armaments) playing an important tactical role in the closing stages of the war. The strategic bomber also made good at last, the British and American heavy bomber fleets playing a decisive role in the defeat of Germany and Japan.

At sea also aircraft played the dominant role. Long-range patrol aircraft helped eliminate the threat posed by the submarine, and carrier-borne strike aircraft, armed with armour-piercing bombs and torpedoes, and protected by

Top: A French Morane-Saulnier 'Bullet' of 1915 vintage, with deflector plates to stop the propeller from being shot off.
Above: Captain Baron Manfred von Richthofen with his own flight on the Western Front. The 'Red Baron', who claimed 80 kills before he himself was shot down, flew several Fokker Dr Is — but never an all-red one, as is popularly believed. His all-red plane was an earlier Albatros.

5

6

4

3

2

1

17

16

18

high-performance fighters, proved more than a match for conventional naval forces.

Performance increased greatly during World War II, speeds rising as high as 450 mph (725 kph) in the case of fighters. Bomb loads rose considerably, and significant advances were made in two fields that were to revolutionize air warfare.

These two factors were electronics and gas turbine (jet) propulsion. The first enabled a massive extension of the faculties of seeing and hearing, as it were ; and the second ushered in a new era in performance, speeds rapidly pushing through the 500 mph (805kph) barrier towards the 'sound barrier' and beyond. Thus, whereas the pilot in the days up to the end of World War II was able to assimilate and act on all the important factors of flying and fighting as they occurred, the new technology made it impossible for him to do so, but on the other hand provided 'intelligent' machines that can do the basic tasks for themselves, leaving the pilot to determine the tactics and decide on the course of action to be undertaken by his machines. So that although fighting aircraft, in which category the helicopter must now be included, has increased in sophistication almost beyond recognition since World War II, tasks and functions remain basically the same as those evolved during World War I. Nevertheless, present-day aircraft are a far cry from those early 'warbirds'.

Left : Fokker Dr I triplane produced in 1917. It was highly manoeuvrable but inclined to break up if subjected to too much stress.
Below : Fokker D VII.
1. *Balanced elevators*
2. *Characteristic 'comma-shaped' rudder*
3. *Throttle*
4. *Plywood panel decking, fabric covered, to rear of cockpit*
5. *Horn-balanced ailerons*
6. *Twin fixed 'Spandau' machine-guns, 500 rounds each*
7. *160hp Mercedes D IIIA water-cooled in-line engine*
8. *'Car-type' honeycomb radiator*
9. *Fuel tank*
10. *Metal panels forward of cockpit*
11. *Constant-chord wings with 3-ply leading edge*
12. *Wire threaded through copper eyelets to form characteristic 'scalloped' trailing edge*
13. *'One piece' lower wing – continuous through fuselage*
14. *760mm × 100mm wheels*
15. *Aerofoil lifting surface covering axle*
16. *Welded steel tube fuselage*
17. *Tail skid springs*
18. *Ash tail skid*

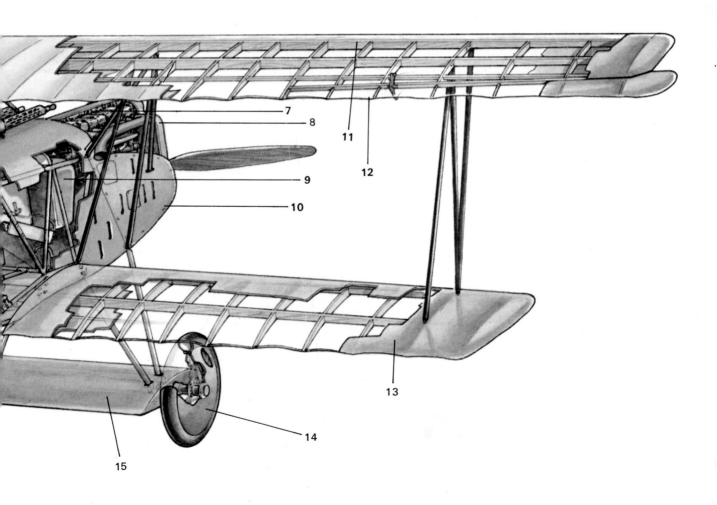

Top : Captain William Avery Bishop RFC ended World War I with 72 victories. A Canadian, Bishop scored most of his successes in the Nieuport B1566, in which our picture shows him seated.

Centre : March 1918, German Albatros D Vs of Jagdstaffel 23b occupy a captured British airfield at Favreuil.

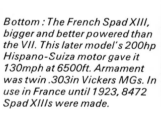

Bottom : The French Spad XIII, bigger and better powered than the VII. This later model's 200hp Hispano-Suiza motor gave it 130mph at 6500ft. Armament was twin .303in Vickers MGs. In use in France until 1923, 8472 Spad XIIIs were made.

World War I (1914-1918)

Before World War I there was little to differentiate 'civil' from 'military' aircraft — the important factor in selection of a type in the latter category being not conformity to strict specifications so much as a relatively robust airframe and engine coupled with the ability to sustain flight.

Although there were still a number of 'birdcage' or 'stick-and-string' designs still in evidence right into the early stages of the war, it is worth noting that in the years 1910-1914 great advances were made in basic design, particularly with a view to improving performance by means of careful streamlining. Notable in this respect were the French Deperdussin *Monocoque*, and the British Sopwith Tabloid and Royal Aircraft Factory SE 2 and 4. All were capable of speeds in excess of 100 mph (160 kph) at a time when average speeds rarely rose above 75 mph (120 kph), and in fact the Deperdussin, with its faired undercarriage and monoplane wings, was more the precursor of design trends of the 1920s than those of World War I. The two British biplanes, however, showed what might be expected of the next generation of high-performance types.

Fighters

As noted above, the major task envisaged for aircraft in the opening stages of World War I was reconnaissance, and this task fell within the capabilities of most of the current types. The results were promising, and it soon became apparent that it would be useful to prevent the enemy obtaining similar help. But how was this to be done? A few adventurous pilots had taken to shooting at their opposite numbers with rifles, shotguns and pistols, but significant results could hardly be achieved in this manner. In tractor aircraft, moreover, it was difficult to shoot forwards, as the propeller was in the way. What was needed was a means of firing a machine gun, fixed along the fuselage axis, directly forwards, so that all the pilot had to do was aim his aircraft at his opponent and fire the gun.

The legendary French airman, Roland Garros, came up with the first 'practical' solution: a machine gun was fixed to the forward fuselage of his Morane-Saulnier Type L scout, and wedge-shaped steel deflectors were attached to the rear of the propeller blades where any bullets might strike them, most of the burst going through the gap between the blades, however. In the spring of 1915 Garros was ready, and soon shot down five German aircraft.

Forced down by engine failure behind the German lines, however, Garros' plane was an inspiration to the Germans, who told the talented Dutchman working for them, Anthony Fokker, to rush the idea into production. Fokker's designers went one better, and produced an interrupter gear, in which a mechanical linkage prevented the gun firing when a propeller blade was in front of the muzzle. This obviated the need for deflectors, and also removed the problem of vibration when a bullet struck such a deflector. The new gear was installed on the otherwise unremarkable Fokker *Eindekker* to produce the world's first true fighter and ushered in the days of the 'Fokker Scourge', when Germany dominated the skies over the Western Front.

The Allies had no comparable interrupter gear, so until they could devise one, they had to rely on pusher types,

Above: In its very early days, aircraft detection was based on sight and sound without electronic help. Here a German officer is being given a 'listen' through a cone sound-detector which would amplify the engine noise from an approaching plane. In the same way the angle indicator would give a rough indication of the aircraft's height. Left: E. V. Rickenbacker, outstanding American pilot with 26 victories.

Above : With two 220lb bombs in position, and five 110lb bombs being put into position, the Gotha G V was able to carry over 1000lb of bombs.

Below : SE5a. Work-horse of the RFC, the SE5 had a good combat record and it was in this plane that James McCudden won the Victoria Cross.

which could mount a gun in the front of the fuselage with no fear of hitting the propeller. The best of this type was the Airco de Havilland DH 2, but combat experience soon revealed that the aerodynamic deficiencies of this layout could not be tolerated in a rapidly advancing technological war. The Allies eventually designed a hydraulic synchronising gear that was more flexible than the German mechanical gear, and this was fitted on most Allied fighting types from the middle of 1916 onwards, starting with the

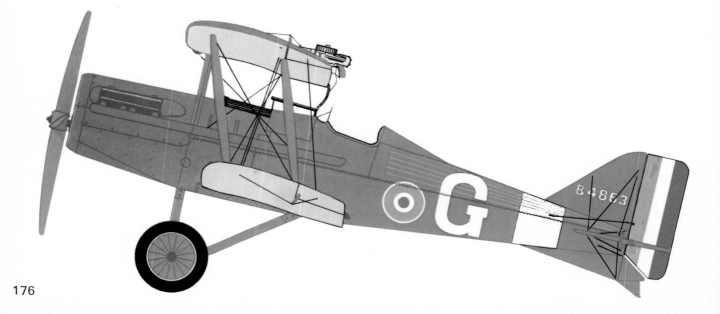

Sopwith 1½-Strutter and Pup. The Germans countered with the two-gun Albatros D I in the spring of 1917. Germany's greatest period of air domination was ushered in with this fighter and the later D II, III and V, which with their guns set the standard for fighter armament right into the 1930s.

The Allies in turn produced the excellent Sopwith Camel, powered by a succession of the magnificent Bentley rotaries, which was supremely agile; the sturdy and dependable Royal Aircraft Factory SE 5 and 5a, powered by water-cooled inlines; and the French Spad 7 and 13, and Nieuport 27 and 28, both basic types being fast, robust and manoeuvrable.

With armament now fixed at two guns by consideration of weight and mass, fighter development now depended on engine power to provide the factors most needed by high-performance combat aircraft: speed, rate of climb and ceiling. At the same time, designers had to try to retain the manoeuvrability of earlier fighters, especially in rates of turn and roll, in machines that now weighed some 2,000 lb (900 kg), compared with 1916 types that weighed 1,200 lb (550 kg). On the whole they were quite successful, producing fast, sturdy fighters that were still very agile, and capable of climb rates of 1000 feet per minute (305 metres per minute) and altitudes approaching 20,000 feet (6,100 metres). 1914 scouts could climb at about half that speed, and attain a ceiling of some 12,000 feet (3,660 metres) on power about two-fifths the 250 hp available to most fighters in 1918.

Exemplary of the last generation of wartime fighters are the Fokker D VII and the Martinsyde F 4 Buzzard, the latter of which was capable of some 150 mph (240 kph). Thus during World War I fighter speeds had nearly doubled, and a considerable armament was now standard in compact aircraft powered by large water-cooled inlines, which had taken over from the rotary as the most popular type of aircraft powerplant, the rotary being at its theoretical limit at powers about 300 hp, and presenting dangerous problems with torque at such powers.

Bombers

The use of bombs in war preceded that of machine guns, the first bombing raid being made in November 1911 by an Italian against Turkish positions in Libya. In the course of

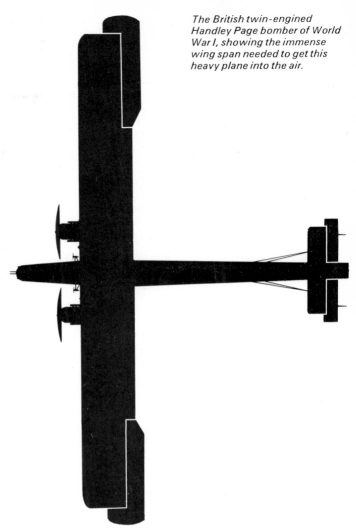

The British twin-engined Handley Page bomber of World War I, showing the immense wing span needed to get this heavy plane into the air.

Below: Nieuport 17, a delightful and manoeuvrable sesquiplane flown by the 'aces' Ball and Bishop. The Sioux insignia was the emblem of the Lafayette Escadrille.

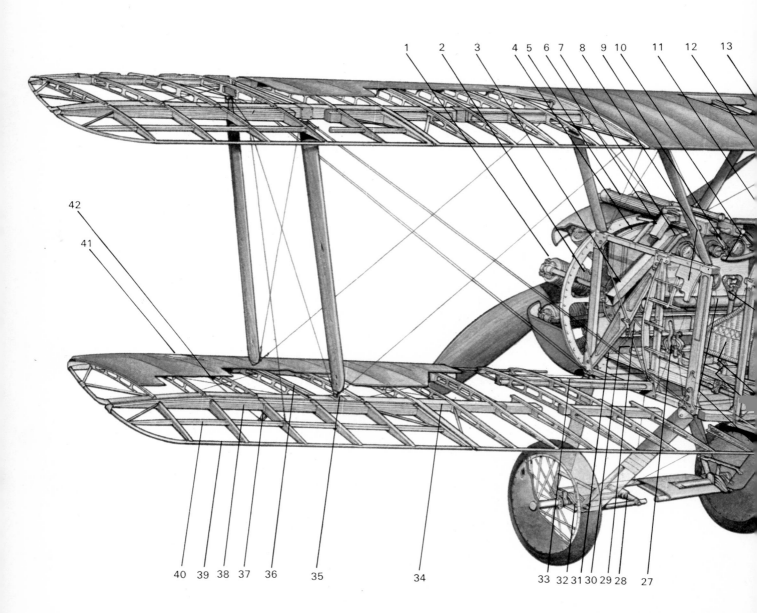

A 'remake of a remake of a remake' Camel F1. This aircraft, in the RAF Historical Museum, Hendon, London, is an exact replica of the World War I fighter. For the stickler for accuracy the main fault is the serial number which is a prefabrication. The original serial number of this particular aircraft is as yet unknown. Otherwise the Camel is just as it was in its heyday in the skies of the Western Front during World War I.

Engine
130hp Clerget 9z
110hp Le Rhône
100hp Gnome Monosoupape
150hp BR1
Wing span (both wings) 28ft
Length
18ft 9in (Clerget)
18ft 8in (Le Rhône)
19ft (Gnome)
18ft 6in (BR1)
Height
8ft 6in (Clerget, Le Rhône, BR1)
8ft 9in (Gnome)

Sopwith Camel F1
1. Bentley BR1 150hp motor
2. Firewall (not shown)
3. Cartridge disposal chute
4. Castor-oil tank
5. Twin .303in Vickers air-cooled MGs
6. Link chute
7. Mount for MGs
8. Plywood decking
9. Cocking handles for twin MGs
10. Instrument panel
11. Auxiliary fuel tank
12. Main fuel tank
13. Open centre-section
14. Control column
15. Intermediate formers
16. Rubber shock cord
17. Steerable ash tail-skid
18. Steel tube outline/nose ribs
19. Fairleads
20. Ash longerons
21. Control cables

22. Tank bearer
23. Turn-buckles
24. Wicker seat
25. Seat bearer
26. Carburettor air intake
27. Throttle quadrant
28. Undercarriage axle hinge point
29. Rear engine mount
30. Rudder bar
31. Foot-board
32. Bungee shock-absorber straps
33. Ash front spar (routed)
34. Solid ash rear spar on lower wing only
35. Mild steel fittings
36. Compression strut
37. Aileron control horn
38. Spruce aileron spar
39. Steel tubing round wing edge
40. Spruce sub-spar
41. Inspection window
42. Wire drag bracings

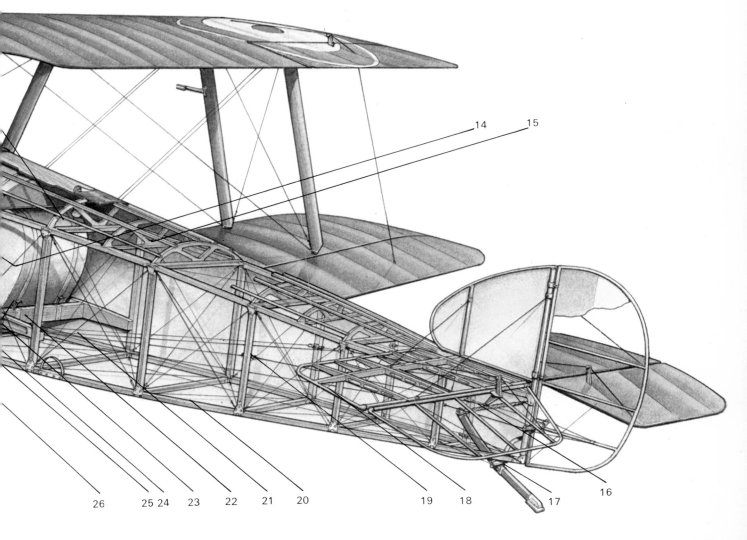

Below: The team whose Vickers airframe and Rolls-Royce engine combination led to the brilliant combat performance of the Spitfire. R. J. Mitchell the designer (left) and F. H. Royce (right).

the two-year war fought by Italy to gain possession of Libya a fair amount of aerial work was undertaken, a factor that is often ignored by air historians. Thus by the outbreak of World War I some real progress had been made towards the development of true bombing aircraft. The most notable of these were the series of multi-engined aircraft that were built by the Italian pioneer Caproni, and the world's first four-engined bomber, the Russian Sikorsky *Ilya Muromets*, as it was renamed after the beginning of the war. In France, bombing was the special province of the Voisin series of aircraft, all ungainly pusher biplanes, but capable of carrying an acceptable load of bombs.

From its earliest days bombing fell into two categories, heavy and light. As already noted, the Italians and Russians had led the way with the Caproni and Sikorsky bombers. The Germans and British were quick to follow, the former with their Gotha, AEG and *Riesen* (giant) aircraft, and the latter with three biplanes from the Handley Page drawing boards.

The two main German twin-engined bombers were the AEG G IV and the Gotha G V, both of which had bomb loads in the order of 1,000 lbs (455 kg), speeds of 100 mph (160 kph) and ranges of 500 miles (1,600 km). Both types appeared in the autumn of 1916, and the Gotha in particular played an important part in the German bombing of England, which led directly to the formation of a unified and independent Royal Air Force by the amalgamation of the Royal Flying Corps and Royal Naval Air Service in

Spitfire Mk I. No. 19 Squadron, Duxford, August 1940.
1. Glycol header tank
2. Rolls Royce Merlin III, 1030hp
3. Coolant pipes
4. Rudder pedals
5. Fuel tanks
6. Heel-board
7. Reflector sight
8. U/c control levers
9. Voltage regulator
10. Harness to anchorage
11. Radio access
12. Identification light
13. Rear access hatch
14. Rudder
15. Castoring tail wheel
16. Elevator
17. IFF aerial
18. Control lines
19. Radio
20. Flare chute
21. Crowbar
22. Pilot's access door
23. Compass
24. U/c hydraulic ram
25. U/c leg mounting
26. Hinged cover acting as flap position indicator
27. Port flap
28. Access panels to machine-guns
29. Port aileron
30. Gun fork-mounting
31. Port-outer .303in Browning MG (8)
32. Underside wing access hatches to ammunition
33. Wheel well
34. Stiffener rails
35. Oil tank

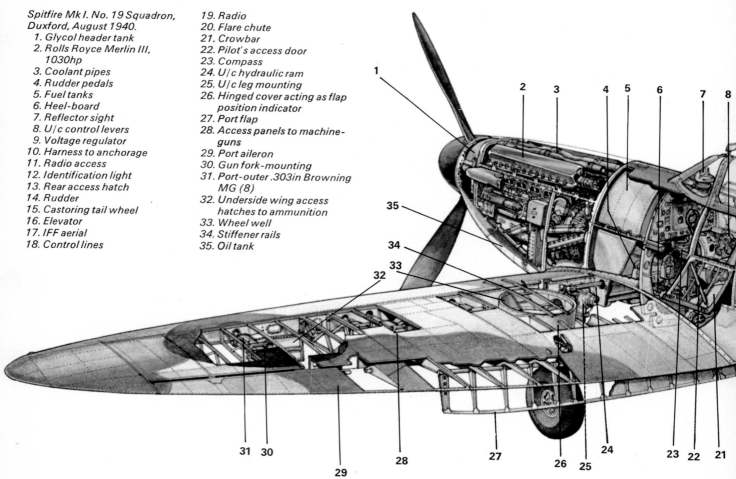

April 1918. Most remarkable of Germany's bombers, however, was the series of R aircraft, vast multi-engined bombers that were not to be exceeded in size by production aircraft until after World War II. The best of these aircraft was the Zeppelin-Staaken R VI, which could carry a 4,000 lb (1,800 kg) bomb load over 700 miles (1,125 km) at a speed of 80 mph (130 kph). Wing span was 138 feet 5½ inches (42.2 m), and the whole series typified by the R VI was a technical *tour de force* in aeronautical engineering unequalled in World War I.

Britain's answers to these aircraft were the Handley Page 0/100, 0/400 and V/1500. The 0/100 and 0/400 were basically the same aircraft with different engines, and constituted Britain's main bombing force from 1916 to 1918. Bomb load was 2,000 lb (900 kg). Just entering service as the war ended was the V/1500, a four-engined machine intended to bomb industrial targets in Germany. Its maximum speed was almost 100 mph (160 kph) and range 1,200 miles (1,930 km), and the payload a very useful 7,500 lb (3,410 kg). This last would have made the V/1500 the world's first true strategic bomber had it been available in large numbers in 1918.

In the field of light bombing, the British and French fared better than the Germans, as exemplified by the two best single-engined bombers of the war : the Airco de Havilland DH 4 and up-engined 9A, and the Breguet 14. Both types were as fast as contemporary fighters, had an excellent defensive armament and could carry 500 to 600 lb (230 to

Below : The British Hawker Hurricane. Although slower than its companion, the Spitfire, the Hurricane was nevertheless an excellent combat fighter.

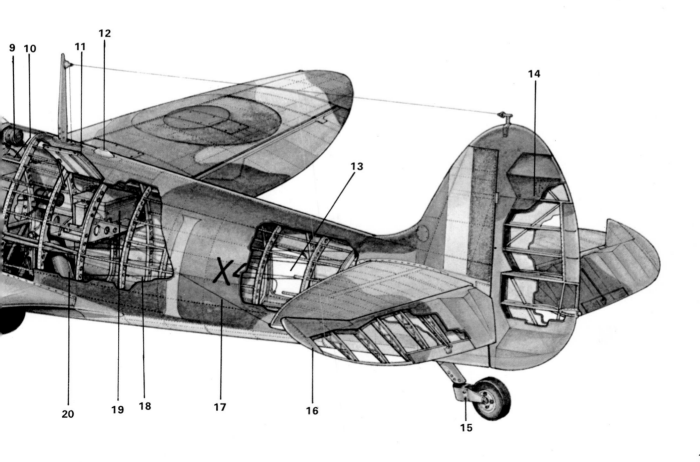

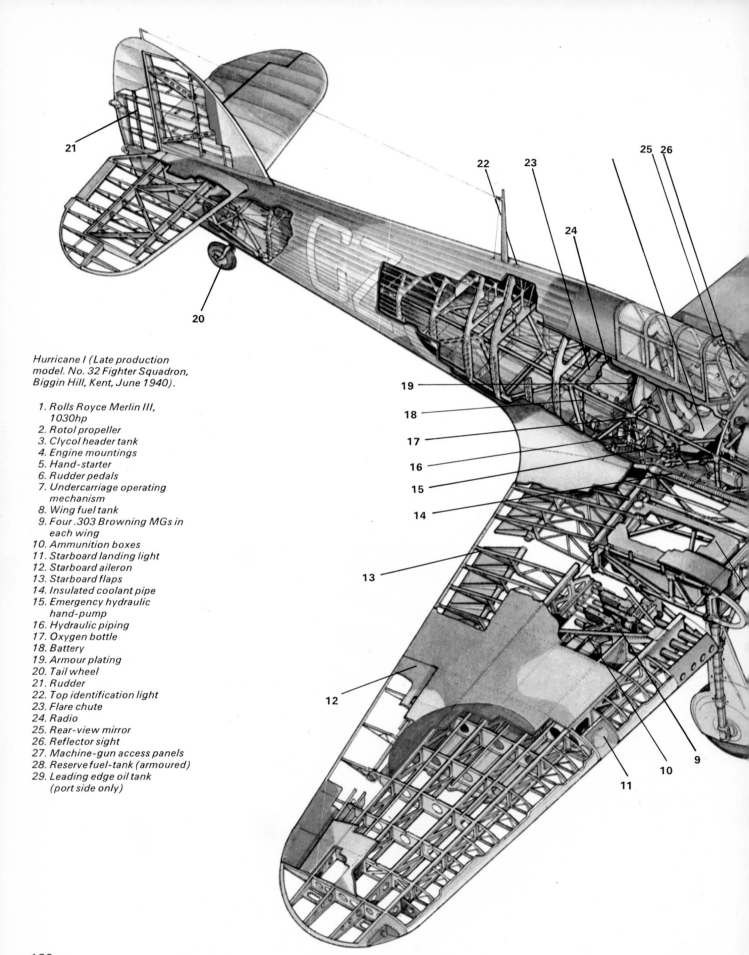

Hurricane I (Late production
model. No. 32 Fighter Squadron,
Biggin Hill, Kent, June 1940).

1. Rolls Royce Merlin III,
   1030hp
2. Rotol propeller
3. Clycol header tank
4. Engine mountings
5. Hand-starter
6. Rudder pedals
7. Undercarriage operating
   mechanism
8. Wing fuel tank
9. Four .303 Browning MGs in
   each wing
10. Ammunition boxes
11. Starboard landing light
12. Starboard aileron
13. Starboard flaps
14. Insulated coolant pipe
15. Emergency hydraulic
    hand-pump
16. Hydraulic piping
17. Oxygen bottle
18. Battery
19. Armour plating
20. Tail wheel
21. Rudder
22. Top identification light
23. Flare chute
24. Radio
25. Rear-view mirror
26. Reflector sight
27. Machine-gun access panels
28. Reserve fuel-tank (armoured)
29. Leading edge oil tank
    (port side only)

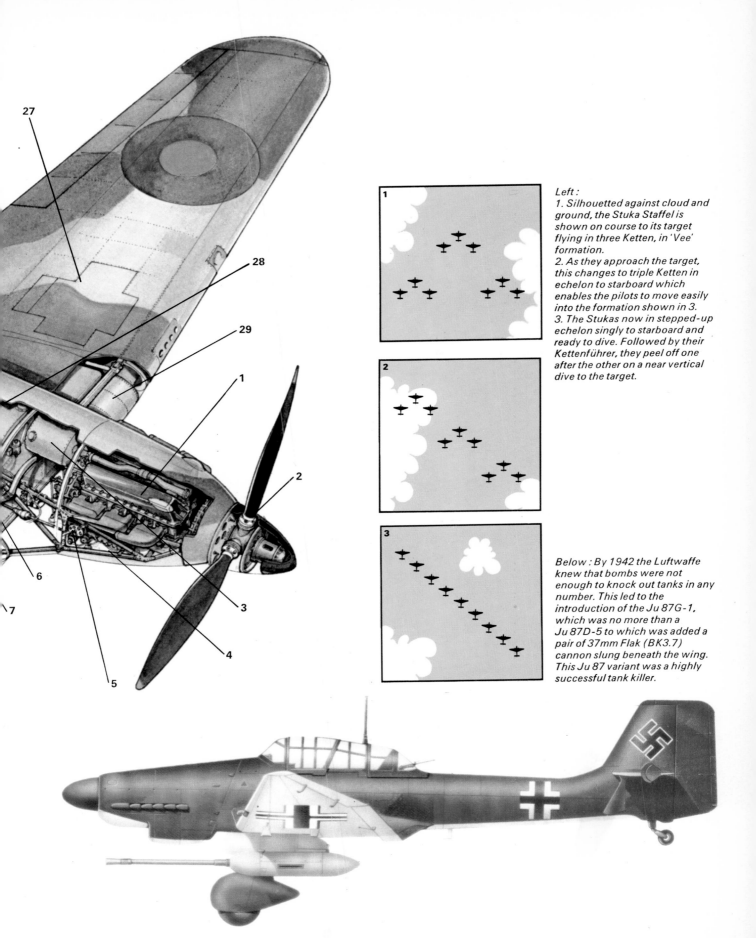

Left:

1. Silhouetted against cloud and ground, the Stuka Staffel is shown on course to its target flying in three Ketten, in 'Vee' formation.

2. As they approach the target, this changes to triple Ketten in echelon to starboard which enables the pilots to move easily into the formation shown in 3.

3. The Stukas now in stepped-up echelon singly to starboard and ready to dive. Followed by their Kettenführer, they peel off one after the other on a near vertical dive to the target.

Below: By 1942 the Luftwaffe knew that bombs were not enough to knock out tanks in any number. This led to the introduction of the Ju 87G-1, which was no more than a Ju 87D-5 to which was added a pair of 37mm Flak (BK3.7) cannon slung beneath the wing. This Ju 87 variant was a highly successful tank killer.

Right: Cockpit of the Do 217E series. The pilot's seat has been removed.
Notably there is no co-pilot's position, the observer being trained to control the aircraft in emergency. Flying controls and blind-flying panel are in front of the odd-shaped controls on the left. On the screen in front of the pilot is the Revi C12 reflector sight, and above this, suspended from the roof, a dive-bombing sight. A large radio-compass is to the lower right of the instrument panel.

Right: A Do 217E-2 releasing an Hs 293 glider bomb, a weapon designed to attack armoured targets.

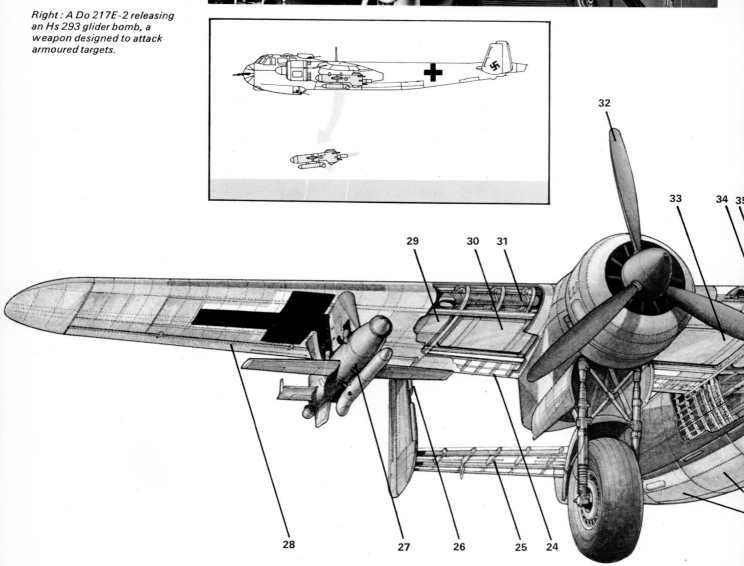

270 kg) of bombs. Operating in the tactical role, these two aircraft fulfilled a very useful, but not vital, part in the final Allied victory.

The Germans did not make much use of the light bomber as such, concentrating instead on the ground-attack type. This class of machine was intended to be a manoeuvrable, two-seater but single-engined biplane capable of supporting the men on the ground from low altitude with bombs and machine gun fire. Best of these were the Halberstadt CL IV, the Hannover CL IIIa, and the Junkers CL I and J I. The two Junkers aircraft pioneered the use of metal in aircraft, the corrugated metal covering contributing considerably to the strength so needed in this type of aircraft. (The CL I was in fact a monoplane.) These ground-support planes, as we would now designate them, proved very useful machines, and paved the way for the type of close-support work by aircraft that became so important a factor in World War II.

The British, who used fighters to support their ground forces with machine gun fire and light bombs, also developed special low-level attack aircraft, the operations of fighters having shown the need for heavier armament and armour protection. The best example of this type of British aircraft was the Sopwith Trench Fighter (TF) 2, which appeared in limited numbers in 1918. Derived from the Snipe fighter, the Salamander had 2,000 rounds of ammunition for each gun, compared with the fighter's average of about 200, and had 650 lb (295 kg) of armour protection. Ammunition capacity and armour protection were to be factors that became vitally important in close-support aircraft in World War II.

Below : Dornier 217E-5
Power : Two BMW 801C 14-cyl 2-row radials giving 1,580hp at take-off : 1,380hp at 15,100ft
Armament : 1 fixed forward-firing 15mm MG151 cannon 1 13mm MG131 (500rnds) in dorsal turret
1 free-mounted 13mm MG131 (1,000rnds) in ventral step
1 7.9mm MG151, free-mounted, forward-firing
2 7.9mm MG81s, remote-controlled, aft-firing in tail cone
Max speed : 273mph at sea level
Cruising speed (with max bomb load) : 258mph at 17,060ft
Service ceiling (without bomb load) : 29,530ft
Service ceiling (with max bomb load) : 24,600ft
Weight (empty) : 19,522lb
Weight (max overload) : 36,299lb
Span : 62ft 4in
Length : 59ft 8½in
Height : 16ft 6in
Wing area 613.542sq ft
1. Pilot's back armour
2. Pilot's seat
3. Flying controls
4. Control column
5. Instrument panel
6. Rudder pedals
7. Hot air ducts
8. Leading edge heating duct
9. Front spar (port)
10. Jettisonable port-fuel tank

(counter-balance for Hs 293 on starboard wing)
11. Fuel tank (port outer) holding 35 galls
12. Engine cooling fan
13. Oil cooler
14. Port BMW 14-cylinder radial engine
15. Under-carriage control mechanism
16. Bomb-aimer's window
17. Jettison chute for used shell-cases
18. Miniature joystick for control of Hs 293
20. Radio equipment and auto-pilot
21. Bomb bay
22. Bomb racks (not used when carrying Hs 293)
23. Bomb doors
24. Starboard flap
25. Tailplane
26. Inward-facing leading-edge slot on starboard fin
27. Hs 293 missile
28. Starboard slotted aileron
29. Starboard outer fuel tank (35 galls)
30. Oil tank (55 galls)
31. Starboard hot air duct
32. Propeller
33. Starboard inboard fuel tank (175 galls)
34. Cabin heating pipe
35. Fuel tank (242 galls)
36. Rear-gunner's seat
37. Bomb-aimer's rest seat

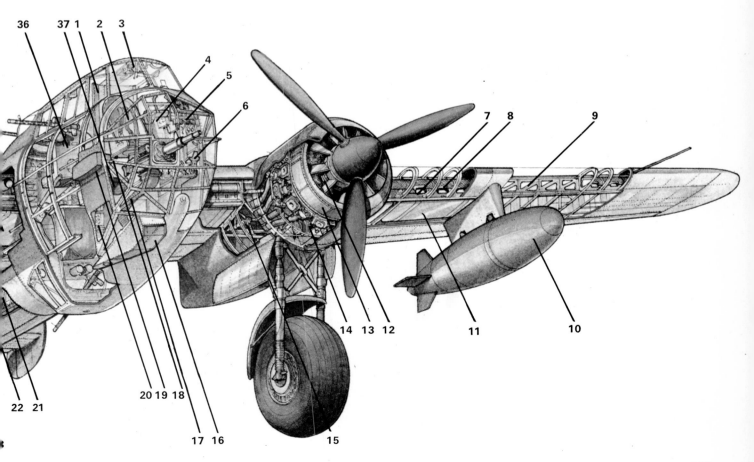

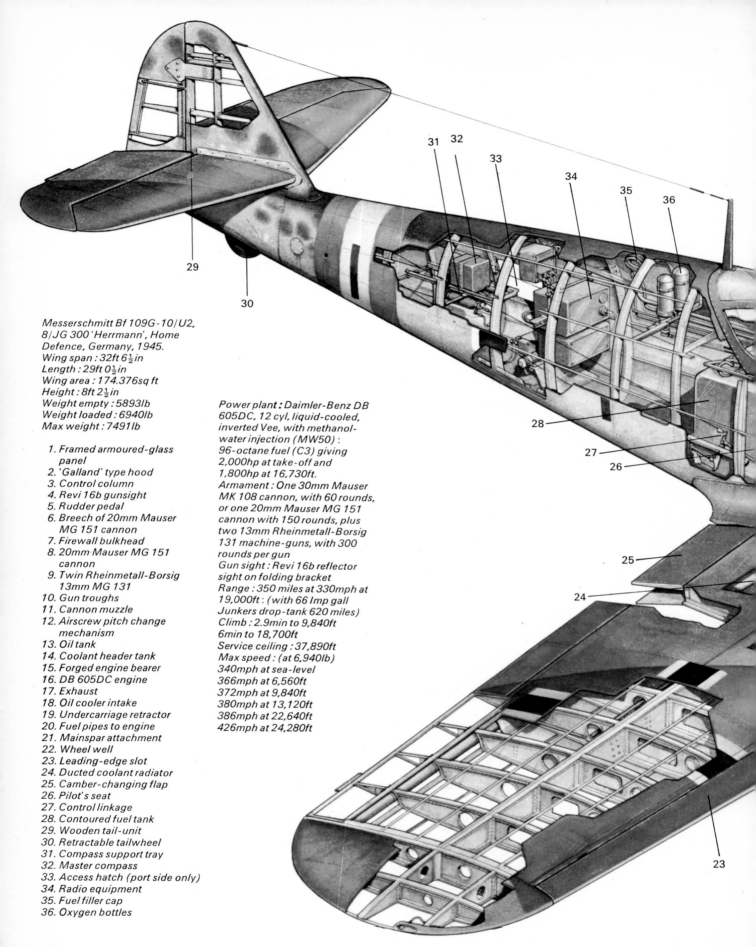

Messerschmitt Bf 109G-10/U2,
8/JG 300 'Herrmann', Home
Defence, Germany, 1945.
Wing span : 32ft 6½in
Length : 29ft 0½in
Wing area : 174.376sq ft
Height : 8ft 2½in
Weight empty : 5893lb
Weight loaded : 6940lb
Max weight : 7491lb

Power plant : Daimler-Benz DB
605DC, 12 cyl, liquid-cooled,
inverted Vee, with methanol-
water injection (MW50) :
96-octane fuel (C3) giving
2,000hp at take-off and
1,800hp at 16,730ft.
Armament : One 30mm Mauser
MK 108 cannon, with 60 rounds,
or one 20mm Mauser MG 151
cannon with 150 rounds, plus
two 13mm Rheinmetall-Borsig
131 machine-guns, with 300
rounds per gun
Gun sight : Revi 16b reflector
sight on folding bracket
Range : 350 miles at 330mph at
19,000ft : (with 66 Imp gall
Junkers drop-tank 620 miles)
Climb : 2.9min to 9,840ft
6min to 18,700ft
Service ceiling : 37,890ft
Max speed : (at 6,940lb)
340mph at sea-level
366mph at 6,560ft
372mph at 9,840ft
380mph at 13,120ft
386mph at 22,640ft
426mph at 24,280ft

 1. Framed armoured-glass
    panel
 2. 'Galland' type hood
 3. Control column
 4. Revi 16b gunsight
 5. Rudder pedal
 6. Breech of 20mm Mauser
    MG 151 cannon
 7. Firewall bulkhead
 8. 20mm Mauser MG 151
    cannon
 9. Twin Rheinmetall-Borsig
    13mm MG 131
10. Gun troughs
11. Cannon muzzle
12. Airscrew pitch change
    mechanism
13. Oil tank
14. Coolant header tank
15. Forged engine bearer
16. DB 605DC engine
17. Exhaust
18. Oil cooler intake
19. Undercarriage retractor
20. Fuel pipes to engine
21. Mainspar attachment
22. Wheel well
23. Leading-edge slot
24. Ducted coolant radiator
25. Camber-changing flap
26. Pilot's seat
27. Control linkage
28. Contoured fuel tank
29. Wooden tail-unit
30. Retractable tailwheel
31. Compass support tray
32. Master compass
33. Access hatch (port side only)
34. Radio equipment
35. Fuel filler cap
36. Oxygen bottles

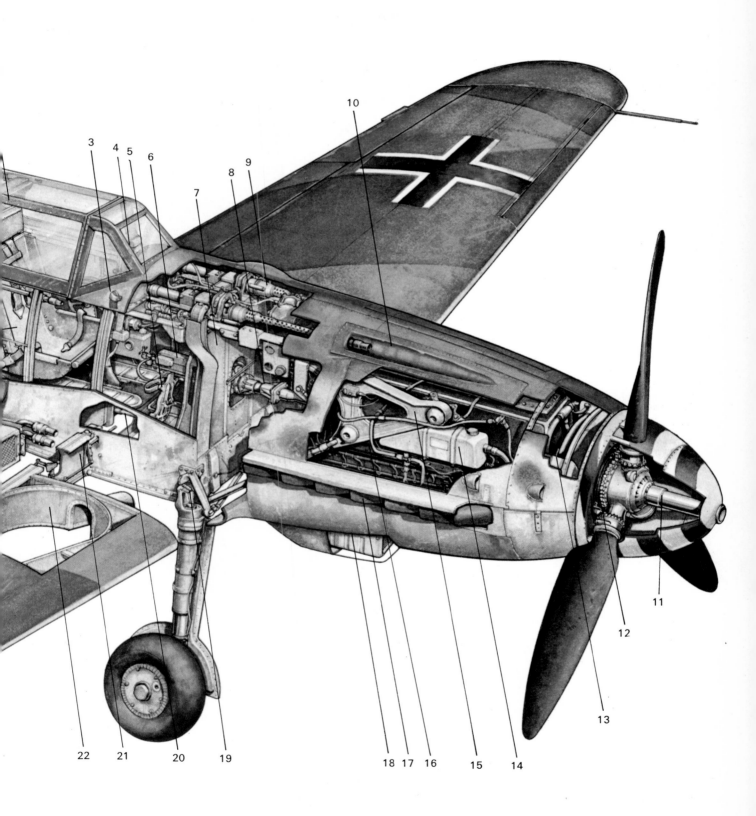

187

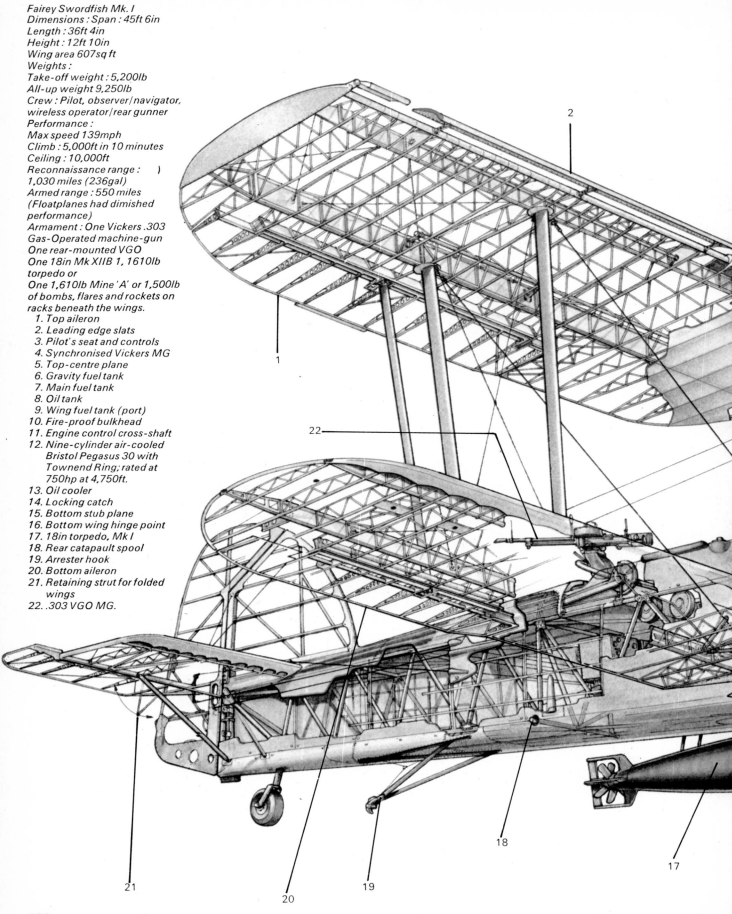

Fairey Swordfish Mk. I
Dimensions : Span : 45ft 6in
Length : 36ft 4in
Height : 12ft 10in
Wing area 607sq ft
Weights :
Take-off weight : 5,200lb
All-up weight 9,250lb
Crew : Pilot, observer/navigator,
wireless operator/rear gunner
Performance :
Max speed 139mph
Climb : 5,000ft in 10 minutes
Ceiling : 10,000ft
Reconnaissance range :   )
1,030 miles (236gal)
Armed range : 550 miles
(Floatplanes had dimished
performance)
Armament : One Vickers .303
Gas-Operated machine-gun
One rear-mounted VGO
One 18in Mk XIIB 1, 1610lb
torpedo or
One 1,610lb Mine 'A' or 1,500lb
of bombs, flares and rockets on
racks beneath the wings.
  1. Top aileron
  2. Leading edge slats
  3. Pilot's seat and controls
  4. Synchronised Vickers MG
  5. Top-centre plane
  6. Gravity fuel tank
  7. Main fuel tank
  8. Oil tank
  9. Wing fuel tank (port)
 10. Fire-proof bulkhead
 11. Engine control cross-shaft
 12. Nine-cylinder air-cooled
     Bristol Pegasus 30 with
     Townend Ring; rated at
     750hp at 4,750ft.
 13. Oil cooler
 14. Locking catch
 15. Bottom stub plane
 16. Bottom wing hinge point
 17. 18in torpedo, Mk I
 18. Rear catapult spool
 19. Arrester hook
 20. Bottom aileron
 21. Retaining strut for folded
     wings
 22. .303 VGO MG.

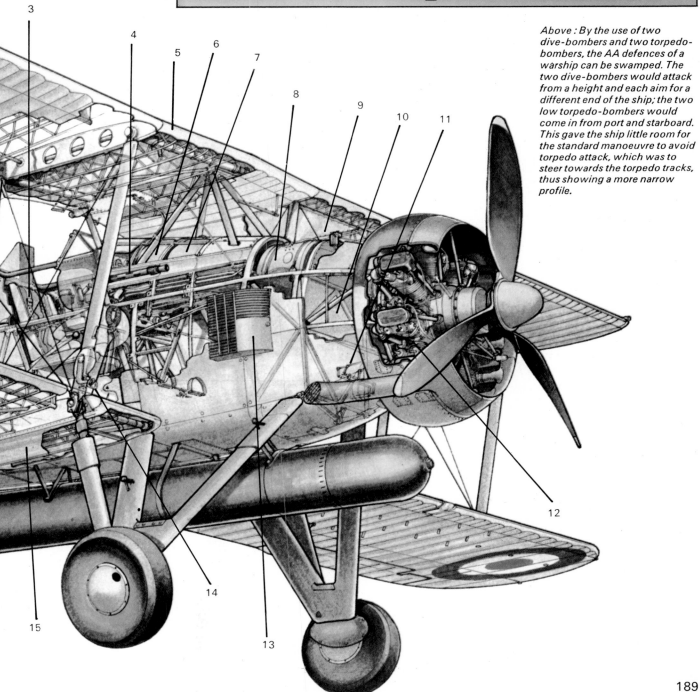

Above : By the use of two dive-bombers and two torpedo-bombers, the AA defences of a warship can be swamped. The two dive-bombers would attack from a height and each aim for a different end of the ship; the two low torpedo-bombers would come in from port and starboard. This gave the ship little room for the standard manoeuvre to avoid torpedo attack, which was to steer towards the torpedo tracks, thus showing a more narrow profile.

3
4
5
6
7
8
9
10
11
12
14
15
13

Opposite page, top : The Ju
88G-1, carrying Lichtenstein
SN-2 radar aerials instead of the
C-1 assembly.
Opposite page, nos. 1-6 :
1. Himmelbett stations in
   Occupied Europe.
2. Fighter orbits and waits as
   'Freya' locks on bomber.
3. 'Wurzburg' radar (green) fixes
   bomber and fighter.
4. Fighter's own 'Lichtenstein'
   radar homes on bomber.
5. The Giant Wurzberg radar
   aerial, range 40 miles.
6. Radio and visual beacons
   Ludwig, Ida, Dora, Otto.

Reconnaissance aircraft

As noted above, it was in the field of reconnaissance and similar functions that aircraft made their greatest contribution to World War I. At first reconnaissance was a simple matter : the observer merely peered over the side of his cockpit to see what was below the aircraft, and jotted down any relevant thing he saw. Despite the distinct lack of trained observers, such reconnaissance swiftly proved itself of use, and soon afterwards the first fighters appeared to try to prevent such reconnaissance. Thus there emerged a need for reconnaissance machines to defend themselves. The solution appeared easy : just arm the observer with a 'flexible' light machine gun of the Lewis type to beat off any attacker. Immediate problems were encountered here, however, for the observer in the commonest types such as the British BE-2 and German Albatros B I normally sat in the front cockpit, between the wings and surrounded by a 'birdcage' of rigging and bracing wires. It was hardly the ideal position from which to pour defensive fire, for there was every likelihood that the observer would shoot away a vital part of his own aircraft. The solution was simple, but took some time to implement : exchange the positions of the pilot and observer, thus giving the latter a clear field of fire over most of the upper hemisphere of his field of vision, as well as downwards on each side of the aircraft.

Better performance was also desirable, and so the new generation of reconnaissance machines were considerably more powerful than their predecessors. But although it was possible to increase performance in matters such as speed, designers had a very tricky job with such aircraft in other respects. In order to make the task of the crew as easy as possible for the primary task of reconnaissance, a certain amount of inherent stability was desirable. Yet in air-to-air combat any measure of inherent stability was a liability. How was the designer to balance these two conflicting requirements ? The answer, particularly on the British side, was that he could not : the Royal Aircraft Factory RE-8, which entered widespread service in 1917, was in many respects too stable to protect itself adequately in combat. Yet when given protection by fighters, it proved an admirable reconnaissance and artillery spotting aircraft, and showed itself to be one of the best and most successful types flown by Britain during World War I. The RE-8 was not fast (there was no particular reason for it to be so), but

Below : The 416mph He
219A-5/R1 carrying both
Lichtenstein SN-2 (large) radar
and the C-1 for close-range
seeking. This night-fighter was
armed with two 30mm MK 108
cannon in the ventral position,
twin wing-root cannon and the
unconventional Schräge Musik
('Jazz Music') upwards-firing
30mm MK 108 cannon.

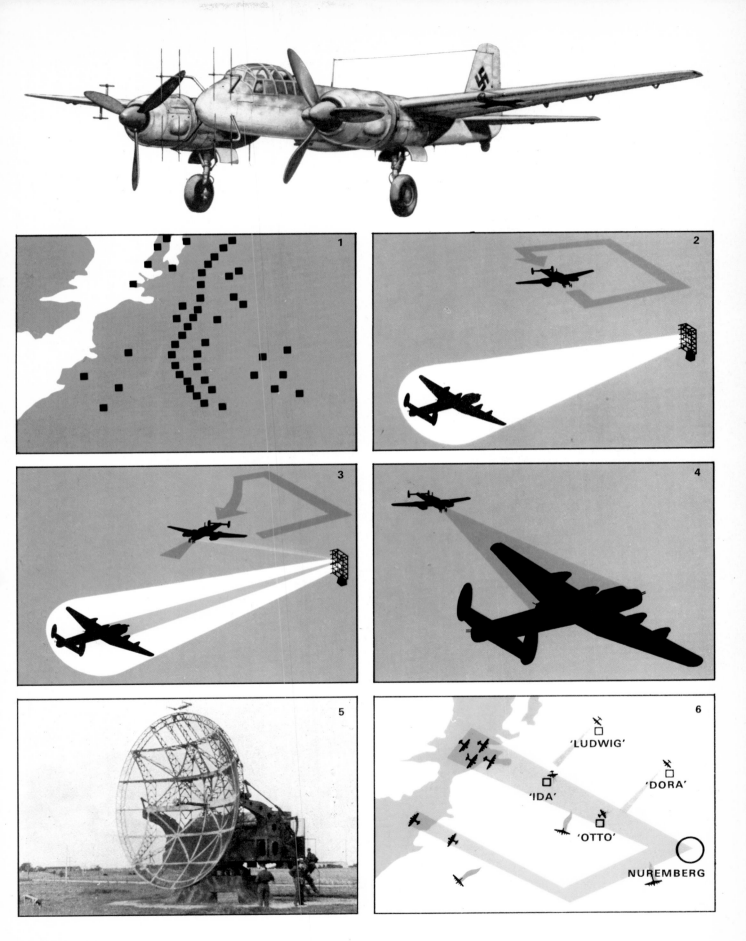

Below : An Oberleutnant in Fliegerbluse and late-pattern one-piece flying suit. He wears night-fighter insignia.

its endurance was good, armament of one fixed gun for the pilot and one or two flexible guns for the observer was adequate, and the payload good, the type being able to carry 260 lb (120 kg) of bombs or one of the clumsy radio sets needed for the essential work of artillery spotting. The Armstrong Whitworth FK-8 fulfilled a similar function at about the same time.

Germany operated a plethora of reconnaissance types, and these served the army exceptionally well. From the Albatros B I, Aviatik B I and LVG B I, all unarmed biplanes in service at the beginning of the war, the Germans quickly moved on to the armed C-class machines, exemplified by the Albatros C I, III and VII (1915-6), the DFW C IV (1916), and the LFG (Roland) C II (1916). These were adequate machines with good armament and range, and in the case of the Roland C II, excellent performance. In the closing stages of World War I the Germans continued to produce first-class reconnaissance machines, all engined with powerful and reliable Mercedes or Benz inline motors.

Although their appearance was often very similar to that of single-engined fighters, these reconnaissance machines were somewhat larger than the fighters, for apart from an extra crewman, they all had to carry radio for artillery spotting or cameras for the photographic reconnaissance roles. Both these items had been reduced in weight and size very considerably by the end of the war, but were still bulky, heavy articles that required a considerable area of wing to provide lift.

Maritime aircraft

Playing an unglamorous and unpublicized part in the war, the maritime air units of the various combatants in fact played a solid part in the fortunes of their countries. Maritime aircraft fall into two categories : those that operate from land, and those that are based on water ; the latter are further subdivided into floatplanes (basically landplanes that have floats in place of wheels on the undercarriage chassis) and flying-boats (aircraft with a boat hull at the bottom of the fuselage).

Land-based aircraft need concern us little, as for the most part they were obsolete aircraft from other theatres fitted out to carry a few small bombs and used as patrol aircraft against submarines, operating in conjunction with small non-rigid airships. Towards the end of the war there emerged the aircraft-carrier, and a few modern types were adapted to fly from the decks of such vessels. The most interesting 'landplane' for maritime use developed during the war, however, was the Sopwith Cuckoo. This was the first torpedo-bomber to be designed for use from a carrier, but few were delivered before the armistice. Nevertheless, it pointed the way to what was to be the carrier's most potent weapon in the next war.

The classic flying-boats of the war were undoubtedly the Curtiss America series, the Franco-British Aviation Type H, the Felixstowe F 2A and the Macchi M5. The first three were fairly substantial patrol flying-boats, but the last was an interesting and quite high-performance fighter for use in the Adriatic. Because of their need to operate from water, all these craft were solidly built, and this stood their crews in good stead in combat, in which small calibre machine gun fire frequently failed to shoot down the larger flying-boats.

Inter war years

The first fifteen years after the end of World War I are usually considered very sterile ones for military aviation. Admittedly, money was in short supply and therefore air force authorities all over the world had to be parsimonious when it came to ordering new types. No enormous orders were placed, but small orders for a variety of fighting types helped air forces to keep up a steady, if slow, progress in the field of aviation.

The important factor, however, was that all the elements needed to make the rapid progress of the middle and late 1930's possible were being developed in a variety of otherwise unremarkable aircraft. Structures, for example, had been mostly of wood, braced with wires, during World War I. There had been exceptions, such as the Fokker welded tubular steel construction pioneered by Reinhold Platz, and the Junkers corrugated iron covering, which so strengthened structures that no bracing wires were needed. Shortly after the end of the war, Short Brothers produced a monocoque aircraft covered in metal, the Silver Streak, which was to prove the true progenitor of later stressed-skin metal monocoque aircraft. Throughout the 1920's a number of constructors on both sides of the Atlantic experimented with metal construction and skinning, paving the way for the designers of the 1930's.

Careful attention also became the norm in the field of streamlining. A few pre-World War I aircraft had shown what might be achieved in this field, and during the war the later Albatros fighters and reconnaissance machines had achieved a fair level of streamlining. But after the war it was the Americans, particularly the Curtiss company, that began to make great strides in the art of streamlining. The performance of Curtiss aircraft, with their beautifully cowled engines, soon impressed the Europeans, and the British and Italians soon began to overhaul the Americans. Streamlining entered the military field with aircraft such as the Fairey Fox, but the greatest strides were made in racing aircraft such as the Supermarine and Macchi series of floatplane racers for the Schneider trophy. The culmination of streamlining on the post-war type of fighter was on the British Hawker Hart.

At the same time, the Americans also made great strides in developing a modern bomber, first with the Boeing YB-9 in the early 1930's, and then with the Martin B-10B,

Top : A Bf 110G-4b/R3 complete with Lichtenstein SN-2 long-range radar and FuG 212C 1,200-yard range radar. The aircraft is fitted with two 66 Imp. gall. drop tanks below the outboard wing-panels. Above : Insignia of the German night-intruder force – 'Englandblitz'. Lightning strikes at a feeble map of England.

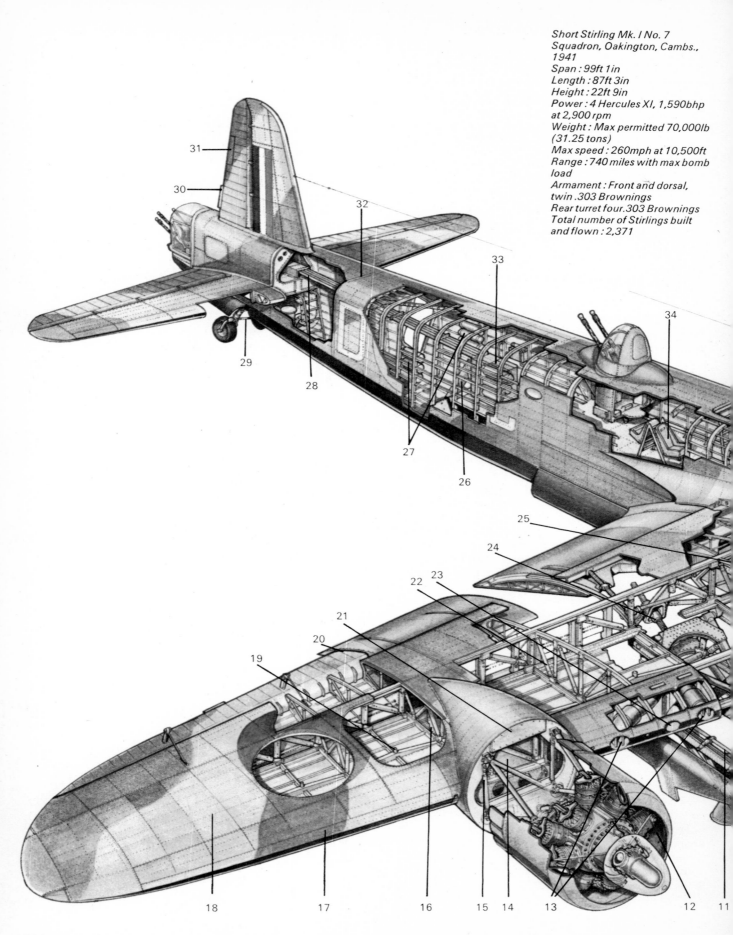

Short Stirling Mk. I No. 7
Squadron, Oakington, Cambs.,
1941
Span : 99ft 1in
Length : 87ft 3in
Height : 22ft 9in
Power : 4 Hercules XI, 1,590bhp
at 2,900 rpm
Weight : Max permitted 70,000lb
(31.25 tons)
Max speed : 260mph at 10,500ft
Range : 740 miles with max bomb
load
Armament : Front and dorsal,
twin .303 Brownings
Rear turret four .303 Brownings
Total number of Stirlings built
and flown : 2,371

1. Pilot's compartment and controls
2. Parachute stowage
3. Pitot heads
4. Stairway
5. Bomb-bays (3)
6. Cabin-heating pipe
7. Bomb-doors
8. Leading-edge fuel tank, not self-sealing (used for maximum-range sorties only)
9. Motor-support beam
10. Undercarriage doors
11. Undercarriage operating rods
12. Starboard-outer Bristol

Hercules XI 14-cyl air-cooled radial
13. Oil-cooler inlets (two on each wing)
14. Starboard-outer engine oil tank (25.5 gall)
15. Engine support strut
16. Watertight bulkhead
17. Armoured leading edge and cable-cutter
18. Detachable watertight outer wing section
19. Self-sealing fuel-tank attachment
20. Gouge-type flaps

21. Nacelle armour
22. Lattice-braced ribs
23. Heater air inlet
24. Undercarriage operating mechanism
25. Starboard wing bomb-cells
26. Flare chute
27. Flare stowage
28. Ammunition runway to rear turret
29. Retracting twin rear wheels
30. Trim tabs
31. Servo tabs
32. Fuselage joint
33. Ammunition stowage

34. Access ladder to dorsal dorsal turret (with seats)
35. Emergency exit and ladder
36. Sliding doors
37. Electric motor flap drive
38. Oxygen bottles
39. D/f loop
40. Dinghy stowage
41. Astro-navigation hatch
42. Gallay steam air heater
43. Self-sealing fuel tanks (2,692 galls of 100 octane were carried in 14 tanks and wing bomb-cells)
44. Flame-damping exhaust

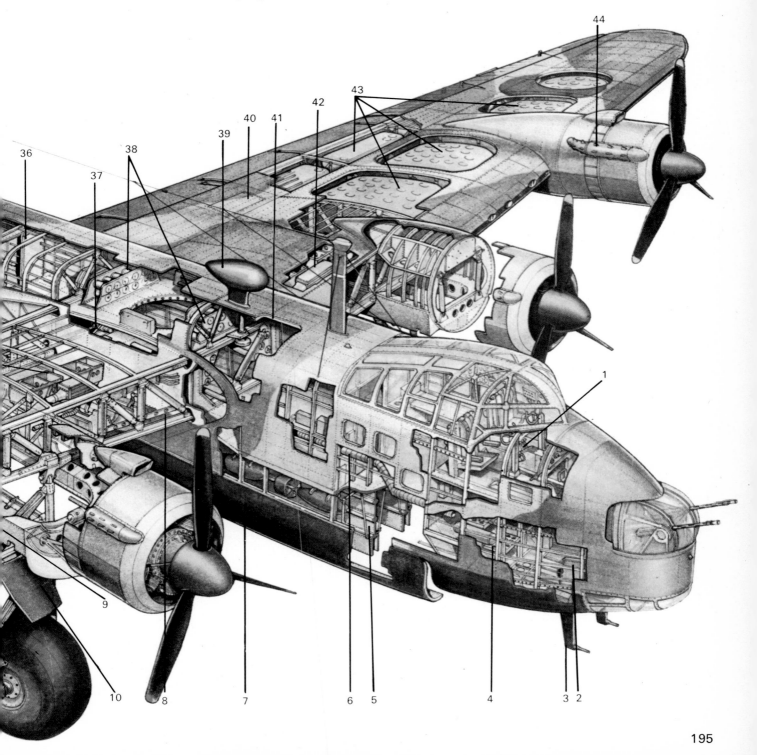

which was fast enough at 215 mph (345 kph) to outfly most contemporary fighters. The American lead in this basic type of aircraft was confirmed by the introduction of the modern all-metal airliner in the early 1930's. Here for the first time the design philosophy of the low-wing, all-metal, two-engined aircraft with a retractable undercarriage and good streamlining found its expression.

Thus structures and aerodynamics had shown great improvements during the 1920's and 1930's. Engines, too, had advanced significantly. The rotary had reached its peak at the end of World War I, leaving the water-cooled inline as the main high-powered engine type. Such engines were relatively heavy, however, and much was expected from the new generation of air-cooled radial engines about to enter service. These had the advantage that although their frontal area was considerably greater than that of inline engines, their power-to-weight ratios were significantly superior. Development work on both types of engine continued at a fairly fast pace in the 1920's, and although the Americans had the excellent Curtiss D-12 inline, they gradually became the chief protagonists of the radial. In Britain Rolls-Royce and Napier produced some remarkable inlines for both racing and service use, whilst Bristol matched the Americans in developing powerful and advanced radial engines. In France both engines were experimented with, but France was even more loathe to

North American B-25J Mitchell
 1. *Fixed twin .5in MGs*
 2. *Flexible ammunition belt*
 3. *Cockpit heater*
 4. *Pilot's controls*
 5. *Pilot's and co-pilot's seats*
 6. *Twin .5in MGs in dorsal turret*
 7. *Bomb bay*
 8. *Fuel cells*
 9. *Ammunition boxes for waist guns*
10. *Rudder trim-tab*
11. *Elevator*
12. *Elevator trim-tab*
13. *Rear-gunner's compartment*
14. *Twin rear .5in MGs*
15. *Port rudder*
16. *Rudder-operating mechanism*
17. *Walkway to rear-gunner's compartment*
18. *Flexible .5in waist gun*
19. *Fuel cells*
20. *Aileron-operating quadrant*
21. *Aileron*
22. *Aileron trim-tab*
23. *Engine mountings*
24. *Firewall*
25. *Main landing gear*
26. *Port Wright Cyclone R2600-29 14-cylinder air-cooled radial engine of 1,700hp*
27. *Fixed twin .5in MGs in side blisters*
28. *Crew access ladder*
29. *Heating and ventilation ducting*
30. *Rudder pedals*
31. *Nose wheel*
32. *Ammunition boxes for fixed MGs*
33. *Flexible nose .5in MG*

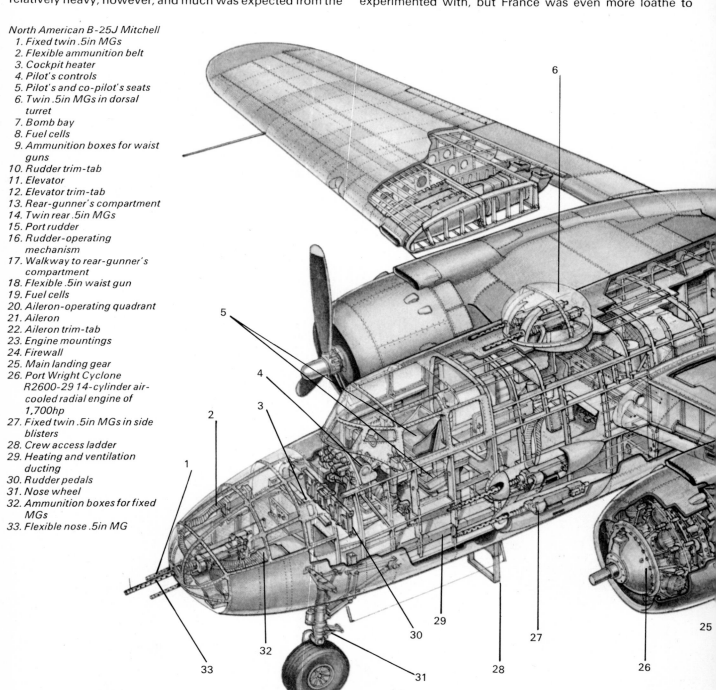

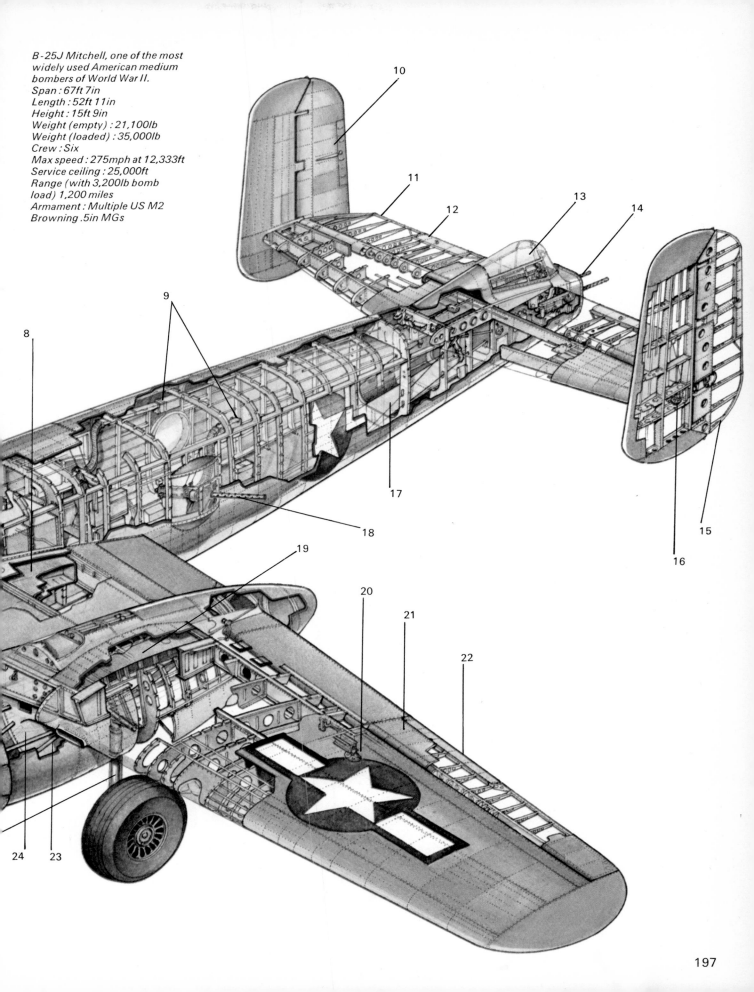

B-25J Mitchell, one of the most
widely used American medium
bombers of World War II.
Span : 67ft 7in
Length : 52ft 11in
Height : 15ft 9in
Weight (empty) : 21,100lb
Weight (loaded) : 35,000lb
Crew : Six
Max speed : 275mph at 12,333ft
Service ceiling : 25,000ft
Range (with 3,200lb bomb
load) 1,200 miles
Armament : Multiple US M2
Browning .5in MGs

spend money on military matters, and by the 1930's had definitely fallen from the front rank of aviation nations. Italy at first concentrated on inlines, with a series of beautiful Fiat water-cooled engines showing the way. But in the 1930's the Fascist government decided that radials offered greater advantages, and ordered all aero engine manufacturers to concentrate on this type of motor. It cost Italy heavily, for during World War II she had to build German inlines under licence, having thrown away all the advantages she had held in this field. Germany, forbidden by the terms of the Treaty of Versailles in 1919 from building military aircraft, had lost considerable impetus in the 1920's, but in the 1930's she came back with some first-class inlines, conventional petrol ones in the case of Daimler-Benz, and diesel ones from the big Junkers concern.

Thus the 1920's had provided the technical background that made advance on a major scale possible in the 1930's. We have already seen how the United States pioneered the way for the development of modern bombers with aircraft such as the Martin B-10B and the Douglas and Boeing airliners. This basic type of aircraft quickly became the norm in military circles, with such aircraft as the British Vickers Wellington, Handley Page Hampden and Armstrong Whitworth Whitley; the German Heinkel He 111, Dornier Do 17 and later the Junkers Ju 88; in Russia the Tupolev SB-2; in Italy the Savoia-Marchetti SM-79; and late in the day in France the Liore et Olivier Le0 45 series. These were all medium bombers, but other developments were also under way: dive-bombers and heavy strategic bombers.

Curtiss had undertaken much development work with the dive-bombing notion in the 1920s, with emphasis on its application to naval aircraft, and by the end of the 1930's the US Navy was well advanced in the theory of dive-bombing, and had some interesting types in service or being designed. The Germans, however, saw the dive-bomber as 'flying artillery' to support their rapidly moving ground forces, spearheaded by armoured formations with which conventional artillery units would not be able to keep up. This type of tactics was experimented with and proved in the Spanish Civil War, in which the Germans and Italians helped the Nationalists under General Franco. The basic German dive-bomber was the Junkers Ju 87, the so-called 'Stuka'.

Russia had considered strategic bombing by four-engined aircraft late in the 1920's, and the Tupolev design bureau had produced a series of large aircraft, culminating in the great ANT-6 early in the 1930's. But then came a change of policy in favour of tactical use of Russian airpower, and this early lead in heavy bombing was thrown away. The United States was also interested in this type of bombing, and designs by Boeing, Consolidated and Douglas materialized in the late 1930's. The designs of the first two companies went into production as the Boeing B-17 Flying Fortress and the Consolidated B-24 Liberator, powerful four-engined aircraft capable of carrying some 8,000 lb (3,635 kg) of bombs over great ranges. At the same time great advances were made in the provision of adequate bomb-sights. Britain too was interested in heavy bombing, and a trio of four-engined bombers was under development in the late 1930's: the

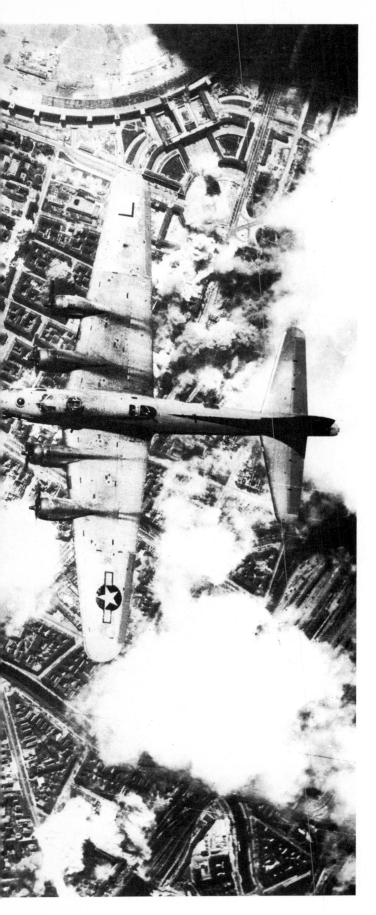

Short Stirling, the Handley Page Halifax and the Avro Lancaster, the last a four-engined version of the unsuccessful Avro Manchester twin-engined bomber.

In the field of fighters it was Russia that led the world in the early 1930's, with the introduction of a new type of fighter, the Polikarpov I-16. This was a small, stubby aircraft powered by a large radial, but for the first time on a production fighter it featured an enclosed cockpit, cantilever monoplane wings, a retractable undercarriage and an armament including provision for cannon and rockets. Both these weapons had been experimented with during World War I, principally by the French, but now, in the middle 1930's, they became an accepted feature on fighter aircraft.

Other nations had already been designing such fighters, and the I-16 was soon followed by the German Messerschmitt Bf 109, the British Hawker Hurricane and Supermarine Spitfire, the French Morane-Saulnier MS 406 and Bloch 151, and the American Curtiss P-40 series. With the exception of the Bloch fighter, all these types were powered by inline engines, whose high power combined with low frontal area recommended them for short-range aircraft. At this time radials found more favour as powerplants for heavier, long-range aircraft, as they were more economical in fuel than inlines.

The scene was thus set for World War II with aircraft that were of cantilever construction, with enclosed cockpits and retractable undercarriages, of metal construction for the most part, and with speeds in the 250 to 350 mph (400 to 565 kph) range. Armament on fighters comprised either a mixture of cannon and machine guns, as on French and German aircraft, or a large number of machine guns, as on British and American aircraft. In general, performance was radically improved, with ceilings now raised to about 35,000 feet (10,670 m) by the use of various types of engine supercharging developed in the 1920's and 1930's.

World War II (1939-1945)

Fighters

The two chief fighter variants in use at the beginning of the war were the light interceptor fighter, exemplified by the Bf 109 and Spitfire, and the heavier, two-engined escort or 'destroyer' fighter such as the Messerschmitt Bf 110 and slightly later Bristol Beaufighter. The two-engined fighter proved not very suitable for air-to-air combat involving single-engined fighters, and was subsequently allocated a different role.

Early fighter combat immediately made it clear that apart from improvements in performance, usually associated with improved powerplants to produce higher speeds, ceilings and rates of climb, fighters needed protection from enemy fire in the form of armour protection for the pilot and engine and self-sealing fuel tanks to prevent these from leaking and catching fire when hit by enemy action. Several of the single-engined types in service in 1939 were still flying in 1945, and the development of aircraft can be gauged

Top left : A Lancaster cockpit. To the right of the wheel is the throttle quadrant, and above it the boost and rev counters.
Bottom left : Lancasters of 50 Sqdn, code letters VN.
Left : Bombs explode far below the starboard wing of a B-17 Fortress during a daylight raid on Berlin, 29 April 1944.

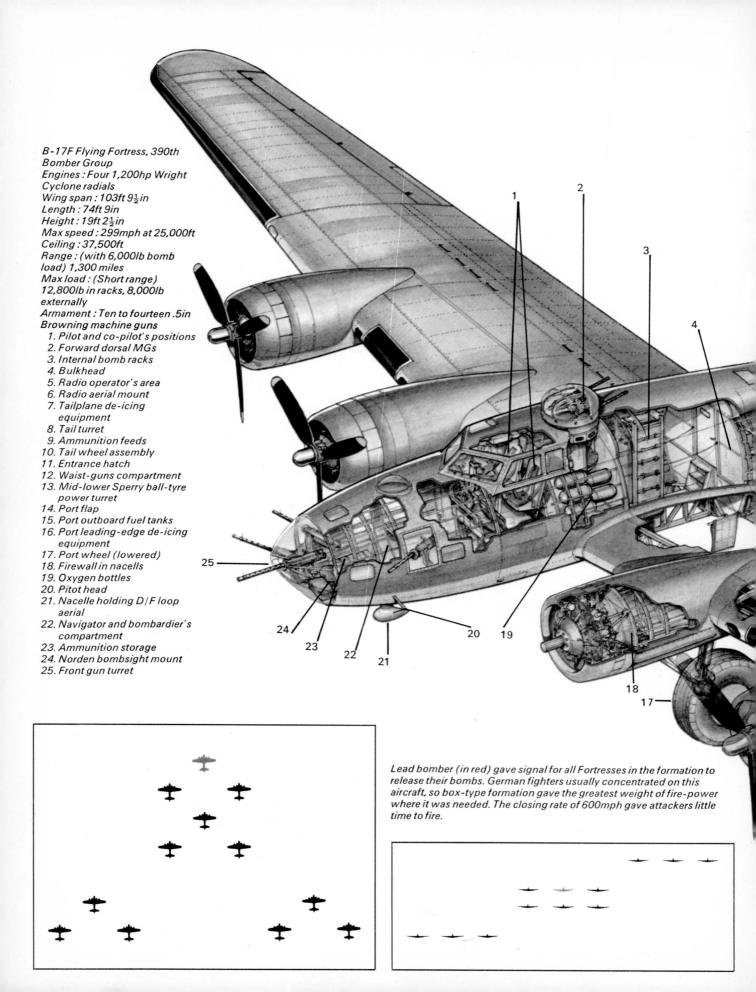

B-17F Flying Fortress, 390th
Bomber Group
Engines : Four 1,200hp Wright
Cyclone radials
Wing span : 103ft 9½in
Length : 74ft 9in
Height : 19ft 2½in
Max speed : 299mph at 25,000ft
Ceiling : 37,500ft
Range : (with 6,000lb bomb
load) 1,300 miles
Max load : (Short range)
12,800lb in racks, 8,000lb
externally
Armament : Ten to fourteen .5in
Browning machine guns

 1. Pilot and co-pilot's positions
 2. Forward dorsal MGs
 3. Internal bomb racks
 4. Bulkhead
 5. Radio operator's area
 6. Radio aerial mount
 7. Tailplane de-icing
    equipment
 8. Tail turret
 9. Ammunition feeds
10. Tail wheel assembly
11. Entrance hatch
12. Waist-guns compartment
13. Mid-lower Sperry ball-tyre
    power turret
14. Port flap
15. Port outboard fuel tanks
16. Port leading-edge de-icing
    equipment
17. Port wheel (lowered)
18. Firewall in nacells
19. Oxygen bottles
20. Pitot head
21. Nacelle holding D/F loop
    aerial
22. Navigator and bombardier's
    compartment
23. Ammunition storage
24. Norden bombsight mount
25. Front gun turret

Lead bomber (in red) gave signal for all Fortresses in the formation to
release their bombs. German fighters usually concentrated on this
aircraft, so box-type formation gave the greatest weight of fire-power
where it was needed. The closing rate of 600mph gave attackers little
time to fire.

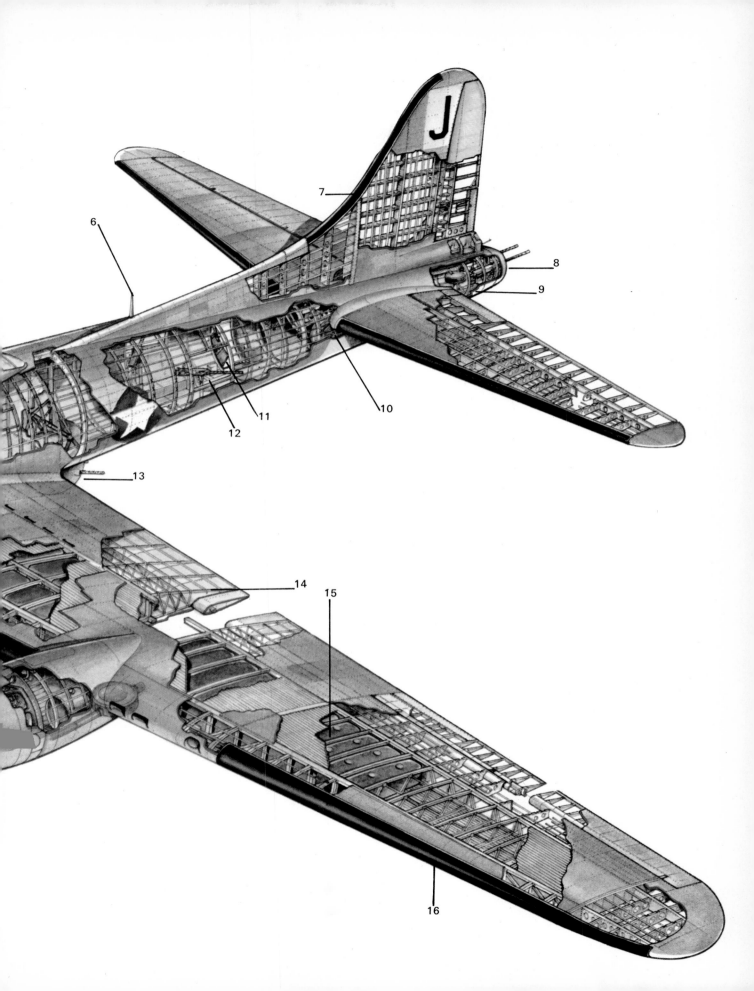

Above : Improved power enabled
the F and G models of the P-38
Lightning to carry more
armament or drop-tanks. Top
speed was over 400mph and
range 450 miles.
Right : P-47 Thunderbolt of 82
Fighter Squadron, 78th Fighter
Group. The engine cowling's
checkerboard design was first
used in April 1944. It was armed
with eight .5in Brownings.

Right : B-17 Flying Fortress,
prime instrument in the air
attacks on Germany by the US
8th AAF. Protected by ten to
fourteen .5in Browning MGs and
capable of carrying a 20,000lb
bomb load at short range.

Top left : This photograph, taken from a gun camera of an American Thunderbolt, shows a second Thunderbolt (right) going in to finish an attack on a Bf 110.

Top right : Pilot Bob Fuller and some of his crew lived after AA fire had ripped off the port wing of 'Wee Willie', a B-17 of 91st Bomber Group.

Left : Probably the best fighter plane of World War II, the P-51 Mustang had a top speed of over 420mph. Its armament of six .5in Browning MGs, plus a range of 950 miles, made it an ideal fighter for escorting bombers.

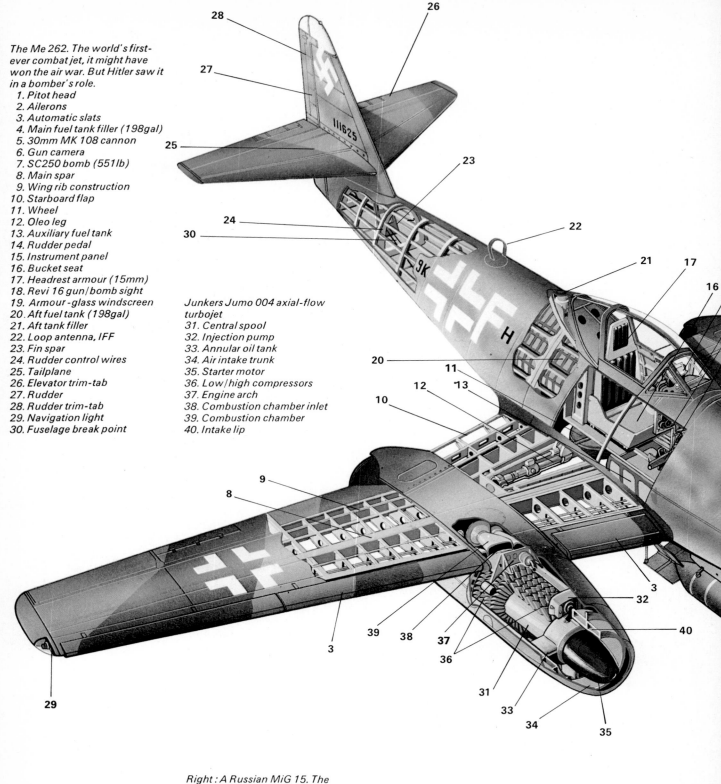

The Me 262. The world's first-ever combat jet, it might have won the air war. But Hitler saw it in a bomber's role.

1. Pitot head
2. Ailerons
3. Automatic slats
4. Main fuel tank filler (198gal)
5. 30mm MK 108 cannon
6. Gun camera
7. SC250 bomb (551lb)
8. Main spar
9. Wing rib construction
10. Starboard flap
11. Wheel
12. Oleo leg
13. Auxiliary fuel tank
14. Rudder pedal
15. Instrument panel
16. Bucket seat
17. Headrest armour (15mm)
18. Revi 16 gun/bomb sight
19. Armour-glass windscreen
20. Aft fuel tank (198gal)
21. Aft tank filler
22. Loop antenna, IFF
23. Fin spar
24. Rudder control wires
25. Tailplane
26. Elevator trim-tab
27. Rudder
28. Rudder trim-tab
29. Navigation light
30. Fuselage break point

Junkers Jumo 004 axial-flow turbojet

31. Central spool
32. Injection pump
33. Annular oil tank
34. Air intake trunk
35. Starter motor
36. Low/high compressors
37. Engine arch
38. Combustion chamber inlet
39. Combustion chamber
40. Intake lip

Right: A Russian MiG 15. The appearance of these planes over North Korea in 1951 was initially the cause of consternation to the UN pilots. However, the excellent qualities of the plane were not equalled by the skills of their pilots.
Far right: An American F-86 Sabre jet, also used in Korea.

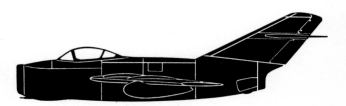

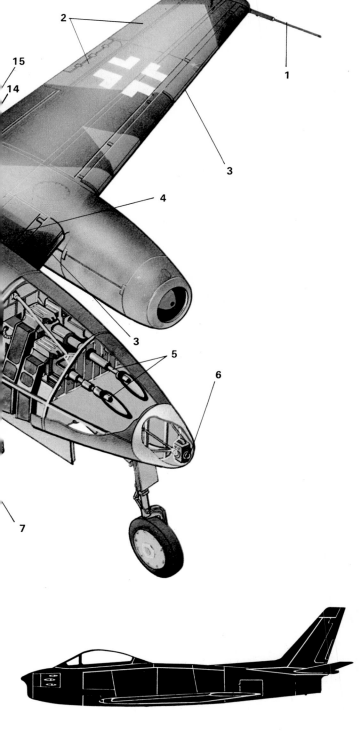

from their development during the war. Armament was naturally increased, with larger calibre machine guns and cannon becoming the norm, but at the same time protection was increased, and performance raised from some 350 mph (565 kph) on 1,000 hp to 450 mph (725 kph) on about 2,000 hp. Ranges were also improved by the introduction of underwing fuel tanks that could be jettisoned when empty. The classic examples of fighters that underwent this type of development were Britain's and Germany's standard fighters, the Spitfire and Bf 109. New fighters were also introduced in the war, and these included the magnificent and versatile Focke Wulf Fw 190, North American P-51 Mustang and Republic P-47 Thunderbolt. The Russians, preoccupied with tactical air operations in support of the army, developed simple but robust fighters which were in every way the match for German fighters at the low altitudes at which the Russians operated.

The need for pure interceptors lessened as the war progressed, so many fighters found themselves adapted to the role of fighter-bombers, with engines adapted for low-altitude operations and the capability of delivering up to 2,000 lb (910 kg) of bombs or a mixture of bombs and rockets. The fighter-bomber was soon a vitally important weapon, especially over Russia and the European fronts. The classic fighter-bombers were the Hawker Typhoon and Tempest. Designed as interceptors, their high-altitude performance was disappointing, but they proved fast, manoeuvrable and capable of carrying heavy underwing loads at low altitude, and were used almost exclusively as fighter-bombers in the second half of the war. In the field of interceptor types, finally, the introduction of the British Gloster Meteor and German Messerschmitt Me 262 jet fighters in 1944, with speeds in the order of 500 mph (805 kph) showed what might be expected from the next generation of fighters.

The heavy fighter of the opening stages of the war was soon evolved into two major roles : bomber-destroying by night, the classic examples being the Messerschmitt Bf 110, Bristol Beaufighter and fighter versions of the de Havilland Mosquito; and as strike fighters, particularly in the maritime role, classic examples of these being again the Beaufighter and Mosquito, in different marks, and the German Junkers Ju 88. The Americans also entered this field, converting many of their medium bombers, principally North American B-25 Mitchells and Martin B-26 Marauders into strike aircraft. In night-fighting and maritime strike operations, small radar sets on board aircraft came to play a dominant role as the war moved towards its conclusion.

Bombers

With the exception of the United States, which did not enter hostilities until 1941 in any case, most of the combatants in World War II started the war with only medium bombers. These underwent transmogrifications similar to those enjoyed by fighters to improve their combat capabilities, speeds rising by up to 100 mph (160 kph) to the region of 350 mph (565 kph) by the end of war. Few new bombers of note entered service after the beginning of hostilities except the extraordinary British de Havilland Mosquito, which was unarmed, made of wood and so fast that no contemporary fighters could catch it; and the Russian Petlyakov Pe-2, a sturdy and versatile two-

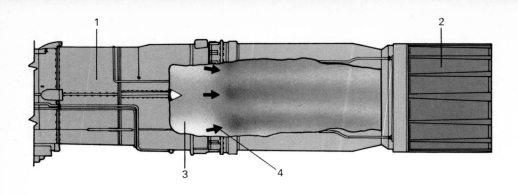

Left : F4 Afterburner
1. Engine
2. Variable area exhaust nozzle
3. Jet stream
4. Injection of 'neat' fuel into jet stream

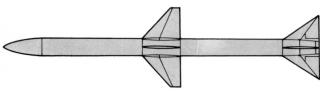

Left : Sparrow III missile
One of the most widely-used and successful US weapons.
Length 12ft : Launch weight 400lb : including 60lb high explosive warhead : Speed Mach 2 : Range over 8 miles.

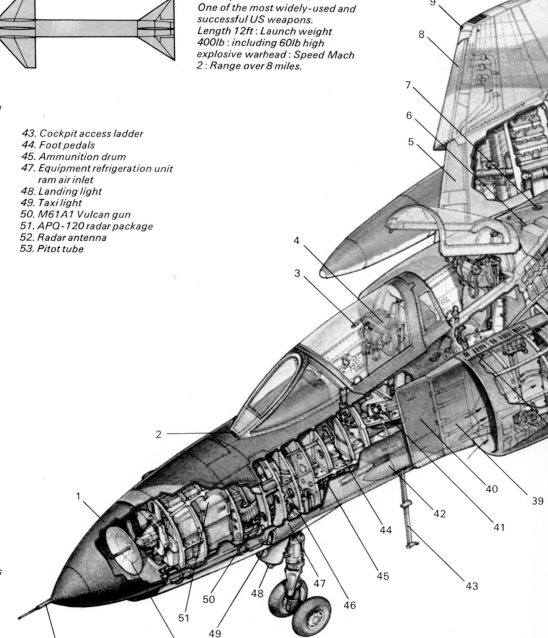

US F4 Phantom, a carrier-based strike aircraft.
1. Radome hinged door
2. Rain removal air nozzle
3. Face-curtain ejector handle
4. Mk. 7 ejection seats
5. Centre leading edge flap
6. IFF antenna
7. Fuselage light
8. Outboard leading edge flap
9. Starboard wing-tip position light
10. Starboard join-up light
11. Fuel vent and dump mast
12. Airflow spoilers
13. General Electric J79-GE-17 engines (two)
14. Fuselage fuel cells (seven)
15. Cooling air duct
16. Anti-collision light
17. Ram air inlet
18. Tail light
19. Rudder
20. Fuel vent mast
21. Drogue chute compartment
22. Slotted stabilator
23. Stabilator actuator
24. Fuel tank cooling air exit
25. Arrester hook
26. Variable area exhaust nozzle
27. Afterburner
28. Trailing-edge flap
29. Port aileron
30. Wing fold actuator
31. Air duct
32. Main landing-gear jack pad access door
33. External wing tank (370 US gallons)
34. Speed brake
35. AIM-9D Sidewinder missiles
36. Wing fuel cell
37. Inboard leading-edge flap
38. Upper variable ramp bleed air louvre
39. Variable ramp
40. Fixed ramp
41. Throttle controls
42. AIM-7E Sparrow III missiles

43. Cockpit access ladder
44. Foot pedals
45. Ammunition drum
47. Equipment refrigeration unit ram air inlet
48. Landing light
49. Taxi light
50. M61A1 Vulcan gun
51. APQ-120 radar package
52. Radar antenna
53. Pitot tube

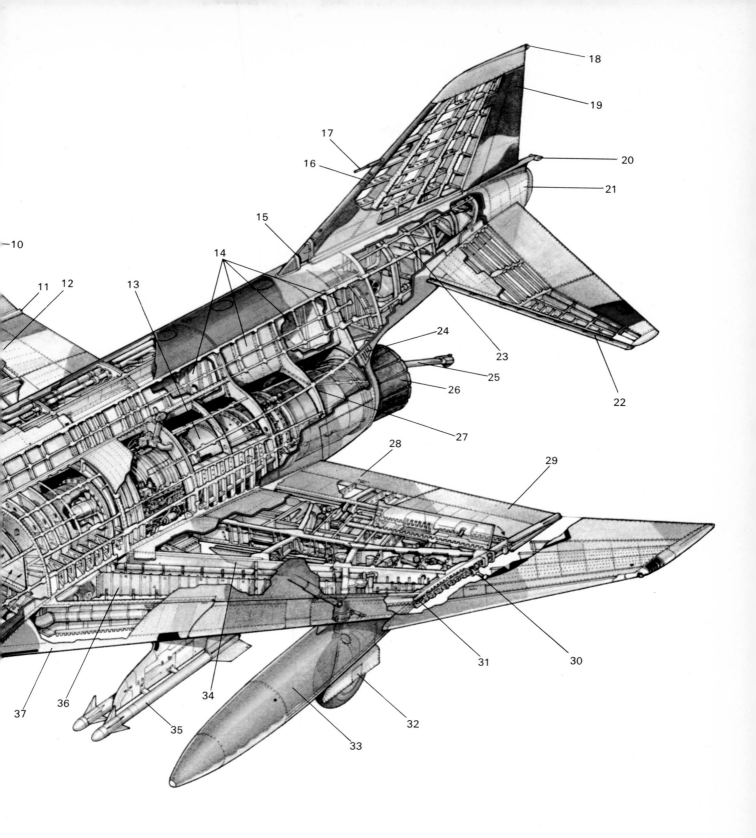

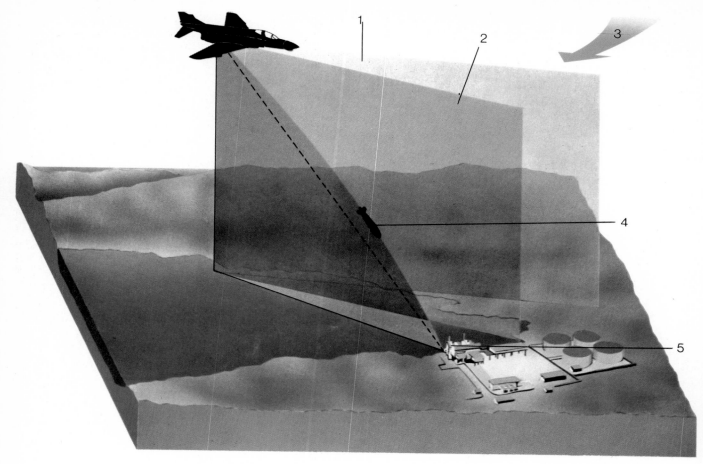

Above : Bomb aiming. The aircraft is continuously deflected from its apparent path by the wind and the bomb itself will also drift from the original launch direction. The calculations for these effects are made on a small computer and are based on the velocity and direction of the aircraft, range, air density and also various constants such as the orientation of the launching equipment. The bomb release line and the calculated aiming reference are shown on a screen in the plane and when these coincide the bomb is released automatically.

1. Apparent direction of aircraft
2. Actual direction of aircraft after drift
3. Wind
4. Final trajectory of dropped bomb
5. Target

engined machine that served Russia remarkably well throughout the war.

Other major types have already been mentioned, leaving only the Ju 87 and the Ilyushin Il-2 to be mentioned. The 'Stuka' performed with distinction in the early campaigns, but the losses suffered by the type in the Battle of Britain showed that its use in theatres where the Germans did not enjoy total air superiority was out of the question unless heavy losses were to be accepted. This was the case over the Eastern Front. On this front one of the most important types was the Il-2, the 'Shturmovik', a single-engined ground-attack machine of extremely strong construction. This was armed with heavy-calibre cannon, rockets and bombs, and rarely operating at altitudes above 1,600 feet (490 m) it proved an absolute scourge for the German armoured forces from late 1942 onwards.

In the sphere of heavy, strategic bombing, the British and Americans reigned supreme, the former by night and the latter by day. The British had started with daylight raids over Germany, but losses had been so severe that they decided instead to concentrate their efforts on mass night raids to destroy whole areas. Based on the Halifax and Lancaster four-engined bombers, capable of carrying loads upwards of 12,000 lb (5455 kg) into Germany, raids by forces of over 1,000 bombers became frequent occurrences in the German night from 1942 onwards. With radar aids these missions became more effective in 1943 and by 1944 were straining German industry and communications to the limit.

The Americans prepared daylight raids by large forces on pinpoint targets. Such was the armament of American bombers such as the B-17G and B-24H that flying in stepped-up box formations, the bombers could provide each other with great defensive fire and thus keep down losses to German fighters. Daylight was essential for the pinpoint raids against the small, vital targets considered the best targets by the Americans. The United States' third major four-engined bomber was the Boeing B-29 Superfortress. This was a large, fast aircraft used for the mass destruction of Japan's cities and industrial capacity. With a top speed of 350 mph (565 kph), it could carry bomb loads of 20,000 lb (9,090 kg) over very great ranges.

At the end of the war, it is worth noting, the Germans had a jet bomber (Arado Ar 234) in service, and were pressing ahead with the development of other advanced types.

With the exception of a few Japanese aircraft, reconnaissance in World War II was undertaken by a variety of converted fighter and medium bomber types. With armament removed, the airframe cleaned up as much as possible, extra fuel tanks and cameras fitted, aircraft such as the Spitfire and Lockheed P-38 Lightning roamed over much of Europe, with help from special photographic reconnaissance versions of the Mosquito joining them later.

Maritime aircraft
It was in World War II that maritime aircraft really came of age, especially in the Pacific theatre. As in World War I, maritime aircraft fell into two categories, this time shore-

Top : In the foreground, Royal Air Force Strike Command Phantom of 43 Squadron, RAF Leuchars, shadows a Russian Tupolev Tu-20 Bear bomber over the North Sea. Phantoms form an integral part of Britain's air defence system and northern-based aircraft often 'intercept' Russian long-range reconnaisance aircraft sent to probe Britain's defence.

Above : An F4C rolls and dives towards a target in the north-west mountains of North Vietnam. This method of approaching a target allows the pilot to keep it in sight throughout the attack. The Phantom's lethal load is clearly seen — eight 750lb bombs are slung from the aircraft's underside.

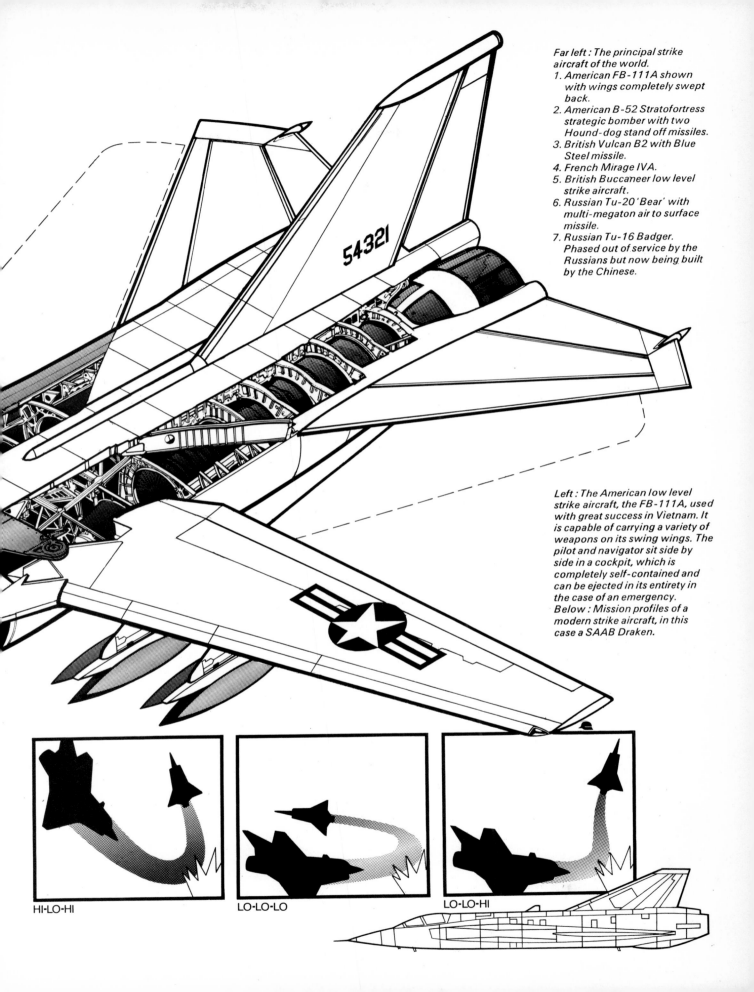

Far left: The principal strike aircraft of the world.
1. American FB-111A shown with wings completely swept back.
2. American B-52 Stratofortress strategic bomber with two Hound-dog stand off missiles.
3. British Vulcan B2 with Blue Steel missile.
4. French Mirage IVA.
5. British Buccaneer low level strike aircraft.
6. Russian Tu-20 'Bear' with multi-megaton air to surface missile.
7. Russian Tu-16 Badger. Phased out of service by the Russians but now being built by the Chinese.

Left: The American low level strike aircraft, the FB-111A, used with great success in Vietnam. It is capable of carrying a variety of weapons on its swing wings. The pilot and navigator sit side by side in a cockpit, which is completely self-contained and can be ejected in its entirety in the case of an emergency.
Below: Mission profiles of a modern strike aircraft, in this case a SAAB Draken.

HI-LO-HI

LO-LO-LO

LO-LO-HI

before contact

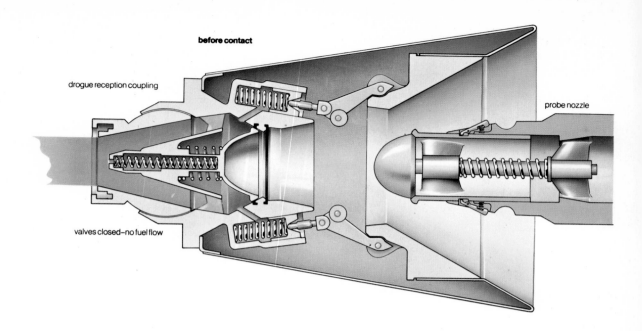

drogue reception coupling

probe nozzle

valves closed—no fuel flow

after contact

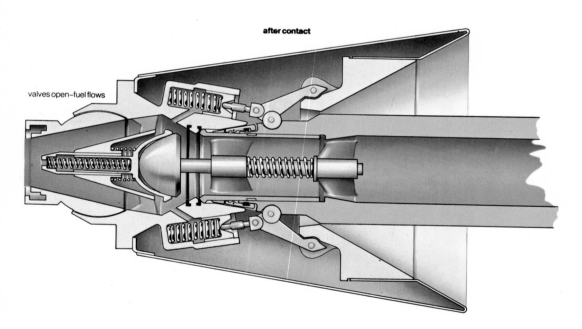

valves open—fuel flows

Above : Diagrams showing the drogue coupling and probe nozzle of a probe and drogue refuelling system, before contact and after contact. The drogue coupling is fitted to the end of the hose trailed by the tanker, and the probe nozzle is mounted on the nose or wing of the receiving aircraft.

Opposite page : Seven of the most widely used combat aircraft.
1. American McDonnel Douglas F4 Phantom.
2. Russian MiG-21 Fishbed.
3. British BAC Lightning soon to be superseded by the Jaguar and the joint European Multiple Role Combat Aircraft.
4. American F-104 Starfighter.
5. French Mirage III used to great effect by the Israeli Air Force in 1967.
6. British Hawker Harrier V/STOL aircraft.
7. Russian Su-9 Fishpot.

based aircraft, both landplanes and seaplanes, for use in the anti-submarine and strike roles, and carrier-based aircraft, for use against other naval forces and land targets beyond the range of land-based aircraft.

The two classic British maritime aircraft were the remarkable Fairey Swordfish and the Short Sunderland. The Swordfish was a biplane torpedo-bomber that was by any standards obsolete by 1939. Yet it soldiered on throughout the war, proving a very versatile and able type. The Sunderland flying-boat played an important part in safeguarding the sealanes across the Atlantic towards Britain.

Japan's greatest naval aircraft was the Mitsubishi A6M 'Zero' fighter. This was the first naval fighter to equal landplanes in performance, and its debut into combat against the Americans came as an enormous shock to the Allies. It was 1943 before they finally got the measure of this remarkably agile fighter.

The main protagonists of naval airpower were the Americans: in a war against Japan this was the only offensive method profitable in the Pacific. The standard fighter at the beginning of the war was the tubby little Grumman F4F Wildcat, which had a just about adequate performance. It was soon succeeded, however, by the F6F Hellcat, and excellent aircraft that was complemented late in the war by the superlative Vought F4U Corsair fighter and fighter-bomber. The Corsair in many authorities' eyes has a good claim to the title of best fighter of the war. As major offensive weapons the US Navy had the Douglas Dauntless dive-bomber and the Grumman Avenger torpedo-bomber.

Post war development

The two major elements in the development of military aircraft from the end of World War II to the present day have been the need to come up with ever more sophisticated aerodynamics to take advantage of the opportunities offered by jet engines, and how best to use the constant advances in electronics.

The jet engine was the first problem to be faced by designers after World War II. Soon new types of fighters were appearing all over the world, as it seemed that the performance needed by this type of aircraft could best be secured by the use of jet engines. Aerodynamically, however, the machines of this first postwar fighter generation showed little advance over aircraft such as the Gloster Meteor, performance being guaranteed by the extra power of the new engines allied to the tried and tested aerodynamics of piston-engined fighters. But by the early 1950's the problem of compressibility began to rear its head as aircraft speeds approached that of sound. The answer lay in the development of swept-back wings to delay the onset of this phenomenon, and types featuring this answer, such as the Mikoyan MiG-15, North American F-86 Sabre and Hawker Hunter, began to appear.

Introduction of jet bombers such as the English Electric Canberra also began in the early 1950's, and although these were at first derived aerodynamically from their piston-engined predecessors, bomber performance soon rivalled that of fighters. Further aerodynamic sophistication, combined with the use of more powerful jet engines

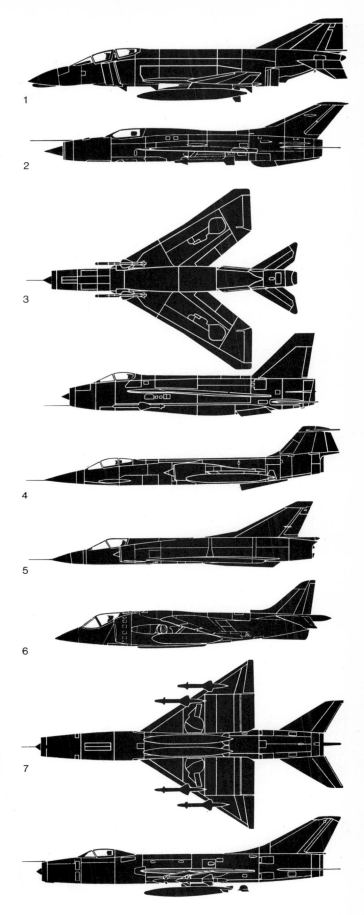

incorporating afterburning or 'reheat' capability, has since raised the performance of modern aircraft of conventional design up to the Mach 2+ region.

As noted above, aircraft designers also had to cope with the rapid advance in electronics. This science has in fact revolutionized air warfare as much as the jet engine. Its first applications were in the field of flight safety and accuracy, in which radar and miniature computers helped to take the load of such tasks from the aircrew, giving them more time for basic decision making. With performance figures for aircraft climbing so fast, however, it was thought in the middle 1950's that the gun was no longer sufficient as fighters' main armament. What was needed was a weapon that could think for itself, and so was born the homing missile. This, with its miniaturized computer 'brain', could be locked onto its target and fired, leaving the pilot of the aircraft to break off the action and retire, or find another target as the case might be. So great were the hopes pinned on the missile, moreover, that the end of the need for manned aircraft was foreseen. As is always the case in such matters, however, electronic counters to the new weapons were swiftly developed, and the electronic air warfare race was on. Crew were still needed in aircraft, it was realized, for only men had the necessary mental equipment for high-speed intuitive decision making.

With the realization that both crew and extremely sophisticated electronics are necessary, and the design of aircraft to meet the new requirements, we have entered a new era of air warfare. No longer is it right to talk of combat aircraft, but rather of aircraft as weapons delivery systems, with the avionic (airborne electronics) as important as the airframe itself. The combination has indeed revolutionized the science of air war, as has been amply demonstrated in the American involvement in the Vietnam conflict and the last two wars between the Arab states and Israel. In these wars the gun has made something of a comeback, albeit in an advanced form with radar and electronic aiming aids, but the main emphasis has been on the missile, for both offensive and defensive purposes. And as much as in anything, in present day aircraft, defence against the missile lies in electronic counter-measures to confuse the attacking hostile 'brain' as in performance and manoeuvrability. It is worth noting, moreover, that offensive loads can now also be delivered with a degree of accuracy undreamed of in World War II. Free-fall bombs are placed with pinpoint precision with the aid of radar and computers, and advanced weapons, both bombs and missiles, can be guided onto special targets by a variety of advanced means, including homing onto the reflections of a laser beam shone onto the target by the attacking aircraft, and control from the aircraft with the aid of a television camera mounted in the nose of the weapon.

Electronics have also been responsible for another development, that of all-weather aircraft. In World War II and before, poor weather frequently grounded aircraft, with the result that ground operations were seriously affected. But now radar can replace the pilot's eyes, and computers can react with the speed necessary to keep the aircraft flying in even the most inclement conditions, leaving the pilot and crew to make the fighting decisions. Allied to this field is that of very low level operations.

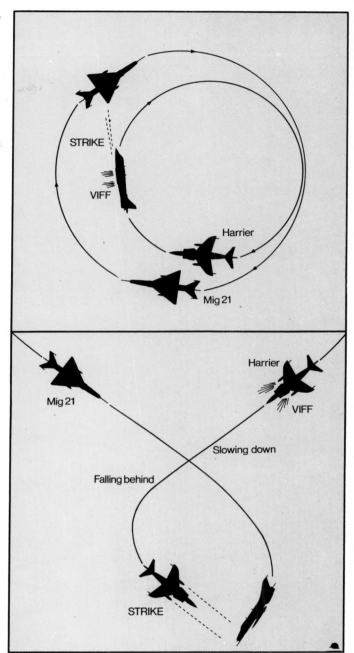

Left : One aircraft using an inertial platform is the Harrier, which uses it as the basis of its inertial navigation and attack system, part of which is the map display in the centre of the instrument panel.
Above : These diagrams illustrate the great manoeuverability of the Harrier over other jet aircraft – in this case a MiG-21, through the use of its vectored thrust nozzles. This technique, known as VIFF (vectoring in forward flight), enables the plane to perform manoeuvres impossible to conventional aircraft.

Top : In a turning manoeuvre, the Harrier can describe a much tighter circle.
Above : On an interception course, both pilots would try to get into a strike position. The Harrier has the advantage of being able to slow down rapidly and fall behind without losing power. If a MiG attempts to perform the same manoeuvre, the loss of power would put him at a considerable disadvantage.

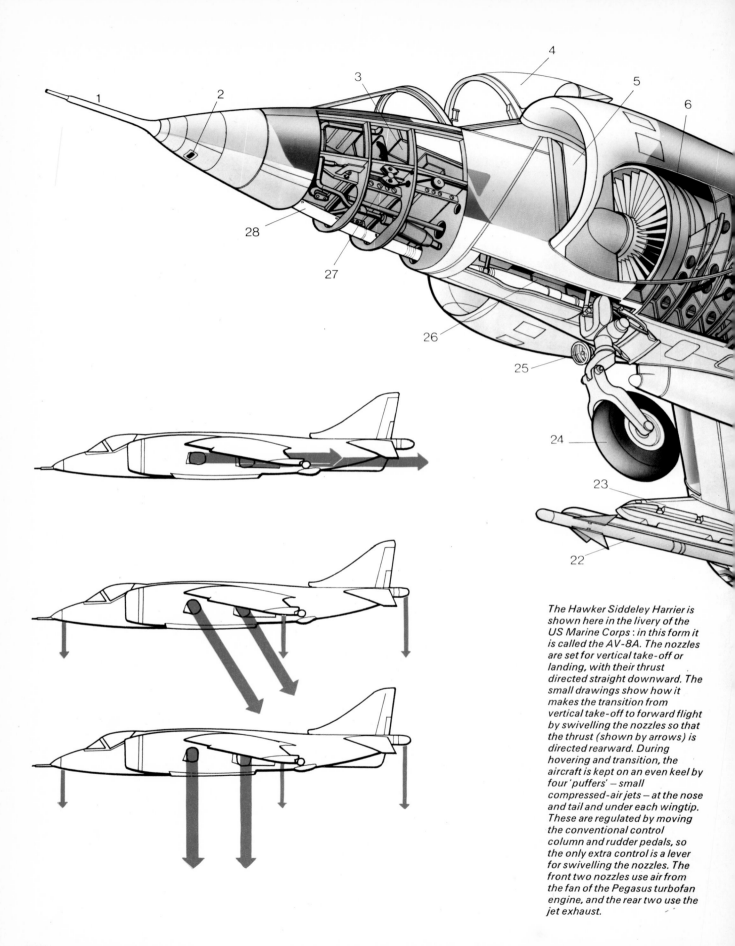

The Hawker Siddeley Harrier is shown here in the livery of the US Marine Corps: in this form it is called the AV-8A. The nozzles are set for vertical take-off or landing, with their thrust directed straight downward. The small drawings show how it makes the transition from vertical take-off to forward flight by swivelling the nozzles so that the thrust (shown by arrows) is directed rearward. During hovering and transition, the aircraft is kept on an even keel by four 'puffers' — small compressed-air jets — at the nose and tail and under each wingtip. These are regulated by moving the conventional control column and rudder pedals, so the only extra control is a lever for swivelling the nozzles. The front two nozzles use air from the fan of the Pegasus turbofan engine, and the rear two use the jet exhaust.

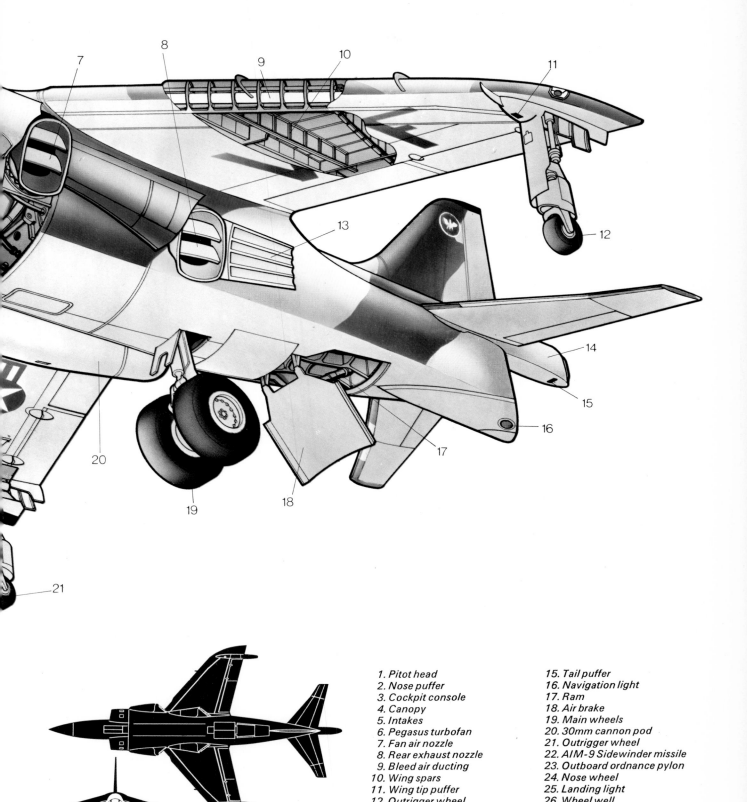

1. Pitot head
2. Nose puffer
3. Cockpit console
4. Canopy
5. Intakes
6. Pegasus turbofan
7. Fan air nozzle
8. Rear exhaust nozzle
9. Bleed air ducting
10. Wing spars
11. Wing tip puffer
12. Outrigger wheel
13. Heat shields
14. Parachute housing
15. Tail puffer
16. Navigation light
17. Ram
18. Air brake
19. Main wheels
20. 30mm cannon pod
21. Outrigger wheel
22. AIM-9 Sidewinder missile
23. Outboard ordnance pylon
24. Nose wheel
25. Landing light
26. Wheel well
27. Rudder quadrant
28. Bleed air ducting

*Above : Royal Marine
Commandos enter a Westland
Wessex HU5 of No. 845
Squadron, Fleet Air Arm aboard
HMS Fearless.*

Whereas in World War II a pilot flying at treetop height would have had to concentrate on avoiding obstacles, present day machines can be flown at very high speed 'on the deck', with the computers flying the aircraft on the basis of the information fed to them by radar looking forwards, downwards and sideways. This is of particular importance in strike operations, where high speed at low level is of considerable importance in evading enemy detection and countermeasures, and securing tactical surprise over the target.

As may be imagined from the above factors, aircraft have increased enormously in complexity and weight since the end of World War II. The avionics, indeed, often cost as much or more than the basic aircraft. This has led to an enormous increase in costs, and now even the two superpowers of Russia and the United States are finding it hard to finance the numbers and types of aircraft needed by their air forces. This cost factor has therefore gradually led to the erosion of the old differentials between aircraft as fighters, bombers or other types of military aircraft. Today aircraft have to be capable of doubling or tripling their roles to make them more cost effective. With the exception of the large strategic bombers employed by the superpowers, aircraft have to be capable of operating as strike aircraft with conventional or nuclear weapons, reconnaissance machines, fighters and even trainers. With even the superpowers having to do this, it is understandable that other countries are finding the burden too heavy on their own. Thus have been born in the 1960's and 1970's international projects such as the British-German-Italian

Multi-Role Combat Aircraft (MRCA), the British-French Jaguar, and the British-French Puma and Gazelle helicopters. It seems almost certain that if aircraft continue to increase in size and complexity, and therefore in cost, multi-national co-operation will become the norm. The basic airframe, the engines and a proportion of the avionics will be standard, with individual national buyers finishing the aircraft to their own particular requirements. The chief problem with this type of co-operation, however, is the formulation of the basic specifications and the apportioning of the costs and building.

Being heavy, modern aircraft need long runways and complex servicing facilities, both of which make them vulnerable to enemy strikes. For if an aircraft cannot take off, what use is it? Thus strenuous efforts have in recent years been made to develop aircraft that can operate from short runways, and also less complex types that require simpler servicing. The former type has been based on two concepts: a variable-geometry wing and V/STOL. Variable-geometry, as used in the General Dynamics F-111, the MRCA and the Tupolev 'Backfire-B', allows the wings to be swept forward to an almost straight line for take-off and landing, thereby enhancing the types' low- and medium-speed characteristics, enabling shorter take-off and landing runs to be contemplated and also increasing ferry ranges, and swept back sharply for high performance during combat.

The Vertical/Short Take-off and Landing concept has found its fullest expression in the Hawker Siddeley Harrier, which uses a vectored-thrust engine. In this, four nozzles through which the engine exhausts may be swivelled downwards to enable the aircraft to take-off and land vertically, then gradually turned towards the rear so that a forward motion is obtained and the wings develop lift to sustain the aircraft in normal flight. Turning the exhausts to a 45° position enables the pilot to make a very short conventional take-off with a heavier load. With this means of flight runways can be obviated entirely, and the aircraft kept in concealment close to the front line. This makes very fast reaction times to tactical needs possible. Moreover, British and American pilots have found that by using the technique known as VIFF (Vectoring in Forward Flight), in which the nozzles are turned in flight, the Harrier's manoeuvrability is considerably improved, often to the point where conventional aircraft could not match it.

The other main form of VTOL in use today is, of course, the helicopter. Of late the performance of helicopters has been much improved, and several nations have developed light attack helicopters armed with guns or missiles. American experience with types such as the Bell Hueycobra in Vietnam, however, suggest that helicopters may be too vulnerable to ground fire for use in any major conflict.

The three main types of aircraft in use today are therefore the manned bomber, the multi-role support aircraft and the 'radical' types such as the Harrier and gunship helicopters. It is likely that the manned bomber will continue as a first-line weapon for some time to come. Although not as potent in destructive potential as surface- or submarine-launched intercontinental ballistic missiles, aircraft still have the capability of great destruction with thermonuclear weapons, and also considerably more flexibility than guided weapons.

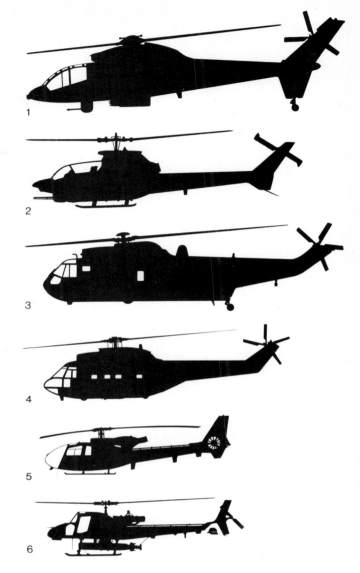

Above: Six examples of helicopters in use today.
1. Sikorsky S-67 Blackhawk anti-tank gunship, USA.
2. Bell Kingcobra gunship, USA.
3. Sikorsky Sea King anti-submarine/rescue, USA.
4. The Anglo-French Aerospatiale/Westland Puma transport/general purpose.
5. The Anglo-French Aerospatiale/Westland Gazelle multi-purpose.
6. Italian Agusta A106 shipboard anti-submarine.

BOMBS & MISSILES

Above : The French tactical nuclear missile 'Pluton', on an AMX chassis. Range 65 miles, launch weight 5335 pounds.

The original difference between a bomb and a missile lay in the way the weapon was delivered and the fact that a missile was not necessarily explosive.

In the twentieth century the terms have a more explicit definition, a bomb referring to the actual explosive device and a missile to the delivery system by which the device is carried.

All the weapons previously covered in this book have been, in one way or another, a form of weapon delivery system. For example, aircraft can fire bullets, drop bombs and carry missiles, while guns, tanks and warships carry out at least one of these functions.

Whereas small arms fire is directed by one individual against another individual or group of men within his immediate range of vision, bombs and missiles are usually controlled and 'fired' by a group of men against large targets (not necessarily human) usually beyond the accurate range of unaided vision. Bombs and missiles are therefore weapons of much greater destructive potential than small arms fire, and over the course of the centuries have been developed from expensive and inaccurate guns into a variety of weapons delivery systems of world-destroying capability. The offensive load can now be delivered with extreme accuracy over enormous ranges, and can consist of relatively simple explosive and chemical agents to potent nuclear weapons.

BOMBS

A bomb can be high-explosive, incendiary, smoke or gas, and is exploded either by percussion or by a timing device. This would include grenades, mines, and the whole range of bombs from armour-piercing, chemical and flying to nuclear weapons.

Grenade

A grenade is a small anti-personnel bomb filled with high explosive and used in close range warfare.

Early grenades of the 14th and 15th centuries were made of bark, glass, clay or earthenware filled with black powder, and were set off by a fuse of corned powder in a quill or a thin tube of rolled metal. Obviously intended to produce an incendiary effect rather than a blast, they were not lethal, and grenades having spherical or cylindrical metal bodies soon succeeded them.

Field use of these grenades tended to be rather dangerous because the fuses were unreliable, the powder burning sporadically and sometimes flashing through to the main filling with disastrous consequences for the thrower. It was not until the early 1900s that more consistent fuses were produced, though the problem of fixing the burning time remained: if it was too long the enemy could throw back the grenade before it went off, and if it was too short the grenade could kill the thrower. Fuses designed to function on impact were slow to perfect, mainly because of the difficulty of making the grenade land nose-first; so handles with trailing tapes were fitted to ensure a proper strike. Arming these fuses, that is changing their state from safe to live, was effected in flight by means of vanes, propellers, springs and inertia sleeves.

During and after World War I many improvements were made and the grenade diversified considerably, being launched from rifles, specially designed weapons and even spring operated guns.

The 1920s and 30s saw the abandonment of the less reliable designs but little progress was made in new developments. It took the renewed hostilities of 1939 to precipitate the next great advance in grenade technology. Progress in development has continued from World War II up to the present day.

Modern anti-personnel grenades comprise three main parts: a pyrotechnic fuse and detonator initiated by the action of a spring-loaded striker on a percussion cap and giving about 5 seconds delay; a filling of high explosive; and a fragmenting case made of wire or engraved steel. As they weigh between 140 and 500 grammes (4.9 to 17.5oz) they can be thrown to about 30 metres or yards, or projected from a rifle to approximately 400 metres. Similar ignition and projection systems are used on smoke, tear gas and signal grenades, but the appropriate filling is usually contained in a simple tinplate body. Anti-tank grenades generally have a shaped charge filling designed to achieve penetration of armour.

Modern grenades can be projected to considerable ranges and can be constructed to produce anti-personnel fragments, to penetrate armour plate, to generate smoke or tear gas, or to fire signal and illuminating flares.

Below: An NCO of the German Grossdeutschland Regiment depicted about to throw a Steilhandgranate; from the cover of the magazine 'German Illustrated'.
This weapon, known to the British Army of World War I as the 'Potato Masher', remained in service until 1945. It was an offensive grenade — one which could be thrown by an attacking soldier safe in the knowledge that he could throw it further than the lethal fragments could fly.

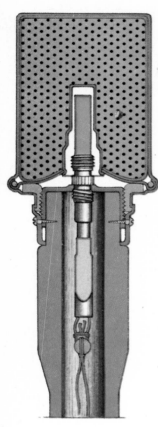

Left : The Stick Grenade
(Steilhandgranate) was known
to the British Army of World War I
as the 'Potato-Masher'. This
model is the Stg24, which
appeared after the war and
remained in service until 1945.
In all important respects,
however, it is the type issued in
1915. The Stick Grenade
operated by having a friction
igniter inside the handle. The end
cap unscrewed to reveal a
porcelain bead on the end of a
length of string.
Pulling the string jerked a
roughened pin through a friction-
sensitive chemical inside the
igniter which flashed and lit the
five-second fuse. This burned
through as the grenade travelled
through the air and – depending
on the thrower's good judgement
– exploded the grenade at the
moment of landing. Unlike
earlier grenades, there were no
serrated iron rings or casings. The
body was made of sheet iron,
which blew into tiny fragments
on bursting. These were lethal at
close range but fairly harmless at
20 yards or more from the burst.

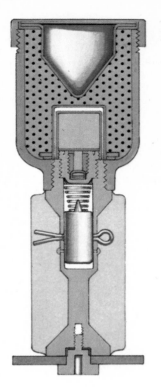

Left : The British 'Grenade, Rifle,
No 68/AT' was one of the first
grenade designs of World War II.
It was also the first 'hollow
charge' grenade to enter service
in any army. This principle relies
on a shaped cavity in an
explosive charge. When
detonated, the cavity acts to
'focus', the detonation force –
blowing a hole through the
target in front of it. The 68
Grenade was produced in the
early days of hollow charge
design. Nobody knew how or
why it worked. The cavity's
shape is not ideal, and there is no
'stand off' (space between bomb
and target to allow focussing
effect to occur).
It could penetrate two inches of
armour plate – remarkable for
1940.

Left : Glass grenades like the one
shown here were used right up to
the 1850s. They were much
lighter than grenades with metal
bodies. On burst they inflicted
savage flesh wounds if they were
properly tempered. Otherwise,
the bomb shattered into
thousands of harmless particles.
Originally they were fused by a
tube pushed into the neck,
containing mealed powder
priming. These had a tendency to
go out before reaching the target.

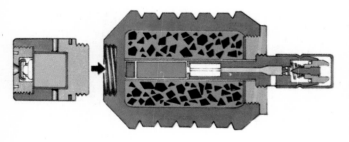

Left : The most common and
versatile of all Japanese
grenades of 1939-45 – the Type
91. In its hand grenade role, it
consisted of a serrated cast iron
body containing explosive, a
central detonator and an igniter
unit – a firing pin held away from
a detonator by a light spring and
secured by a safety pin. To
operate, the pin was removed
and the igniter tip smashed down

on a handy hard surface –
driving the pin into the detonator.
A finned tail unit could be
screwed into a socket at the base
to make a rifle grenade – fired by
a blank charge from a standard
rifle with barrel extension. With a
propellant cartridge screwed into
the base, the grenade became a
mortar bomb – used with the
Type 89 mortar.

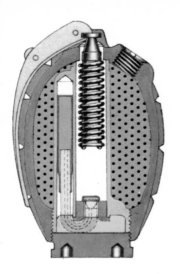

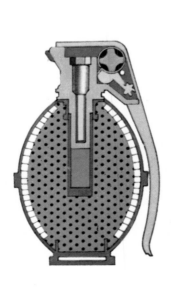

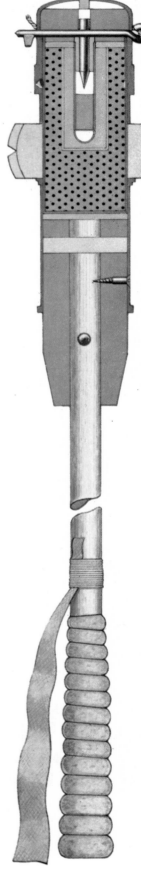

Left : British 'Mills Bomb' patented by Mr. W. Mills of Birmingham and issued in May 1915 as 'Grenade, Hand, No 5'. A defensive grenade, its cast iron case splintered into fragments on burst. Some of these were lethal at long range. The thrower was within lethal range of the blast and needed to take cover. The 'Mills' was operated by a spring-loaded striker. The lever was locked by a safety pin until needed. The thrower held the lever against the body when pulling the pin. The lever flew off in mid-air and the striker dropped – striking a cap and lighting a five second fuse. In 1916, the 'Mills' was adapted to take a 5½ in rifle rod and became 'Grenade, Hand and Rifle No 23'. This was later improved by using a 'cup discharger' launching method. A 2½ in diameter baseplate was fitted to the 'Mills'. It became the 'Grenade, Hand and Rifle No 36'. The 'Mills' retired in the 1970s.

Left : Developed by the French in World War I, the Vivien Bessier grenade was launched from a discharger cup on a rifle's muzzle with a standard ball cartridge. A hole ran through the central axis of the grenade body. The bullet passed through this. Expanding gas behind the bullet sent the grenade to a considerable range. The bullet carried on its journey – depressing a firing pin arm, which lit a five-second fuse detonating the bomb.

Right : The British Army designed 'Grenade, Hand, No 1' of June 1908. Its cap carried a fixed firing pin. Before throwing, this was removed and a mining detonator inserted into a hole in the Lyddite filling. The cap was then replaced – a safety pin preventing contact between pin and detonator. Grooves on the cap, mating with lugs on the body, held the cap in place when the safety pin was pulled out. The 36in braid streamer ensured the grenade landed nose first. The 16in cane handle was cut to 8½ in in the Mark 2 model to reduce accidents in the trenches.

Left : British L2A1 AP Grenade. A coil of notched steel in a thin metal case is used. The filling is RDX/TNT with a 4 second fuse. On burst, the coil breaks into about 1200 equal pieces – moving at 5000fps. The resulting cloud is lethal within five yards. But at 1/200oz, the fragments are safe over 10 yards from the burst. There is a rifle-launching adaptor. This, used with a muzzle-adaptor and blank cartridge, fires the grenade to 150 yards range.

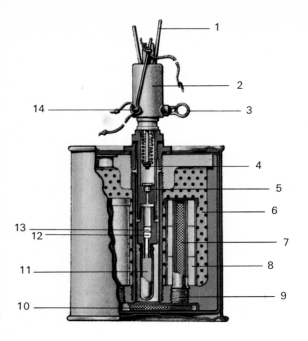

Mine

Mines can be used at sea or on land, and differ from most other weapons in that they are not directed against specific targets.

Land mines

The placing of explosives in the ground, to detonate under an enemy, is a classic siege technique which has been practised since the sixteenth century. The British Royal Engineers earned their old title of 'Sappers and Miners' because 'sapping' was the name for the digging of the trenches under the enemy and 'mining' the placing of explosives in them.

During the American Civil War, the highly successful Petersburg Mine Assault of June 1864 was carried out by the 48th Pennsylvania Infantry Regiment, composed largely of men who were coal miners in civilian life. It took them 34 days to dig a shaft under a Confederate artillery battery. This tunnel was then stocked with 8000lb of black powder, which when blown caused 278 Confederate casualties and left a 30ft deep crater, 170ft by 80ft.

It was, however, the development of mass production techniques which gave the land mine, as we know it today, its place on the battlefield. The first land mines, used by the Germans in World War I, consisted of artillery shells buried, fuse uppermost, in the ground so that they would be initiated by the weight of a tank. Anti-personnel mines and mines specially designed for use against tanks were not introduced until World War II when they were widely used in North Africa and on the Russian front.

The two basic varieties of land mine are the anti-tank mine and the anti-personnel mine. The anti-tank mine is designed to destroy a tank track and suspension but will also devastate any wheeled vehicle that passes over it. A weight of between 300lb and 500lb is needed to detonate an anti-tank mine. The tread of a soldier, therefore, will not detonate them but such mines can be fitted with devices that prevent them being lifted by infantry. The lighter anti-personnel mine is constructed so that it will kill or wound men when detonated by a 4lb weight or less.

Mines are simple in construction. Each mine consists of a main explosive charge in a container, a detonator which sets off the main charge and a firing mechanism which sets off the detonator. The firing mechanism prevents the mine being set off by interference and guarantees immediate detonation. It is activated in one of three ways — pressure, a trip wire, or by radio. The more common firing mechanisms have spring-operated ignition. Here a strong spring drives a striker into a percussion cap, which explodes and sets off the detonator. The diaphragm control, which is also widely used, consists of a thin sheet of springy metal which bulges outwards. Pressure on the bulge, from a vehicle or soldier will make it invert suddenly, detonating the mine.

The shape of the body will depend on the intended target, and the material used will be decided by the degree of fragmentation required and the need to make detection difficult. Thus non-magnetic and non-conducting materials, often plastics, are usually employed for anti-personnel mines. The body of the mine may be fitted with a device to prevent the mine from being lifted and neutralized. In some cases the body will be thrown into the air to allow the mine

Above : The M16 Anti-personnel mine is triggered by foot pressure and has two explosive charges ; one throws the mine into the air and the other propels the projectiles.
1. *Pressure prongs (3)*
2. *Trigger*
3. *Release-pin ring*
4. *Striker*
5. *Percussion primer*
6. *Fragmentation charge*
7. *Detonator*
8. *Booster charge*
9. *Delay element*
10. *Expelling charge*
11. *Flash igniter charge*
12. *Relay charge*
13. *Delay charge*
14. *Locking safety pin*
Right : An automatic mine-laying machine towed behind an armoured vehicle. The machine is being used to lay bar mines 42 inches (107cm) long and weighing 23lb (10.4kg). The mines are made of plastic to avoid detection by conventional mine detectors.

charge to detonate in a more favourable position. The quantity of the explosive charge of a mine will vary from less than one pound (0.45kg) in an anti-personnel mine to more than 20lb (9kg) in a large anti-tank mine. The charge may produce its effect by direct contact with its target or it may propel fragments or a solid projectile. One type of mine uses a shaped charge to propel an incandescent jet of gases at very high speed into the underside of the target.

Anti-personnel mines are either fragmentation or blast mines. Fragmentation mines produce a large number of high velocity fragments and these have a considerable range. Mines of this type include bounding mines, in which the fragmenting projectile is blown into the air and produces its fragments at a height of about six feet (1.8m) so that they radiate out horizontally in all directions; fixed non-directional mines, which are placed on the ground or just below the surface and project fragments upward and outward in all directions; and fixed directional mines, which project fragments in a 60° arc. The US Claymore mine belongs to this last type and contains a curved plate of explosive studded with about three hundred steel projectiles. Blast mines have a very limited range and are effective only against the enemy who has initiated them.

Anti-tank mines contain a heavy explosive charge and are laid below ground level. They are usually initiated by a force of 300 to 400lb (136 to 182kg). Anti-personnel mines are frequently laid with anti-tank mines to make the task of detecting and lifting the anti-tank mines more difficult. The high explosive charge, typically weighing about 12lb (5.4kg), destroys vehicles by blast effect.

Chemical mines are used to disperse chemical agents from fixed locations. They may use either persistent or non-persistent liquids or gases, and are most effective when laid in anti-personnel or anti-tank minefields, which slow down the progress of the enemy and so result in greater exposure to the chemical.

The booby trap mines are anti-personnel, anti-vehicle or both. The essence of a booby trap is cunning, surprise and variety. It can take the form of a baited trap, a snare or a double bluff. Some booby trap mines are anti-personnel, containing small charges operated by normal means, and others are anti-vehicle. A third type uses delayed charges operated by delay mechanisms, aimed at destroying materials or causing casualties.

The anti-personnel booby trap sometimes takes the form of a pressure switch under a floorboard designed to go off under the weight of a man. The charge is placed nearby and both switch and charge are further concealed, often by an everyday object such as a door mat. An anti-vehicle booby trap placed on a railway line might also use a pressure switch.

Minefields are 'anti-tank', 'anti-personnel' or 'mixed' depending on what mine is used. A further classification denotes their task. The additional classifications are 'protective', 'defensive', 'barrier', 'nuisance' and 'phoney' minefields. A protective minefield is laid for the close defence of a position and for maximum effectiveness it must be covered by the small arms fire of the defenders. The intention of such minefields is to slow down the enemy, who may be in vehicles or on foot, at a point where maximum defensive fire can be brought to bear on the attacker. Defensive minefields are laid as a counter to

enemy penetration between defended areas. It is not always possible to cover these with direct fire from small arms but, again for effectiveness, they must be covered by indirect artillery fire. Barrier minefields are designed to canalize the movement of the enemy into a predetermined 'killing zone' where an assault by troops in defensive positions wreaks havoc on the enemy. A nuisance minefield is laid to delay, disorganize and hinder the use of a particular route and is of particular value in the early stages of a defensive battle, before the enemy attacks. Finally a phoney minefield is an area of un-mined ground marked to give the impression that a minefield exists, thereby deceiving the enemy who will waste valuable time searching for non-existent mines.

The density of a minefield is denoted by the average number of mines it contains per metre of front; a minefield 1000 metres long containing 1000 mines would have a density of 1. The density, of course, together with the

minefield's shape, size and strength of mines used directly affects the number of casualties the minefield is likely to inflict.

Mines are not laid uniformly throughout the whole area of a minefield. They are usually laid in clusters in a pattern made up of rows — the precise pattern depends on the method of laying. Laying mines in a pattern is far safer and more effective than simply scattering them. An enemy, faced with a minefield, has three ways of getting through. The minefield can be dug up by hand, explosives may be used or it can be mechanically breached. Hand-breaching is a slow and very demanding task. A more acceptable method is to fire a flexible hose filled with plastic explosive across an anti-personnel minefield and then explode the hose. This detonates the mines in its path, clearing a lane through the minefield. The final method of clearing a minefield is to fix a plough attachment or a roller to a tank. A plough attachment digs through the ground; lifting any mines in its path and pushing them to one side, clear of the tracks. The roller method is similar except that the roller detonates single pressure mines — a skilful layer would fix double action fuses which would defeat this method of clearing.

Naval mines

Mines were first developed for naval use. In 1585 the Dutch succeeded in using a clockwork device to set off explosive charges placed in small boats and rowed out to the enemy Spanish ships. Although mines were used to a limited extent in both the American War of Independence and the American Civil War, it was not until World War I that their use became widespread; a total of about 240,000 mines were laid between 1914 and 1918. During World War I the Germans used mines to considerable advantage against both merchant ships and warships; Field Marshal Lord Kitchener was killed when the cruiser HMS Hampshire struck a mine off the Orkney Islands in 1916. In World War II techniques of laying mines from the air were developed, and this allowed internal waterways such

Above: Many modern mines, such as the Italian VS50 anti-personnel mine, can be sown by helicopters to create immediate danger zones behind enemy lines. A special distributor carried beneath a helicopter can scatter over 2,000 within minutes. Such mines are anti-magnetic and insensitive/resistant to counter measures.

Below : An M48 Patton tank using a mine-exploding roller to clear pressure-activated mines. The roller's high-strength steel construction enables it to withstand much of the shock and blast from detonated mines.

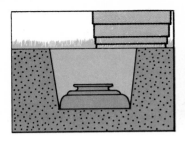

Mine-laying technique. WRONG. Mine is laid too deep. Earth cover may absorb pressure and prevent detonation.

Mine-laying technique. WRONG. Loose-packed earth has not been properly concealed. Mine situation may be seen and avoided.

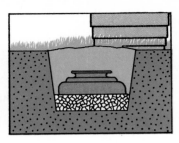

Mine-laying technique. CORRECT. Mine is concealed and at proper depth. Firm rubble at base puts mine at correct height.

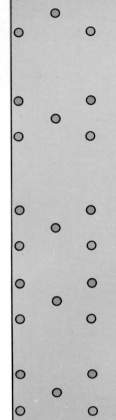

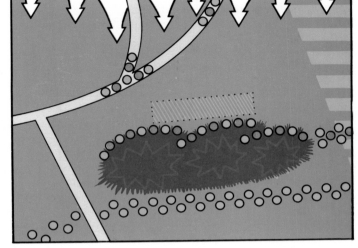

Left : The five minefield types. Blue denotes AT and red AP mines. A 'nuisance' field impedes the initial advance. A 'barrier' one covers the road junction and canalizes enemy movement into a killing zone. A marked but unsown field is 'phoney' and lures the enemy into the thick 'protective' minefield close to the defences. If they are captured, a 'defensive' AT minefield will prevent enemy vehicles exploiting success. Right : A typical cluster pattern in a 'mixed' minefield.

The M6A2

US Heavy Anti-tank mine, of 1956 vintage, measuring 13¼ in wide with a depth of 3⅜ in. Anti-tank mines are much more complex than anti-personnel types. The famous German Teller AT mine of World War II weighed 20lb and contained 12lb of TNT set off by a 240-400lb pressure on the round top plate. Other types need twice as much.

1. Pressure plate
2. Arming plug
3. Fuse retainer spring
4. Belleville spring
5. Second fuse booster
6. Closing cap
7. Bottom activation well
8. Booster for main fuse
9. Boosters
10. Fuse
11. TNT charge
12. Carrying handle
13. Side activation well
14. Second fuse booster

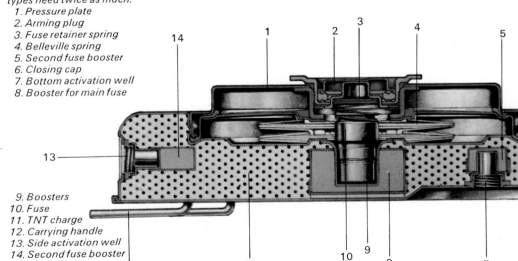

as the River Danube to be mined.

Once laid they can remain active for years, and modern types are difficult to detect and destroy. Mines represent a cheap and effective means of preventing the movement of shipping, and demand from the enemy a considerable effort in clearing lanes and keeping them clear. They have the advantage of attacking a ship in its weakest area under the water line and are rendered particularly effective by the non-compressibility of water, which transmits the blast extremely effectively to the target.

There are basically two types of mine: controlled and independent. Controlled mines are connected by cable to an observation and control station from which they are armed or made safe. They are used exclusively for harbour defence. Independent mines, which are either moored or grounded on the sea bed, are normally actuated by contact, magnetic pressure or acoustic devices. In addition it is to be expected that other techniques may be used in the future.

Contact mines are laid in a 'safe' condition, and when they sink to a pre-set depth the water pressure operates a hydrostatic device which arms the firing circuit. The mine is equipped with contact horns (projections) which, when struck by a ship, pass an electric current to the detonator which sets off the high explosive filling. Magnetic mines make use of the magnetic fields of a ship to trigger the firing mechanism, and the sensitivity of the device is set to ensure that the high explosive filling is detonated in a moment. Pressure mines operate in shallow water and rely on the reduction in pressure produced when a ship passes

Right : Widespread, open-sea mine warfare began off Port Arthur in 1904. On 15 May that year the Russian minelayer Amur sowed mines off the Tiger Peninsula and sank Japan's battleship Hatsuse, 15,000 tons, with 495 crew.
Below : A paravane consists of a torpedo-shaped body having two wing-like planes extending one from each side. During minesweeping operations it is towed from the forefoot of a ship by means of a towing wire attached to a point just above the paravane cutter. The mooring wires of naval mines are cut either by the paravane towing wire or by the cutter, and the mines, which are buoyant, then float to the surface where they can be detonated harmlessly by rifle fire. Paravanes are towed in pairs, one on each side of the ship.
Below: Mine-sweeping
1. mine
2. paravane
3. towing wire
4. mooring wire
5. cutter
6. plane

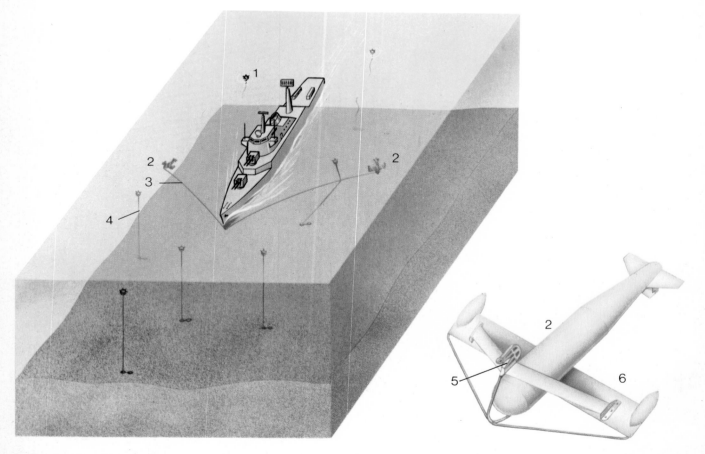

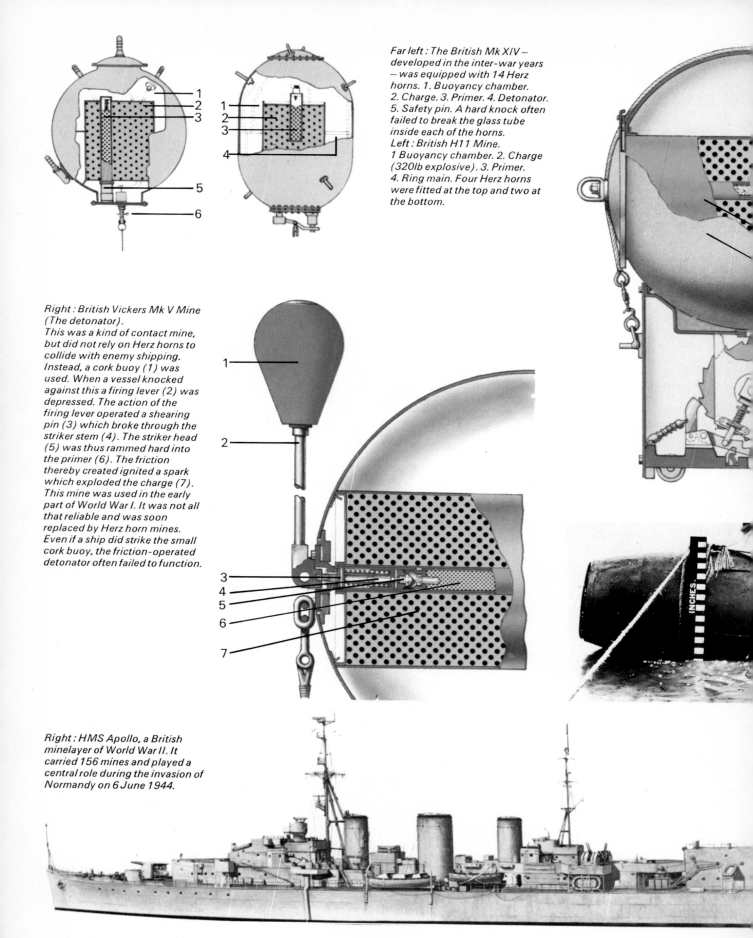

Far left : The British Mk XIV —
developed in the inter-war years
— was equipped with 14 Herz
horns. 1. Buoyancy chamber.
2. Charge. 3. Primer. 4. Detonator.
5. Safety pin. A hard knock often
failed to break the glass tube
inside each of the horns.
Left : British H11 Mine.
1 Buoyancy chamber. 2. Charge
(320lb explosive). 3. Primer.
4. Ring main. Four Herz horns
were fitted at the top and two at
the bottom.

Right : British Vickers Mk V Mine
(The detonator).
This was a kind of contact mine,
but did not rely on Herz horns to
collide with enemy shipping.
Instead, a cork buoy (1) was
used. When a vessel knocked
against this a firing lever (2) was
depressed. The action of the
firing lever operated a shearing
pin (3) which broke through the
striker stem (4). The striker head
(5) was thus rammed hard into
the primer (6). The friction
thereby created ignited a spark
which exploded the charge (7).
This mine was used in the early
part of World War I. It was not all
that reliable and was soon
replaced by Herz horn mines.
Even if a ship did strike the small
cork buoy, the friction-operated
detonator often failed to function.

Right : HMS Apollo, a British
minelayer of World War II. It
carried 156 mines and played a
central role during the invasion of
Normandy on 6 June 1944.

230

Left : British Elia Mine.
This was one of the first mines to see action in World War I. Originally an Italian-produced mine, the British naval authorities first showed an interest in and examined the Elia Mine in 1901. The British improved on the Italian design and the Elia Mine came to replace the more primitive spherical 'service' mine previously in use. The diagram shows the mine on its minelaying carriage. When a vessel collided with the firing lever (1) it was depressed. This action acted as a trigger – firing the pistol (2) which sent a projectile into the primer (3). This action detonated the charge (4). Its 220lbs of TNT produced a huge explosion.

Left : A German magnetic mine of early World War II. As can be seen by the rule alongside it, it was a pretty hefty weapon. Magnetic mines are detonated by their reaction to the magnetic field of ships. Degaussers were used to combat them.

Right : A Type 1 German Naval Mine of the simple contact design. Each of these mines was sunk to a pre-set depth. They incorporated the Hertz horn method of firing. This was invented in 1868 by Dr. Herz of the German Mine Defence Committee. Inside each lead horn (1) was a glass tube containing bichromate solution. When any of the horns was hit by a ship it was bent, the glass tube shattered and the solution came into contact with a zinc/carbon plate to produce an electric battery (2). Current passed into a thin platinum fuse wire in a fulminate of mercury detonator (3) – firing the charge (4).

overhead. The mechanism employs a diaphragm in a chamber which is open to the water. When a ship causes a sudden reduction in pressure, the diaphragm moves towards the low pressure region and fires the detonator. A presure system of this type has also been used to arm acoustic and magnetic mines. Acoustic mines have a microphone which picks up the sound of the propellers and at a given sound level the detonator functions. The growth of encrustation and the drifting of silt gradually make the device less sensitive and later mines frequently used the acoustic system to arm the firing circuit and relied on pressure or a magnetic device to fire the high explosive filling.

Minesweeping Tethered mines are swept by paravanes, which are torpedo-shaped floats towed underwater to one side of the minesweeper. The towing cable deflects the mine to the paravane where the mooring wire is cut. The mine rises to the surface and is then destroyed by rifle or machine gun fire directed at the contact horns. Magnetic mines are set off by two minesweepers steaming abreast, each towing a cable carrying a pulsed current. The magnetic field between the two tows is sufficient to detonate the mine. Pressure mines are very difficult to sweep. In practice an expendable boat towed over them produces some results but is an expensive, slow and unreliable process. Acoustic mines are destroyed by towing a 'hammer box' noisemaker over them.

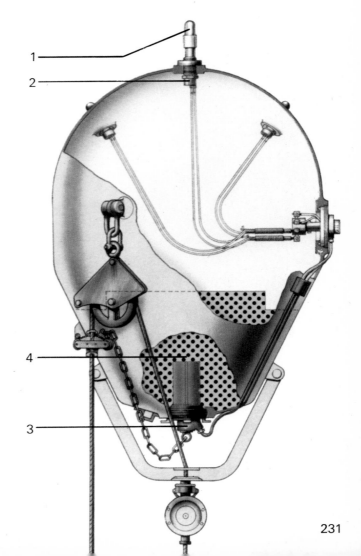

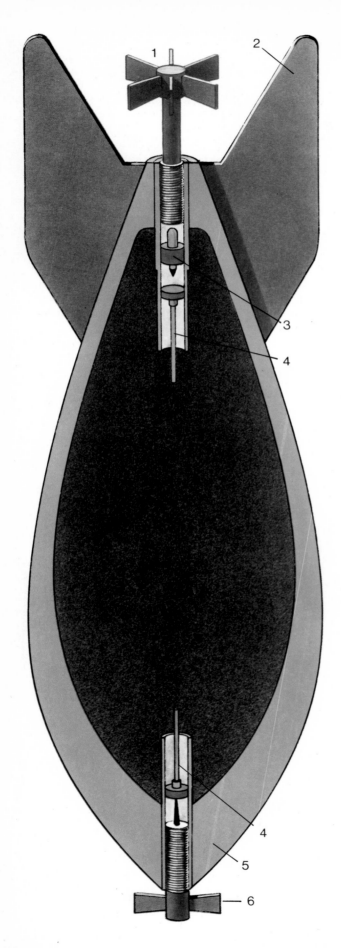

Bomb

A bomb is a hollow case filled with explosive or other destructive chemicals, and exploded by percussion or a timing device. The case may be metal, plastic, concrete or glass, and the shape, size and contents of the bomb depend on its application. Although some bombs are designed to be placed in position or thrown by hand, most modern bombs are delivered from the air by an aircraft or a rocket.

The early aerial bombs of World War I were ordinary shells with fins and new fuses added. Because they were aimed by eye and hand-launched they tended to be small, about 25lb (11kg), and inaccurate. During and after World War I great improvements were made, mounting racks and aiming devices were fitted to aircraft, and a variety of special purpose bombs appeared: fragmentation, incendiary, chemical, illuminating and so on.

In World War II, despite the development of more lethal bombs, the major problem was accuracy. Techniques were developed, such as the use of radio beacons to fix targets and target-illuminating flares for night bombing. The latest improvement in accuracy is the use of lasers to guide the bomb which enables pin-point targets to be hit with certainty. This system was successfully used in 1971 by the United States in Vietnam.

Bomb design A bomb comprises four main parts: a body or case filled with the payload; a fin assembly to stabilize the bomb in flight; one or more fuses; and an assembly to 'arm' the bomb at the moment of release. Arming a bomb is similar to releasing a safety catch. A parachute may also

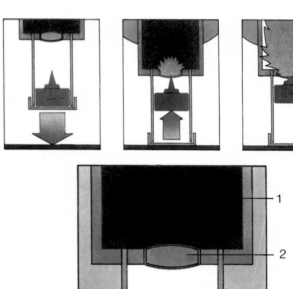

be included to stabilize or retard the bomb's fall to earth. The body usually has an aerodynamically streamlined shape which tapers to a point, or ogive, at the nose, and a wall thickness that depends on the effect required on bursting. The stabilizing fin assembly attached to the tail is often made of sheet metal, and it varies from a simple arrangement for normal trajectories to a complex design with offset aerofoil surfaces to spin the falling bomb.

The fuse must include safety devices for handling and transhipment, and yet must be capable of setting off a large quantity of explosive when the bomb strikes the target, or after a pre-determined delay. A substantial intermediary charge between the fuse and the main filling is incorporated to transmit the shock wave of detonation, and produce the maximum explosive effect. Two fuses are sometimes used to ensure detonation at the target or to provide alternative ways of bombing. They may be fitted in the nose, tail, or centre-body. Once the bombs are installed in the aircraft, by means of lugs on the body, a wire arming system is attached. This arming wire may be released with the bomb, allowing the bomb to drop safe, or may be retained by the aircraft, arming the bomb's fuse mechanism as it is released.

Types of bomb The shape of the bomb often depends on the bombing technique employed. For instance a streamlined 500lb (230kg) bomb dropped from a high altitude, say 10,000ft (3000m), reaches a terminal velocity – at which air resistance prevents it from speeding up further – of about 1000ft/s (300m/s) and strikes at an angle near to 20° to the vertical. Providing the case is

Far left : A general purpose bomb designed to explode after penetrating the upper floors of a building. The firing pin is screwed into contact with the booster charge by the propellers as the bomb falls.
1. *Tail fuse*
2. *Stabilizing fin*
3. *Primer detonator*
4. *Booster charge*
5. *Bomb casing*
6. *Nose fuse*
Below left : The mechanism of a percussion fuse. The safety pin ensures that the firing pin cannot move accidentally and is removed before launch. On impact the firing pin is thrown back into the capsule of fulminate of mercury, causing it and also the booster charge to explode.
1. *Booster charge*
2. *Fulminate of mercury*
3. *Firing pin*
4. *Plunger*
5. *Safety pin*

Below: A large current passes through the bridge wire of an electric detonator, lighting the

surrounding explosive. Impact on the acid horn shatters the glass tube and acid enters the cell, setting up a current. In the typical impact detonator a firing pin hits the priming charge at a speed sufficient to ignite it.
1. *Plastic covered wires*
2. *Detonator tube*
3. *Casing*
4. *Plug*
5. *Solder*
6. *Igniting composition*
7. *Flashing composition*
8. *Bridge wire*
9. *Priming charge*
10. *Base charge*
11. *Lead cap*
12. *Glass tube with acid*
13. *Holes*
14. *Zinc carbon cell*
15. *Wires to firing mechanism*
16. *Main charge*
17. *Secondary charge*
18. *Ignition tube*
19. *Priming charge*
20. *Safety pin*
21. *Detonating pin*
22. *Firing pin*
23. *Primer cap*
24. *Propelling charge*

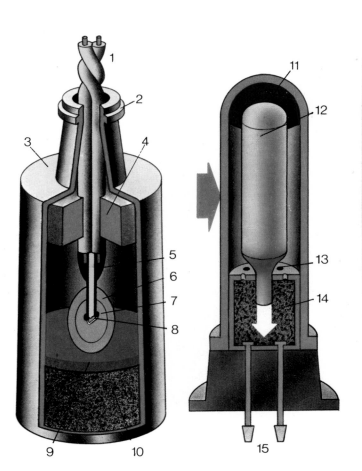

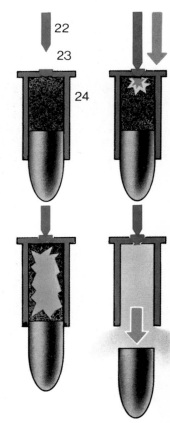

strong enough to withstand impact, the bomb could penetrate several storeys of a normal building or some 20ft (6m) of earth before coming to rest, causing a lot of damage before it detonates. An incendiary bomb, however, does not need to penetrate before ignition, and a lightweight body of poor ballistic shape is used because it has the advantage of restricting terminal velocity to less than 300ft/s (90m/s). Wings and other control surfaces can also be fitted to give certain effects, as in an ingenious bomb designed by Dr Barnes Wallis to destroy dams. When dropped from an exact height and speed, the bomb rotated and skipped along the surface of the water, as a flat stone does on a pond, until it came to rest against the dam wall and sank to the bottom where it exploded.

Depth bombs, which are large high capacity bombs with light cases, are designed for underwater demolition work. They are hydrostatically activated when the right depth is reached, and also have a nose fuse for use against surface targets. Their main purpose is attacking submarines, which can be severely damaged by blast pressure. The bombs are cylindrical, with a flat nose to prevent ricochet. They have an explosive content of about 75% and range from 300 to 700lb (140 to 320kg).

Armour-piercing bombs are designed to penetrate heavy armour and concrete-reinforced structure. They have a high strength steel case, weigh about 1000lb (450kg), are very streamlined with a solid pointed nose, and have a low (5% to 15%) explosive content. The fusing system has a delay to allow deep penetration of the target before detonation.

Flying bombs, or V-1s, invented by the Germans in World War II, contained 2000lb (900kg) of explosive in the body of a ram-jet powered pilotless aircraft. The aircraft fell to earth when the fuel was turned off by an automatic device, and extensive blast-wave damage was caused by detonation of its payload.

Chemical bombs include those filled with war gases, smoke producers, and incendiary materials. The gas generating bombs contain such things as lung irritants, blistering gases, tear gases, irritant smokes, and nerve and blood poisons. Smoke bombs are filled with chemicals such as titanium tetrachloride, hexachlorethane and zinc dust, chlorosulphonic acid and sulphur trioxide, or white phosphorus mixtures. The latter produce an incendiary effect on bursting as well as clouds of dense white smoke. Incendiary bombs often use thermite, a mixture of aluminium powder, iron oxide and magnesium, which reaches a temperature of 2500°C (4500°F) on ignition.

Other types include pyrotechnic bombs, containing chemicals which produce white or coloured light. Photo-flash bombs generate a short burst of high intensity illumination suitable for night photography of ground positions. They contain a photographic flash powder, and are provided with a mechanical time fuse to burst them while still in the air. A similar mixture, but slower burning, is used for battlefield and target illumination, and the bomb includes a small parachute to retard its fall. Another type of target marker contains coloured candles, which are ejected and burn as they fall on to the target.

Leaflet bombs, usually less than 500lb (230kg) in total weight, are cylindrical in shape with a weakened centre section. When the fuse initiates the small bursting charge, the case splits in half to disperse propaganda leaflets over a wide area.

Atomic bombs

Atomic bombs use energy released from the nuclei of atoms. There are two types, the atomic bomb and the hydrogen bomb. Both are so powerful that their power is measured in kilotons and megatons, equivalent to the explosive force of thousands or millions of tons of TNT respectively.

Strictly speaking, the term 'atomic bomb' includes the hydrogen bomb, which also uses atomic power. But in general usage, 'atomic bomb' is reserved for earlier weapons that work by nuclear fission, that is, splitting atoms. The hydrogen bomb works by nuclear fusion, the joining of small atoms together to make larger ones. Both fission and fusion release huge amounts of energy, causing an explosion.

Nuclear fission The huge power of an atomic bomb

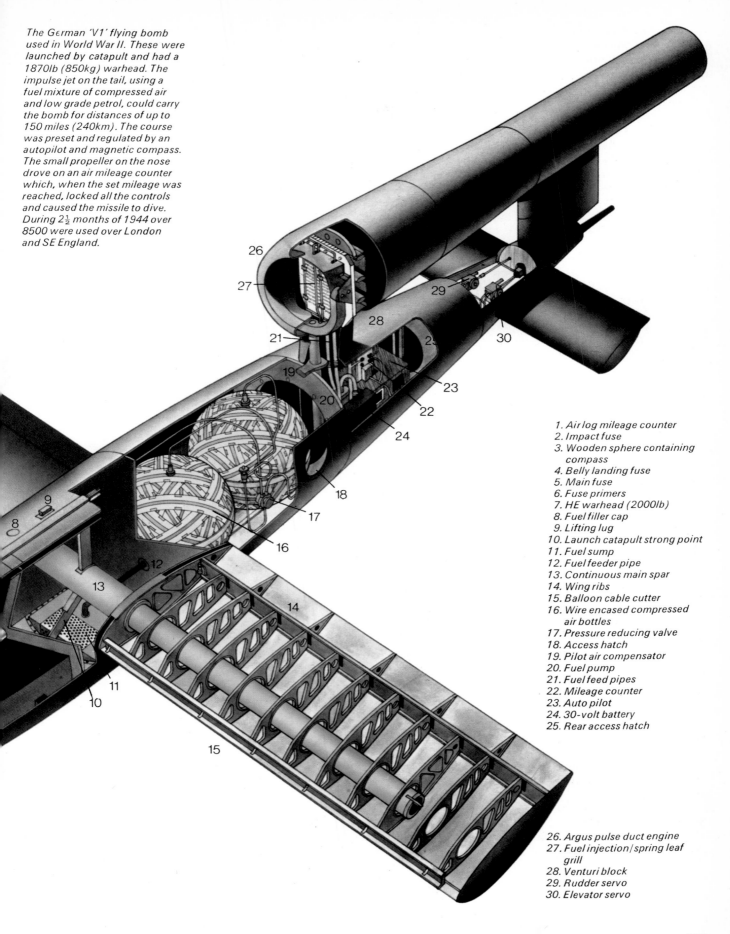

The German 'V1' flying bomb used in World War II. These were launched by catapult and had a 1870lb (850kg) warhead. The impulse jet on the tail, using a fuel mixture of compressed air and low grade petrol, could carry the bomb for distances of up to 150 miles (240km). The course was preset and regulated by an autopilot and magnetic compass. The small propeller on the nose drove on an air mileage counter which, when the set mileage was reached, locked all the controls and caused the missile to dive. During 2½ months of 1944 over 8500 were used over London and SE England.

1. Air log mileage counter
2. Impact fuse
3. Wooden sphere containing compass
4. Belly landing fuse
5. Main fuse
6. Fuse primers
7. HE warhead (2000lb)
8. Fuel filler cap
9. Lifting lug
10. Launch catapult strong point
11. Fuel sump
12. Fuel feeder pipe
13. Continuous main spar
14. Wing ribs
15. Balloon cable cutter
16. Wire encased compressed air bottles
17. Pressure reducing valve
18. Access hatch
19. Pilot air compensator
20. Fuel pump
21. Fuel feed pipes
22. Mileage counter
23. Auto pilot
24. 30-volt battery
25. Rear access hatch

26. Argus pulse duct engine
27. Fuel injection/spring leaf grill
28. Venturi block
29. Rudder servo
30. Elevator servo

comes from the forces holding each individual atom of substance together. Atoms are made up of three kinds of particles: protons and neutrons, which form the nucleus of the atom, and electrons, which spin around the nucleus.

Most naturally occurring elements have very stable atoms which are impossible to split except by using such techniques as bombarding them in a particle accelerator. The metal uranium, however, is one element whose atoms can be split comparatively easily. This is because uranium is an extremely heavy metal and has the largest atoms of any element. There are two isotopes of uranium; an isotope is a form of an element distinguished by the number of neutrons in its atom. Natural uranium consists mostly of the isotope U-238, but mixed in with this is about 0.6 per cent of the other isotope, U-235. This isotope, unlike U-238, is fissionable (its atoms can be split), and so it is the one used for making bombs.

Both isotopes of uranium, and certain other heavy elements, are naturally radioactive, that is, their big, unstable atoms slowly disintegrate in the course of time, which can take thousands of years. Atoms of U-235 can be made to break up much faster than this in a chain reaction. The atoms are forcibly split by neutrons travelling at speeds near that of light. A U-235 atom is so unstable that a blow from another neutron is enough to split it. As it splits it gives off energy in the form of heat and gamma radiation, the most powerful form of radiation and the one which is most harmful to life. It also gives off two or three 'spare' neutrons, which fly out and split other atoms. In theory it is only necessary to split one U-235 atom, and the neutrons given off will split the other atoms, this is why it is called 'chain reaction'. This occurs at great speed, all the atoms splitting within a millionth of a second.

In practice, it is not quite so simple to start a nuclear explosion. There has to be a certain weight of U-235 present before the chain reaction will sustain itself. If there is less than this amount there will be too few atoms to ensure that neutrons from every atom that splits will hit other atoms.

The minimum amount is known as the critical mass. The actual mass depends on the purity of the material, but for pure U-235, it is 110lb (50kg). No U-235 ever is quite pure, so in reality more is needed.

Uranium is not the only material used for making A-bombs. Another material is the element plutonium, in its isotope Pu-239. Plutonium is not a natural element but is made from uranium.

Mechanism of the bomb There is more to an A-bomb than just the nuclear fuel. Fairly elaborate equipment is needed to set it off, and there are also safety devices to make it absolutely impossible to set off by accident.

A bomb cannot be made simply by putting a piece of uranium larger than critical mass into a casing, because this would cause it to go off immediately. Instead, two or more pieces are inserted a safe distance apart and 'assembled', or shot together, to start a chain reaction.

The simplest possible atomic bomb is one of the type dropped on Hiroshima. It is known as a 'gun-type' bomb, and actually does contain a gun. At one end of the barrel there is a 'target', a piece of U-235 slightly smaller than critical mass and shaped like a sphere with a conical

wedge removed from it. This gap in the sphere reaches right down to its centre and faces towards the other end of the barrel.

At the other end of the barrel there is another, smaller, piece of U-235 in the shape of a cone with its point towards the gap in the target. It is the exact shape of the piece missing from the sphere. Together, the two pieces are just over critical mass.

The smaller piece is backed by a charge of ordinary high explosive. When this is set off, the cone is shot into the sphere and the force of the impact welds the two pieces together solidly. The explosion follows instantly.

Plutonium bombs are slightly more sophisticated. Plutonium is even more easily fissionable than U-235, and its critical mass is lower: 35.2lb (16kg) for pure Pu-239.

The mass can be reduced further, to 22lb or 10kg, by making a sphere of this weight of plutonium and surrounding it with non-fissionable U-238, which 'reflects' neutrons back into the centre of the sphere and minimizes loss to the outside.

Plutonium cannot be exploded so easily by a gun-type device. It has to be 'assembled' with much greater speed than uranium or it will not explode properly.

Plutonium is therefore assembled by a technique known as implosion. A number of wedge-shaped pieces of plutonium, which together will build up into a sphere, are arranged at equal inetrvals around a neutron source. Explosive charges of exactly equal weight are placed behind each wedge and all are detonated together. The wedges shoot towards the centre and touch each other at the same moment. This technique was used for the second American atomic bomb, which was dropped on Nagasaki.

Apart from the basic mechanism that starts the chain reaction there has to be some device for setting off the explosive. This depends on the exact nature and use of the bomb. The Hiroshima and Nagasaki bombs were both worked by built-in altimeters, so that they exploded automatically when they had fallen to a certain height above the city.

Today, A-bombs are considered by the major world powers as obsolete weapons. But they are still needed as 'triggers' to set off hydrogen bombs, and have also been used to replace conventional chemical explosives for certain kinds of civil engineering projects.

Hydrogen bombs
A hydrogen bomb is a device in which energy from nuclear fusion reactions between isotopes of hydrogen is released in an uncontrolled, explosive manner. Nuclear fusion is a process in which nuclei of small atoms combine to form the nucleus of a larger atom, and energy is released because the binding energy holding together the particles in the large nucleus is less than the sum of the binding energies holding together the small nuclei. The energy set free by the almost instantaneous fusion of many millions of nuclei results in an explosion of enormous power. Indeed, the hydrogen bomb is the most destructive device ever produced by man.

Fusion Nuclear fusion cannot occur spontaneously. Normally two nuclei will tend to repel each other because they both carry a positive electric charge, so if they are to fuse, they must be forced together. In order to force nuclei together, favourable conditions are required: the nuclei

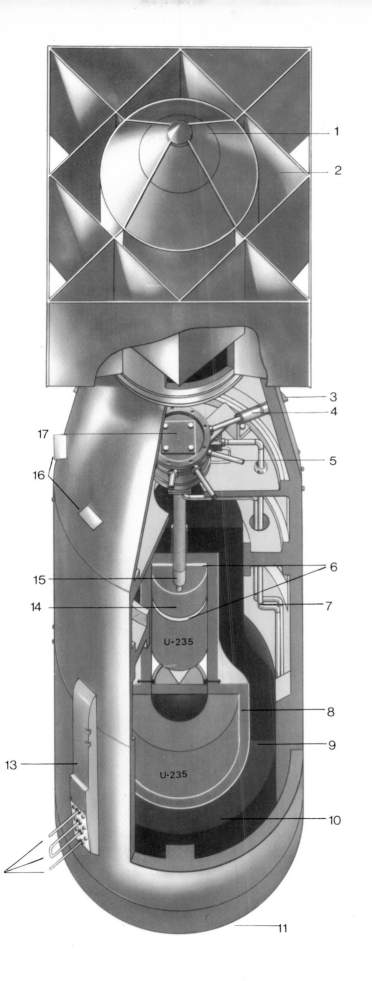

Left : A cutaway view of the U-235 bomb 'Little Boy'.

1. Tail cone
2. Stabilizing tail fins
3. Airstream defectors
4. Air inlet tube
5. Pressure sensors
6. Packing
7. Electronic conduits and fusing circuits
8. Neutron reflector
9. Cast bomb casing
10. Lead shield container
11. Fuses
12. Telemetry monitoring probes
13. Battery stores
14. Conventional explosive charge
15. Detonating head
16. Airstream deflectors
17. Air pressure detonator

U-235

U-235

must be as close together as possible to start with and they must be moving towards each other at very high velocities. High velocities can be achieved by heating the components to temperatures of several hundred million degrees and for this reason the hydrogen bomb is often called a thermonuclear bomb. Once the critical temperature is achieved, fusion will begin, and the energy released will maintain the temperature, then hence the reaction, until either all the fusionable material has been used or the whole reaction mixture has expanded to such an extent that the temperature has fallen below the critical level. This whole process takes place so quickly that it is almost instantaneous.

Two isotopes of hydrogen – deuterium and tritium – are used in hydrogen bombs, rather than ordinary hydrogen. Deuterium occurs in nature, for example as deuterium oxide (D_2O or heavy water) to the extent of about one part in 5000 of ordinary water, from which it can be extracted and purified. Tritium, a radioactive isotope, does not occur naturally and must be produced artificially: it is made by bombarding lithium-6 (an isotope of the alkali metal lithium with atomic weight 6) with neutrons, when it splits into helium and tritium.

Development of hydrogen bombs Primitive hydrogen bombs consisted of an A-bomb and a supply of hydrogen isotopes in liquid form. The A-bomb acted as a trigger by supplying the heat necessary to initiate the fusion reaction. (This is still the only practical means of supplying the enormous heat required, although the possibilities of using lasers as triggers are being explored.) Liquid isotopes were used because atoms are closer together in a liquid than in a gas, but because liquid hydrogen isotopes are very unstable and dangerous, this type of hydrogen bomb could not be stored safely.

Modern hydrogen bombs consist basically of an A-bomb trigger surrounded by a lining of lithium deuteride, a compound of deuterium and lithium (lithium-6). Lithium deuterium nuclei are very close together (atoms are even more closely packed in a solid than in a liquid) so that they are in a favourable position to undergo fusion when heat is supplied. Second, the lithium-6 will produce tritium when bombarded with neutrons, and the tritium can then fuse with the deuterium. Neutrons for this process are supplied by the A-bomb, so that the trigger also has more than one function. In addition to the main reactions – deuterium with deuterium and deuterium with tritium – other fusion reactions may contribute to the explosion. For example, a lithium nucleus can fuse with a deuterium nucleus to release energy.

This type of hydrogen bomb is said to be relatively 'clean' meaning that it produces only small quantities of radioactive debris, or 'fallout'. The fallout, which can remain radioactive for months or years, is composed chiefly of radioactive fission products from the trigger – but only in limited amounts as only a small A-bomb is used – together with unburned tritium. Often, however, a hydrogen bomb is surrounded by a layer of uranium (uranium-238). As well as acting as a 'container' to keep the bomb together and the fusion reaction going a little longer, this uranium, when bombarded by fast neutrons generated by the fusion reaction, is a further source of fission energy. This type of bomb – called a fission-fusion-fission bomb – produces considerable amounts of radioactive fallout, and is therefore described as 'dirty'.

The explosive power of a hydrogen bomb is much greater than that of an A-bomb, for two main reasons. First, because hydrogen is the lightest of all elements, a given mass of deuterium or tritium contains many more atoms than the same mass of uranium or plutonium and thus, weight for weight, there are more deuterium or tritium nuclei available for fusion than there are uranium or plutonium nuclei able to undergo fission. In fact, the complete fusion of a given mass of deuterium would theoretically yield almost three times as much energy as the complete fission of the same mass of uranium-235. Second, the size of a hydrogen bomb, unlike that of an A-bomb, is theoretically almost unlimited. The self-sustaining chain reaction of an A-bomb can only continue if more than a certain mass of fissionable material is present, but when the bomb explodes, much of the fissionable material is blown away unused and, because the required mass is no longer present, the chain reaction stops. In the hydrogen bomb, fusion will continue as long as fusionable material is available, in however small amounts, provided the temperature is high enough, and so a larger proportion of the fusionable material is used. Hydrogen bomb size is therefore limited only by the weight than an aircraft or missile delivery system can carry.

Testing of hydrogen bombs The largest hydrogen bomb ever exploded – by the Soviet Union on 30 August 1961 – was estimated to have had a yield of some 60 megatons (equivalent to 60 million tons of TNT). For comparison, the A-bombs exploded over Japan at the end of World War II had a yield of about 15 kilotons (equivalent to 15,000 tons of TNT).

Although hydrogen bombs have never been used in war, test explosions have many undesirable effects. In particular, radioactive fallout can contaminate food, milk and so on, and could cause serious diseases such as cancer. It was at least partly to minimize such dangers that in August 1963 the United States, the Soviet Union and Britain signed a treaty banning nuclear weapon tests of any type in the atmosphere, in outer space or underwater: such tests are permitted only if they are carried out underground and only if adequate precautions are taken to prevent the escape of radioactive debris into the atmosphere. Since then, many other countries have signed this treaty, even though they are not themselves in a position to carry out nuclear tests. But two countries – France and China – have not yet signed, and are still carrying out tests in the atmosphere, despite strong protests from countries such as Australia and New Zealand who claim that their territories are being contaminated by radioactive fallout.

At the present time, moves are being made to persuade France and China to stop their atmospheric testing and also to limit the size of test explosions carried out underground. While these moves will not themselves affect the numbers of hydrogen bombs currently stockpiled by the nuclear-weapon countries – many thousands of them are already fitted into intercontinental ballistic missiles and carried on long-range bombers and nuclear submarines – it is hoped that limiting and eventually abolishing nuclear testing altogether will be at least a first step in ensuring that these terrible weapons will never be used in war.

Above: When static launch sites were knocked out by Allied bombing, the Germans developed highly mobile arrangements for firing the V2. This V2 is being raised into its firing position from its trailer.

MISSILES

A guided missile is an unmanned self-propelled airborne vehicle or spacecraft which carries a destructive load; it may be remotely guided or direct itself to a preselected target. Whatever its specific purpose might be, a missile consists of an air-frame, with or without wings and fins, housing a motor, control system, guidance system and warhead.

Airframe and motor The configuration and size of a missile are governed by its range and the type of motor used to propel it. Largest of all are intercontinental ballistic missiles (ICBMs), with a range of at least 8000 km (5000 miles), requiring multi-stage rocket motors, which take them to a height of up to 1600 km (1000 miles). The cylindrical propellant tanks for liquid-propellant motors, or cylindrical casings of solid-propellant motors, often form the outer skin of the missile, the individual stages of which are jettisoned after burnout, leaving the warhead to complete the trajectory to impact alone. No wings or fins are fitted, as most of the missile's flight is outside the Earth's atmosphere, where aerodynamic surfaces would be ineffective. Materials used for the rocket casings include maraging steel (alloy steel subjected to a heat treatment to impart toughness), high strength aluminium alloy and glassfibre.

Air-breathing or cruise missiles, designed to travel within the atmosphere, utilize ramjet or turbojet engines. They need air intakes for these engines, and wings or fins to sustain them in flight. Consequently, their design often resembles that of a piloted aircraft. The earliest and best known example was the World War II V-1 flying bomb.

Most other categories of missile have a cylindrical body fitted with cruciform wings and either cruciform tail-fins or nose-mounted foreplanes. Depending on the required maximum speed, the wings may be rectangular, sweptback or delta, sometimes with a chord (the line joining the centres of curvature of the leading and trailing edges of an aerofoil section), many times their span. When such missiles are launched from a tube, or from inside the bomb-bay of an aircraft, it is normal for the wings to be hinged, so that they fold around the body, and to be spring-loaded so that they extend after launch.

Solid-propellant booster rockets are often attached to the body of missiles, particularly those with ramjet or turbojet engines, to give a high initial launch speed. The boosters jettison after burnout.

Control system Missiles which operate within the Earth's atmosphere are able to utilize aerodynamic control surfaces moved by electrical, hydraulic or pneumatic actuators. Either the cruciform wings or the tail surfaces may be pivoted for this purpose. Less frequently, the use

239

German A4 Rocket (V2)

1. Internal carbon guide-vanes
2. External control vanes
3. Electro-hydraulic servo-motors
4. Turbine exhaust
5. Stabilizing fins
6. Hydrogen peroxide tank
7. Liquid oxygen tank
8. Shell construction
9. Servo-operated alcohol valve
10. Front joint ring
11. Conduit
12. Warhead
13. Central explorer tube
14. Control and radio equipment
15. Alcohol tank
16. Double-walled alcohol delivery pipe to pump
17. Rear joint ring
18. Air bottles
19. Tubular frame supporting turbine and pump assembly
20. Alcohol distribution pipe
21. Combustion chamber
22. Chain drive to external control vanes
23. Venturi nozzle

Below : When the threat of the V2 was finally extinguished, great interest was shown by the Americans in the assembly lines of the rocket. Here at Kleitnbodingen, Germany, a partly completed rocket shows the unfinished engine compartment at the base.

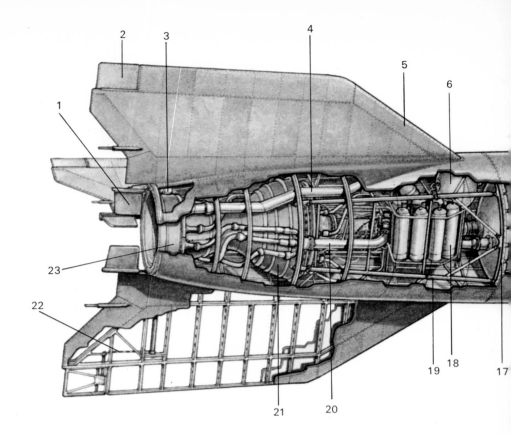

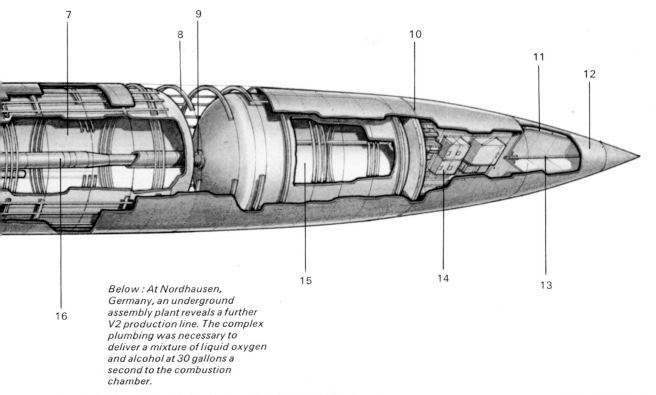

*Below : At Nordhausen,
Germany, an underground
assembly plant reveals a further
V2 production line. The complex
plumbing was necessary to
deliver a mixture of liquid oxygen
and alcohol at 30 gallons a
second to the combustion
chamber.*

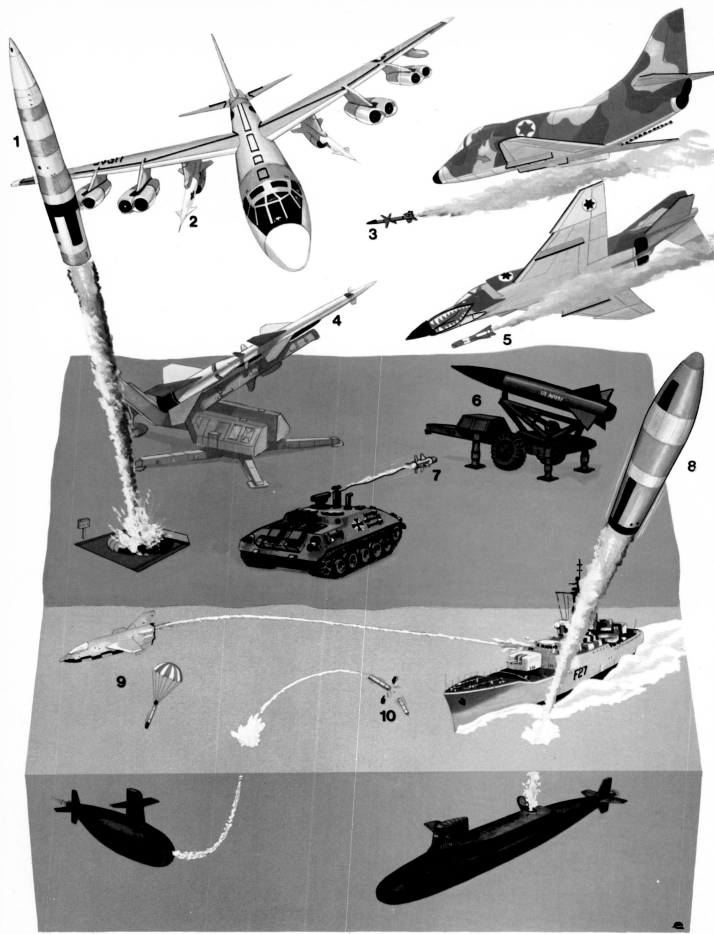

of wing-mounted ailerons or elevons, or pivoted vertical and horizontal tail surfaces, or a combination of both, provides an even closer similarity to the control surfaces of a piloted aircraft.

An alternative to aerodynamic control is some form of vectored thrust, which is effective in both atmosphere and space. In large missiles, such as ICBMs, it is usual to gimbal the nozzles of the rocket motors, thus steering the missiles by changing the direction of thrust. A similar deflection of thrust can be achieved by liquid injection on one inner wall of the nozzle, or by blanking off part of the nozzle. This last technique, employing 'pivoted 'semaphores', is particularly suitable for close-range air-launched anti-aircraft missiles, which must have high manoeuvrability to match that of the target.

Guidance system The most important component of a missile is the system which ensures that it hits the correct target. Some guidance systems are self-contained within the missile; these often have the advantage of being less susceptible to enemy electronic countermeasures (ECM) or jamming. Others involve continuous monitoring of the

Left : Ten types of missile currently in service.
1. Minuteman (USA), three-stage solid-fuelled intercontinental ballistic missile, thermonuclear MIRV (multiple independently-targetable re-entry vehicles) warhead.
2. Hound Dog (USA), air-to-surface thermonuclear missile, turbojet-powered, inertial guidance and star-tracking systems.
3. Shrike (USA), supersonic air-to-surface anti-radar missile, solid propellant rocket, high-explosvie warhead, homes on enemy radars.
4. SAM-2 (USSR), surface-to-air missile. Two-stage rocket (solid and liquid), radio-guided and detonated (also has conventional fuses).
5. Maverick (USA), tactical air-to-surface missile, solid-

propellant rocket. Self-homing TV system with camera in nose locks on to target automatically once aimed, leaving pilot free to turn away.
6. Lance (USA), surface-to-surface artillery missile, liquid-propellant rocket powered, nuclear or high-explosive warhead.
7. HOT (France & Germany), anti-tank missile, wire-guided, two-stage solid-propellant rocket motor.
8. Poseidon (USA), underwater-to-surface ballistic missile, solid-propellant rocket, thermonuclear MIRV warhead.
9. Ikara (Australia), long-range anti-submarine missile, solid-propellant rocket powered, carries torpedo to target and drops it by parachute.
10. Subroc (USA), underwater-to-underwater missile, solid-propellant rockets, inertial guidance system. Fired from submarine, surfaces, travels to target, drops nuclear depth bomb.

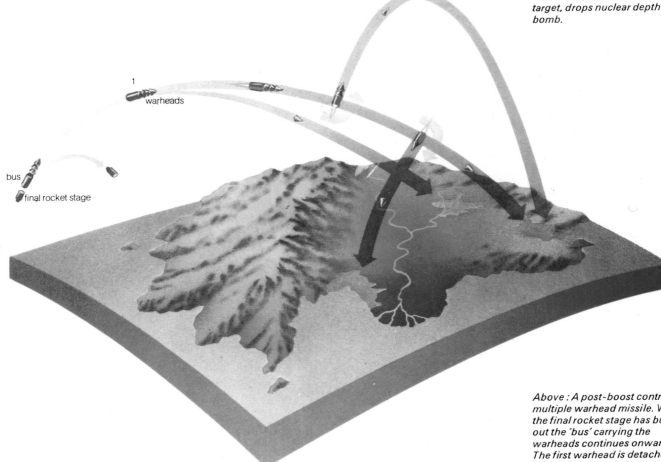

1
warheads

bus
final rocket stage

missile's position, and course corrections, during flight.

One of the simplest forms of guidance for short-range missiles is wire guidance. As the missile travels towards its target, it trails one or two fine wires which unwind from bobbins and continue to link it with the operator's controls. He can steer it into the target, using a thumbstick or

Above : A post-boost controlled multiple warhead missile. When the final rocket stage has burned out the 'bus' carrying the warheads continues onwards. The first warhead is detached at 1. The bus then performs a series of manoeuvres by firing its own rocket motor and another warhead is ejected at each stage. The warheads can either be aimed at different targets or at the same target after a predetermined time lapse.

miniature aircraft-type joystick to generate electrical signals which are transmitted over the wires to the missile's control system. The weight of the wire limits range to about two miles, and both target and missile must be visible to the operator. Tracking flares attached to the missile help him follow its path as distance from the launcher increases, especially in poor light or rough country.

At a small cost in complexity, it is possible to dispense with the wires by transmitting signals by radio between the operator and the missile (radio command guidance). This increases the danger of enemy ECM interference, requiring use of a range of signal frequencies, one of which must be selected and fed into the missile electronics before launch, so that it will ignore signals on all other frequencies. Devices to afford further protection (ECCM: electronic counter-countermeasures) can also be built into the missile.

If the missile is to be fired against a target beyond visual range, a cathode ray viewer rather like a TV screen is used. The precise position of the target, if fixed and known, can be set up on the screen. The missile can then be tracked by radar in flight, and its 'blip' steered into the target. Greater accuracy can be achieved by fitting a small TV camera into the nose of the missile. Then, as it approaches the target, the controller receives a TV picture of the target area and can steer the missile to a precisely-chosen pinpoint. Such techniques have enabled controllers in aircraft to hit a particular bridge support or part of a ship beyond visual range.

An advantage of such a system is that the launch aircraft can turn back towards its base once the missile has been launched, without any loss of control over the flight path. This permits launch and control over 'stand-off' ranges, beyond the reach of the target's close defences.

Another TV guidance technique entails 'locking' the camera onto the target before launching the missile, which will then home automatically on where the camera is aimed, by means of onboard electronics.

Radar tracking is used widely for surface-launched anti-aircraft missiles, advantages being that it can, if required, eliminate the need for manual steering and is fully effective

Left: A Minuteman ICBM being launched from its underground silo. The smoke ring is formed by exhaust from the rocket motor passing up between the missile and the silo wall after ignition.

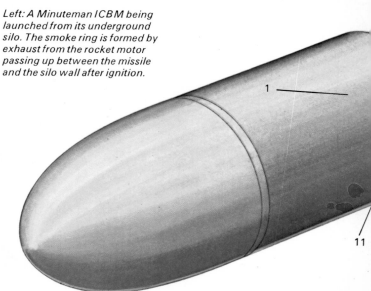

Left : With a roar of booster-jets, one SS11 B1 leaves a Scout ATH. The infra-red flare can be seen glowing at the rear of the missile on its wire-guided path towards the tank. Low scrub cover, used by the ATH on its 'stalk' of the tank, can be seen to the left.

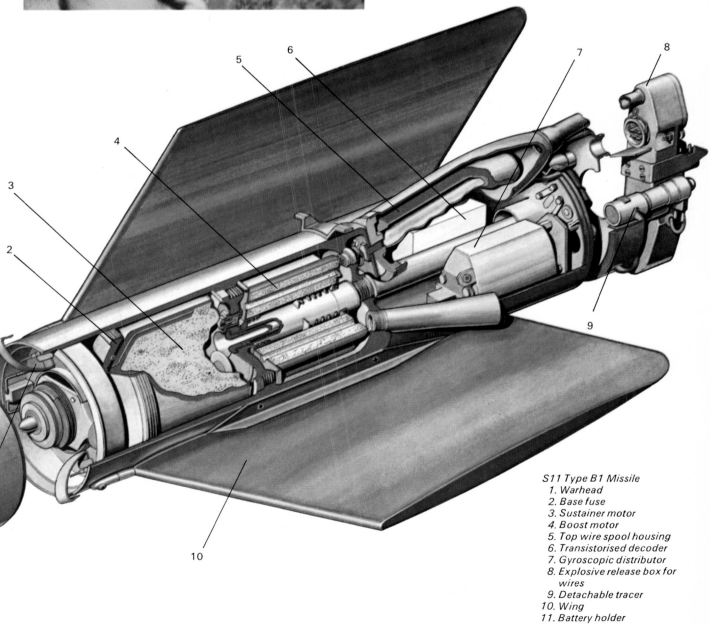

S11 Type B1 Missile
1. Warhead
2. Base fuse
3. Sustainer motor
4. Boost motor
5. Top wire spool housing
6. Transistorised decoder
7. Gyroscopic distributor
8. Explosive release box for wires
9. Detachable tracer
10. Wing
11. Battery holder

Above: A selection of aircraft weapons including cannon, bombs, and missiles. Air-to-air missiles usually have high-explosive warheads, and air-to-surface missiles are either high-explosive or nuclear.

in bad weather or at night. The automatic system requires two radars, to track the target and missile respectively. Radar information is fed into a computer, which causes signals to be transmitted to the missile so that it will intercept the target. This is called radar command guidance.

Only one radar is needed for beam-riding guidance. After the radar has been locked onto the target, a missile is launched and guided into the radar beam. It locks onto the beam and flies along it to the target. Semi-active homing is somewhat similar. This involves 'illuminating' the target with a radar, causing radar signals to be reflected back from it. The missile then homes onto the source of the reflected signals. Active homing differs in that the missile both transmits and receives the signals, making it independent of radar transmitters on the ground or in a launch aircraft.

Active homing missiles tend to be comparatively large and complex. By comparison, those which employ passive homing are among the simplest of all, requiring no transmitters of any kind although they are self-contained. Typical are missiles fitted with an infra-red heat-seeking head. This locates any source of heat emission, such as the exhaust of an aircraft jet engine, and homes onto it. Another homing technique uses laser designators to achieve high effectiveness even in a rapidly changing combat environment. A controller on the ground, or in an aircraft, locates a target and directs a laser beam onto it. The missile then picks up the reflected laser beam and homes onto the source of the reflections.

The most advanced system of all is inertial guidance, being self-contained in the missile, unjammable and extremely accurate. It uses accelerometers and gyroscopes to measure every slight change of direction of the missile during flight. If any change would take it off its predetermined course to the target, the guidance system moves the controls to put it right.

Warhead Missiles can carry almost any kind of military warhead, including those associated with chemical or biological warfare. Anti-tank wire-guided missiles, for example, can be fitted with interchangeable armour piercing types able to penetrate 600mm (24in) of steel, high-explosive or anti-personnel fragmentation types. The largest Soviet ICBMs can carry a 25-megaton thermo-nuclear warhead, a cluster of individually-targeted thermonuclear warheads able to manoeuvre to elude the defences, or a 'space bomb' that can be put into orbit and directed down onto its target at will. Small nuclear warheads can be fitted to almost any class of missile. High-explosive types are normally fitted with both contact and proximity fuses.

The effectiveness of ICBMs has been increased by the development of multiple re-entry vehicles (MRVs) and multiple independently targetable re-entry vehicles (MIRVs). MRVs have several small warheads carried by one missile, which are released in controlled sequence as the missile passes over the target (rather like an aircraft dropping bombs), thus spreading the damage over a wider area. MIRVs take this idea a stage further by ejecting the warheads from the 'bus' (main missile) at predetermined times, with different directions and velocities, so that one ICBM can attack several separate targets.